JUDGING STATE-SPONSORED VIOLENCE, IMAGINING POLITICAL CHANGE

How should state-sponsored atrocities be judged and remembered? This controversial question animates contemporary debates on transitional justice and reconciliation. This book reconsiders the legacies of two institutions that transformed the theory and practice of transitional justice. Whereas the International Military Tribunal at Nuremberg came to exemplify the promise of legalism and international criminal justice, South Africa's Truth and Reconciliation Commission promoted restorative justice and truth commissions. Bronwyn Leebaw argues that the two frameworks share a common problem: Both rely on criminal justice strategies to investigate experiences of individual victims and perpetrators, which undermines their critical role as responses to systematic atrocities. Drawing on the work of influential transitional justice institutions and thinkers such as Judith Shklar, Hannah Arendt, José Zalaquett, and Desmond Tutu, Leebaw offers a new approach to thinking about the critical role of transitional justice – one that emphasizes the importance of political judgment and investigations that examine complicity in, and resistance to, systematic atrocities.

BRONWYN LEEBAW is currently an assistant professor in the political science department at the University of California, Riverside. Her interest in transitional justice, restorative justice, and human rights has led her to South Africa, Bosnia-Herzegovina, and The Hague, Netherlands. Leebaw has published several articles on these topics in journals such as *Perspectives on Politics, Human Rights Quarterly,* and *Polity.*

T0384762

JUDGING
STATE-SPONSORED VIOLENCE, IMAGINING
POLITICAL CHANGE

BRONWYN LEEBAW

University of California, Riverside

CAMBRIDGE
UNIVERSITY PRESS

CAMBRIDGE UNIVERSITY PRESS
Cambridge, New York, Melbourne, Madrid, Cape Town,
Singapore, São Paulo, Delhi, Tokyo, Mexico City

Cambridge University Press
32 Avenue of the Americas, New York, NY 10013-2473, USA

www.cambridge.org
Information on this title: www.cambridge.org/9780521169776

First published 2011

Printed in the United States of America

A catalog record for this publication is available from the British Library.

Library of Congress Cataloging in Publication data
Leebaw, Bronwyn Anne.
Judging state-sponsored violence, imagining
political change / Bronwyn Anne Leebaw.
p.   cm.
ISBN 978-1-107-00058-2 (hardback) – ISBN 978-0-521-16977-6 (paperback)
1. International police.   2. Transitional justice.   3. Political violence.   4. Crimes against
humanity.   5. Intervention (International law)   6. Truth commissions – South Africa –
History.   7. War crime trials – Germany – Nuremberg.   I. Title.
KZ6374.L44   2011
342.08–dc22   2010039406

ISBN 978-1-107-00058-2 Hardback
ISBN 978-0-521-16977-6 Paperback

To Teo, Nadia, and John

Contents

Acknowledgments

I have many extraordinary people to thank for their role in helping me complete this project. I am grateful to the professors at UC Berkeley who worked with me on this project at its earliest stages. The late, dearly missed Michael Paul Rogin was an incredible mentor and aided me in formulating the ideas that would come to frame this project. Hanna Pitkin patiently read through multiple early drafts of core chapters and provided encouragement when it was most needed. Wendy Brown, Bob Kagan, and Robert Post all provided essential support, thoughtful comments, and challenging criticism that deepened my thinking on these issues in crucial ways. I am also grateful to professors Beatriz Manz, Theodor Meron, Nancy Scheper-Hughes, and Paul Thomas for insightful comments that informed my thinking.

I learned a great deal about transitional justice through my work with Eric Stover and Harvey M. Weinstein at the UC Berkeley Human Rights Center, and through ongoing conversations with many individuals that were involved at the Human Rights Center while I was there, especially Patrick Ball, Laurel Fletcher, Laurie Lola Vollen, and Gilles Peress.

I am grateful to the many scholars, leaders, and activists based in South Africa who took time out of their demanding schedules to meet with me during my visits – the first of which was many years ago. The late Peter Biehl, Linda Biehl, Richard Goldstone, Rhoda Kadalie, Dumisa Ntzebeza, Fazel Randera, Fiona Ross, Hugo Van der Merwe, Charles Villa-Vicencio, Nomfundo Walaza, and many others, generously shared their thoughts with me. The Centre for the Study of Violence and Reconciliation in Johannesburg and the Trauma Center for Survivors of Violence and Torture in Cape Town allowed me to make use of their facilities. Hylton Alcock, Mary Galvin, Mike Metelits, and Nicky Nathan opened their homes to me on my visits and showed me around. My deepest thanks go to the many people, too numerous to name, in South

Africa, Bosnia-Herzegovina, and the Hague, Netherlands, who gave their time in interviews and discussions about transitional justice institutions.

I am grateful to the Institute for the Study of World Politics and the Hewlett Foundation for grants that supported my work on this project. I also want to thank the University of California, Riverside, for providing grants, sabbatical leave, and maternity leave, which made it possible for me to complete this book. I am especially grateful to Shaun Bowler and Monique Davis-Brooks for their assistance and patience in helping me navigate the logistics of leave taking. Prior to the current budget crisis, UC Riverside was able to hire an incredible pool of talented young scholars that have established a fantastic and nurturing intellectual community here. As fellow members of a working group on Gandhi's legacy, Farah Godrej, June O'Connor, and David Biggs contributed to my thinking on reconciliation and resistance. In the department of political science, I have been lucky to have colleagues that are thoroughly engaging, inspiring, and unpretentious. Chris Laursen provided thoughtful feedback on the manuscript and saved me from some embarrassing mistakes. A special thanks to David Pion Berlin, Juliann Allison, and Feryal Cherif, who have been involved in organizing the departmental human rights colloquium. I am also grateful to my students, graduate and undergraduate alike, for what they have taught me about the themes that animate this book.

This book has benefited a great deal from the thoughtful comments and counsel of colleagues that I have had the fortune to meet at conferences over the years. As discussants on various conference panels, W. James Booth, John F. Burke, Javier Couso, Mark Drumbl, Victor Peskin, Naomi Roht-Arriaza, and Brad Roth provided extremely valuable feedback. As fellow panelists or participants in conferences, Stephen Esquith, Chimène Keitner, Helen Kinsella, Nesam Mcmillan, David Mendeloff, Daniel Philpott, Jamie Rowen, Chandra Sriram, Andrew Valls, and Leslie Vinjamuri commented on drafts or presentations of this work in ways that enriched my thinking. Dean Mathiowetz not only provided intellectual nourishment from the very beginning, but also detailed comments and criticisms that greatly improved Chapter 4. I am especially grateful to Ruti Teitel for her constructive feedback and generous encouragement. I am also grateful to Amy Ross for taking the time to share her wisdom and experience when I was beginning this project, and to Peter Agree for his support and insight along the way. All of these people have contributed to my thinking on the ideas developed in this book. Of course, any errors and limitations of the book are mine alone.

I am deeply grateful to my editor at Cambridge University Press, John Berger, and to the anonymous reviewers who provided incredibly thoughtful and constructive feedback on my original manuscript. For advice and encouragement throughout the process, I am grateful to Tracy Fisher, Jennifer Hughes, Hong Anh Ly, Bronwen Morgan, Karthick Ramakrishnan, and Brinda Sarathy. Wayne Leebaw, Ellen Leebaw, and Danya Leebaw provided an endless supply of moral support. Finally, I am especially grateful to John Cioffi, for his love and his wisdom, and to our children, Teo and Nadia, for joyfully slowing me down.

1

Introduction: Transitional Justice and the "Gray Zone"

A torturer informs a prisoner that no matter how loud she screams no one will ever hear her cries. Perceived enemies of the state are "disappeared," buried in mass graves, and forgotten. Episodes of repression, atrocity, and political violence are customarily downplayed or avoided in the history lessons that are taught to schoolchildren. Hannah Arendt characterized such strategies as efforts to establish "holes of oblivion into which all deeds, good and evil, would disappear."[1] She added that these efforts would never be entirely successful because "one person will always be left alive to tell the story."

In recent decades, institutions designed to recover such stories, and to challenge efforts to consign evidence of past atrocities to "holes of oblivion," have proliferated to numerous countries around the world. International war crimes tribunals have hired forensic scientists to reconstruct the stories that are told by the bones found in the mass graves of Bosnia-Herzegovina and Rwanda. An International Criminal Court has been developed to hold individuals accountable for egregious violations of human rights and humanitarian law. Truth commissions have been created in more than thirty-five countries to investigate patterns of political violence and abuses. These institutions have sent teams of investigators to the remote regions of Peru, the townships of South Africa, and the villages of East Timor and Sierra Leone to take testimony from survivors of political violence. They have compelled people who are responsible for torture, mass rape, "ethnic cleansing," and genocide to come forward with evidence and confessions. A growing number of leaders are facing pressure to address past wrongs through apologies, reparations, and reform.

In contemporary theoretical and policy debates, efforts to reckon with past political violence as part of a process of political change are now widely referred

---

[1]   Hannah Arendt, *Eichmann in Jerusalem* (New York: Penguin, 1965), 232.

to as forms of "transitional justice."[2] This term was first used by Ruti Teitel as a way to characterize legal mechanisms for addressing wrongs committed under a prior regime in the context of liberalizing regime change. In the early 1990s, the term was generally associated with strategies adopted by successor regimes in Latin America, Eastern Europe, and Africa to address past human rights abuses while advancing democratization. Over time, transitional justice scholarship and policy have come to encompass extralegal responses to past abuses, along with an expansive conception of "transition" that includes many forms of political change and conflict resolution.

Following the end of the Cold War, international organizations became increasingly involved in developing transitional justice institutions in the context of ongoing conflicts or as part of negotiated settlements. At the same time, transitional justice became increasingly identified with the aspirations of the human rights movement and with the development of human rights institutions, especially war crimes tribunals and truth commissions. Transitional justice is championed as a critical and transformative response to political violence, which aims to expose previously hidden abuses, challenge denial, establish accountability, and advance political reform. The expansion of transitional justice institutions and practices is widely viewed as a victory in the struggle for justice and memory as against the powerful forces of denial and forgetting.

Yet the expansion of transitional justice has also been fraught with ambiguities and perplexities. What sets transitional justice apart from "ordinary" justice has less to do with the context of *transition* than with the political nature of the wrongs that these institutions seek to address. Transitional justice is often referred to as a response to "atrocities" or "past abuses," yet the meaning of these terms is contested and varies tremendously in different contexts. The atrocity of the Rwandan genocide, for example, is something quite different than the institutionalized racism, political exclusion, and entrenched

---

[2] Ruti Teitel, *Transitional Justice* (Oxford and New York: Oxford University Press, 2000); Jon Elster, *Closing the Books: Transitional Justice in Historical Perspective* (Cambridge: Cambridge University Press, 2004); James A. McAdams, ed., *Transitional Justice and the Rule of Law in New Democracies* (Notre Dame, IN: University of Notre Dame Press, 1997); Naomi Roht-Arriaza and Javier Mariecruzana, eds., *Transitional Justice in the Twenty-First Century: Beyond Truth versus Justice* (New York: Cambridge University Press, 2006); Chandra Sriram, *Confronting Past Human Rights Violations* (London and New York: Frank Cass, 2004); Chandra Sriram, "Transitional Justice Comes of Age: Enduring Lessons and Challenges," *Berkeley Journal of International Law* 23, no. 2 (2005): 101–18; Jonathan Van Antwerpen, "Moral Globalization and Discursive Struggle: Reconciliation, Transitional Justice, and Cosmopolitan Discourse," in *Globalization, Philanthropy, and Civil Society*, ed. David Hammack and Steven Heydemann (Bloomington, IN: Indiana University Press, 2009); Bronwyn Leebaw, "The Irreconcilable Goals of Transitional Justice." *Human Rights Quarterly* 30, no. 1 (2008): 95–118.

repression of South Africa's apartheid regime. What they have in common is their *systemic* character. Both cases involved injustices and killings that were authorized and ordered by political authorities, and both involved the widespread participation, complicity, and acquiescence of a large component of the population.

Mass complicity is a defining feature of systematic political violence and takes many forms. It may be the active, enthusiastic participation of the zealot or the quiet acquiescence of the timid bystander. Complicity may be secured by force or subtle coercion. Auschwitz survivor Primo Levi described the use of "Special Squads" comprised of Jewish concentration camp victims to participate in the gassing of other Jews as an attempt to shift the burden of guilt back onto victims, "so that they were deprived even of the solace of their innocence."[3] Children and teens have been forced to participate in atrocities against their own communities in a number of conflicts from Central America to Sierra Leone. The first defendant to face charges before the International Criminal Tribunal for the former Yugoslavia, Drazen Erdemovic, claimed that he too was a victim of forced complicity. In his testimony before the court, Erdemovic insisted that he had attempted to refuse his orders to shoot the unarmed men. "[A]t first I resisted," he stated, "and Brano Gojkovic told me if I was sorry for those people that I should line up with them; and I knew that this was not just a mere threat but that it could happen."[4] Complicity is not always coerced, however, and frequently takes the form of passive or unquestioning acceptance.

Levi referred to these various forms of complicity as "the gray zone," a space between victims and perpetrators, peopled with "gray, ambiguous persons" that exist in every society, but may become available as "vectors and instruments" for a criminal system.[5] The "gray zone" poses practical challenges to official efforts to judge and remember past abuse. Those who were complicit or acquiescent in past atrocities may still retain military or political power. They may continue to cherish the ideologies or mythologies that were invoked to justify past brutalities. They may be heavily invested in denying that such abuses ever occurred, or they may simultaneously justify and deny past abuses.[6]

The "gray zone" complicates and challenges basic assumptions about what judgment and remembrance ought to entail in the aftermath of politically

3 Primo Levi, *Survival in Auschwitz*, trans. Stuart Woolf (New York: Collier, 1993), 53.
4 *Prosecutor v. Drazen Erdemovic, Sentencing Judgment* (March 5, 1998).
5 Levi, *Survival in Auschwitz*, 49.
6 For an analysis of the various denials employed by those engaged in massive atrocity, see Stanley Cohen, *States of Denial: Knowing about Atrocities and Suffering* (Cambridge: Polity Press, 2001).

authorized abuses and killings. Transitional justice institutions do not simply apply a set of commonly accepted legal standards to the task of judging past violence. Rather, they are engaged in a process of redefining what constitutes justice and injustice, one that challenges previously accepted or officially mandated views.[7] Transitional justice institutions cannot simply rely on a set of commonly accepted norms for guidance. Instead, they are engaged in a process of reimagining the very basis of political community. These dimensions of transitional justice raise a difficult set of questions that are relevant not only in the context of regime change or negotiated settlement, but that also apply more generally to various policies or programs designed to judge, investigate, and commemorate systematic political violence. Who is guilty when ordinary people commit extraordinary acts of brutality? What is the basis for judging atrocities that were authorized or compelled by political authorities? What is the relationship between the commitment to remember past abuses and the goal of advancing political reform to ensure their prevention in the future?

This book offers a new way to think about the legacies of two institutions that have profoundly influenced contemporary responses to these questions: the International Military Tribunal at Nuremberg and the South African Truth and Reconciliation Commission. Whereas the Nuremberg Trials inspired the development of legalistic responses to politically authorized atrocities, South Africa's Truth and Reconciliation Commission has served as a major influence for restorative approaches to transitional justice that aim to "heal the wounds of the past" through dialogue, testimony, or ritual. Human rights legalism and restorative justice present distinctive, even conflicting theoretical approaches to defining the terms of justice and memory in the aftermath of atrocities. However, the two frameworks share a common problem. Both are premised on the view that crime constitutes a discrete deviation from the shared norms or standards of a political community. Therefore, human rights legalism and restorative justice have judged and commemorated political violence in relation to the experiences of individual victims and perpetrators, while avoiding and obfuscating the "gray zone."

The individualistic focus of these frameworks has been a strategy for depoliticizing transitional justice in contexts characterized by persistent, volatile, conflict over the very terms of judgment and memory. Depoliticization is embraced as a way to establish the legitimacy of transitional justice institutions, the integrity of their investigations, and their contributions to political reconciliation. However, depoliticization has also undermined the critical role of transitional justice as a challenge to denial, as a basis for exposing the systemic dimension of past wrongs, and as a basis for advancing an ongoing process of change.

7   Teitel, *Transitional Justice*, 6.

Returning to theoretical debates on judgment and memory in the aftermath of Nazism and apartheid, this book locates and develops an alternative approach to transitional justice that moves beyond this victim-perpetrator framework to develop strategies for investigating complicity in, as well as *resistance to*, past injustices. In order to develop such strategies, I contend, it will be important to counter the prevailing logic of depoliticization associated with contemporary transitional justice by acknowledging, affirming, and critically evaluating the role of political judgment in our moral responses to political violence.

A GREAT LEGALISTIC ACT

In the aftermath of the Second World War, one of the problems confronted by the Allied countries was the question of what to do with surviving leaders of the Nazi regime. President Roosevelt's cabinet was divided over the issue. Secretary of the Treasury, Henry Morgenthau Jr., proposed summary execution for those listed as "archcriminals." Secretary of War, Henry Stimson, lobbied against this plan with a proposal for the United States to participate in an international tribunal for chief Nazi officials. Eventually, Stimson would prevail with a proposal to put leaders of the Nazi regime on trial in a court of law.[8]

The International Military Tribunal at Nuremberg would be the first international criminal court and the first to try leaders for "crimes against humanity." Of course, the Allied powers that occupied Germany were responsible for their own wartime atrocities. In filmed interviews with Erol Morris, former Defense Secretary Robert McNamara recites figures on the staggering loss of human life that resulted from the firebombing of Japanese cities, which he had helped plan while working under General Curtis LeMay. McNamara acknowledges that if the Allies had lost the war, he and his colleagues would justifiably have been tried as war criminals.[9] Nevertheless, the Nuremberg Trials were championed as a spectacle of restraint and evidence of the law's power to "stay the hand of vengeance and voluntarily submit their captive enemies to the judgment of law."[10] The trials were also seen as a basis for challenging denial regarding the extent of Nazi atrocities. Chief Prosecutor, Justice

[8] Telford Taylor, *The Anatomy of the Nuremberg Trials: A Personal Memoir* (New York: Knopf, 1992), 32–4.
[9] *The Fog of War: Eleven Lessons from the Life of Robert S. McNamara*. Directed by Erol Morris (Sony Pictures Classics, 2004).
[10] Justice Robert Jackson, "Opening Statement to the International Military Tribunal," *Trial of the Major War Criminals before the International Military Tribunal. Volume II. Proceedings: 11/14/1945–11/30/1945* (Nuremberg: IMT, 1947), 98–102.

Robert Jackson, famously announced that the trials would provide "undeniable proofs of incredible events."[11]

While the historical importance of the Nuremberg Tribunal is unquestionable, it is reasonable to wonder whether Nuremberg remains relevant for contemporary transitional justice debates. The International Military Tribunal at Nuremberg was developed under conditions of total occupation and unconditional surrender. In contrast, contemporary transitional justice institutions are generally established in contexts where the outgoing regime retains a significant degree of power or control. Yet the Nuremberg Tribunal continues to inform contemporary *ideas* regarding the meaning and role of justice in the aftermath of political violence. As Judith Shklar put it, establishing the Nuremberg Tribunal was a "great legalistic act."[12] "For those who believe in human rights," adds Gary Jonathan Bass, "Nuremberg remains legalism's greatest moment of glory."[13] The International Military Tribunal at Nuremberg was established under conditions that were historically unique and unlikely to be repeated, yet it continues to inspire the prominent view that a *just* response to political violence is a *legalistic* one.

In her classic work on the theme, Judith Shklar characterized legalism as the "ethical attitude that holds moral conduct to be a matter of rule following and moral relationships to consist of duties and rights determined by rules."[14] Shklar saw legalism as an ethos, as well as an ideology. As an ethos, legalism holds that the court and the trial epitomize moral perfection, and that a bright line must be established between law and politics. From the vantage point of the legalist, the distinction between law and politics is a basis for constraining abuses of power by transcending ideology altogether. Shklar countered this view by arguing that legalism must also be understood as an ideology with distinct political preferences.

A particular variant of legalism, which I refer to as "human rights legalism," has been at the center of evolving debates on transitional and global justice. With Nuremberg as a major source of inspiration, human rights legalism not only insists upon the promotion of *law* and courts in general, but on the centrality of *criminal* law in the aftermath of atrocities and political violence.[15]

---

[11] Jackson, "Opening Statement."

[12] Judith N. Shklar, *Legalism: Law, Morals, and Political Trials* (Cambridge, MA: Harvard University Press, 1964), 1.

[13] Gary Jonathan Bass, *Stay the Hand of Vengeance: The Politics of War Crimes Tribunals* (Princeton, NJ: Princeton University Press, 2001), 203.

[14] Shklar, *Legalism*, 1.

[15] Mark Drumbl, *Atrocity, Punishment, and International Law* (New York: Cambridge University Press, 2007).

"Nuremberg stands for the proposition that the most appropriate form of judgment is the trial," writes Ruti Teitel, "and the most appropriate forum of judgment is the International Military Tribunal."[16] Human rights legalism holds that formal standards of international criminal law provide the basis for judging political violence, whether criminal trials occur at the domestic or international level. Criminal trials focus narrowly on the task of establishing individual guilt and must provide due process guarantees to defendants. In this view, international law provides a basis for transcending the conflicts and divisions associated with judging "the gray zone." By prosecuting individuals in accordance with due process guarantees, human rights legalism aspires to challenge the demonization of groups based on attributions of collective criminality and to channel the desire for revenge into support for measured punishment bounded by fair procedures.

This set of ideas has had a powerful influence on the development of contemporary transitional justice institutions. In the post–Cold War era, legalism has animated the development of ad hoc international criminal tribunals to oversee prosecution for atrocities committed in the former Yugoslavia and Rwanda, as well as the development of the International Criminal Court.[17] Hybrid courts, which combine international and domestic oversight, have been developed in Sierra Leone, East Timor, and Cambodia. International organizations and powerful states have tended to criticize or condemn transitional justice practices that are not compatible with legalism.[18] Human rights organizations have been critical of administrative purges and lustration processes, for example, because these responses to political violence generally involve significant punishment without due process guarantees. For the same reason, human rights groups have been concerned about Rwanda's decision to use quasi-traditional *gacaca* courts as a way to process complaints against some 100,000 alleged *genocidaires* that had been awaiting trial in detention for more than a decade.[19] Proponents of human rights legalism also tend to oppose the use of amnesties or political pardons as strategies for negotiating an end to civil wars. It is a specifically legalistic definition of justice that is at the center of ongoing debates that pit the pursuit of peace against the goal of justice. Less obviously, human rights legalism has narrowed the scope of

---

[16] Ruti Teitel, "Nuremberg and Its Legacy: 50 Years Later," in *War Crimes: The Legacy of Nuremberg*, ed. Belinda Cooper (New York: TV Books, 1999), 44.

[17] Bass, *Stay the Hand of Vengeance*; Drumbl, *Atrocity, Punishment, and International Law*.

[18] Drumbl, *Atrocity, Punishment, and International Law*.

[19] See for example, Amnesty International, *Rwanda: A Question of Justice* (London: Amnesty International Secretariat, 2002), or more recently, Kenneth Roth, "The Power of Horror in Rwanda," *Los Angeles Times*, April 9, 2009, Opinion Section.

inquiry associated with transitional justice policy and practice. These institutions have tended to focus on violations of civil and political rights, which are amenable to a legalistic response, while avoiding economic and social injustices, which are held to require broader political solutions.[20]

Critics of human rights legalism have argued that the demand for criminal trials clashes with pragmatic responses to conflict that might serve to minimize backlash from nationalists and apologists.[21] Others contend that legalism defines justice narrowly in accordance with an idealized Western approach to criminal prosecution, superseding social and economic justice, as well as alternative approaches to criminal justice.[22] Such scholars have opened an important debate about the limitations and problematic implications of human rights legalism. However, they have generally focused on legalistic institutions and policies, with less attention to the network of ideas associated with legalism. South Africa's Truth and Reconciliation Commission became significant in transitional justice debates because it developed a critique of human rights legalism and offered an alternative way to think about the basis of judgment and the role of official remembrance in the aftermath of political violence.

A DIFFERENT KIND OF JUSTICE

It is often observed that the UN's adoption of the 1948 *Universal Declaration of Human Rights* became possible only as a result of global outrage in response to Nazism.[23] Yet the human rights movement was also profoundly influenced by global outrage in response to the racism, dispossession, exploitation, and violent repression that was institutionalized by South Africa's apartheid system.

---

[20] Kenneth Roth, "Defending Economic, Social, and Cultural Rights: Practical Issues Faced by an International Human Rights Organization," *Human Rights Quarterly* 26, no. 1 (2004): 63–73; Zinaida Miller, "Effects of Invisibility: In Search of the Economic in Transitional Justice," *International Journal of Transitional Justice* 2, no. 3 (2008): 266–291. For a discussion of the way in which human rights activists are developing new strategies for addressing private harms and social injustices, see Alison Brysk, *Human Rights and Private Wrongs: Constructing Global Civil Society* (New York: Routledge, 2005).
[21] Jack Snyder and Leslie Vinjamuri, "Trials and Errors: Principle and Pragmatism in Strategies of International Justice," *International Security* 28 (2003/4): 5–44.
[22] Kieran McEvoy, "Beyond Legalism: Toward a Thicker Understanding of Transitional Justice," *Journal of Law and Society* 34, no. 4 (2007): 411–440; Drumbl, *Atrocity, Punishment and International Law*; Rama Mani, *Beyond Retribution: Seeking Justice in the Shadows of War* (Cambridge: Polity Press, 2002); Brad Roth, "Peaceful Transition and Retrospective Justice: Some Reservations. A Response to Juan Méndez." *Ethics & International Affairs* 15 (2001): 45–50.
[23] Johannes Morsink, *The Universal Declaration of Human Rights: Origins, Drafting, and Intent* (Philadelphia: University of Pennsylvania Press, 1999).

Apartheid was legally entrenched with the victory of the National Party in 1948, shortly after the signing of the UDHR. South Africa was seen as a "test case" for those who sought to use human rights in the struggle against racism and colonialism.[24] The African National Congress incorporated human rights language into the text of the historic Freedom Charter in 1955. The transnational network that developed to oppose the South African regime is widely viewed as a model for contemporary human rights activism and evidence of its success.[25]

In 1994, the black majority of South Africa finally achieved full political equality. In South Africa's first democratic elections, the African National Congress was transformed from a guerilla movement into the ruling political party. South Africa's relatively peaceful transition to majority democratic rule was widely viewed as a "small miracle." Among the compromises that facilitated this transition was a decision to grant amnesties to those responsible for past human rights abuses on the grounds that they would agree to provide public confessions outlining the details of their acts. Inserted into South Africa's interim constitution was a statement intended to set the tone for the transition: "there is a need for understanding but not for vengeance, a need for reparation but not for retaliation, a need for *ubuntu* ["humaneness"] but not for victimization." In the immediate aftermath of the transition, South Africa's parliament passed legislation to establish a Truth and Reconciliation Commission (hereafter TRC) that would oversee the process of dealing with apartheid-era violence.

Truth commissions are temporary institutions designed to investigate patterns of political violence and abuse.[26] In contrast with commissions of inquiry, truth commissions are generally established in the immediate aftermath of a regime change or as part of a negotiated settlement to end a civil war. Truth commissions are usually defined as public institutions, established either by

---

[24] Paul Gordon Lauren, *The Evolution of International Human Rights: Visions Seen* (Philadelphia: University of Pennsylvania Press, 1998), 213.

[25] See Audie Klotz, *Norms in International Relations: The Struggle Against Apartheid* (Ithaca, NY: Cornell University Press, 1995); William Korey, *NGOs and the Universal Declaration of Human Rights: "A Curious Grapevine"* (New York: St. Martin's Press, 1998); Lynn Graybill, *Truth and Reconciliation in South Africa: Miracle or Model?* (Boulder, CO: Lynne Rienner, 2002).

[26] Priscilla Hayner, *Unspeakable Truths: Confronting State Terror and Atrocity* (New York and London: Routledge, 2001). For a more recent comparative analysis of truth commission procedures, see Mark Freeman, *Truth Commissions and Procedural Fairness* (Cambridge: Cambridge University Press, 2006). See also Eric Wiebelhaus-Brahm, *Truth Commissions and Transitional Societies: The Impact on Human Rights and Democracy* (New York: Routledge, 2009); Ernesto Verdeja, *Unchopping a Tree: Reconciliation in the Aftermath of Political Violence* (Philadelphia: Temple University Press, 2009).

domestic authorities or by the United Nations. However, in Brazil, Guatemala, and other countries, private organizations have launched investigations similar to those undertaken by truth commissions.[27] Truth commission investigations encompass not only the causes, but also the consequences and legacies of political violence. Their approaches to investigation vary significantly, but they nearly always involve a process of taking statements and testimony from victims.[28] Truth commissions do not have the power to prosecute alleged perpetrators of abuse. However, many truth commissions, including South Africa's TRC, are designed to give information to prosecuting authorities.[29] Upon completing their investigations, truth commissions develop reports and issue recommendations for reparation, institutional reform, prosecution, or commemoration.

Human rights advocates once saw truth commissions as a pragmatic alternative in contexts where prosecuting those responsible for past injustices would be preferable, but limited, impractical, or unfeasible. South Africa's TRC challenged this view with the claim that it was not merely a next best alternative to trials, but rather a basis for advancing a "different kind of justice": *restorative justice*.[30] South African leaders associated with the TRC were not opposed to international criminal justice. In fact, many went on to become staunch supporters of the International Criminal Court.[31] However, they challenged the basic theoretical assumptions animating human rights legalism and offered restorative justice as an alternative.[32]

---

[27] On the *Nunca Mais* project in Brazil, see Lawrence Wechsler, *A Miracle, A Universe: Settling Accounts with Torturers* (Chicago: University of Chicago Press, 1990); On unofficial truth projects, see Louis Bickford, "Unofficial Truth Projects," *Human Rights Quarterly* 29, no. 4 (2007).

[28] See Audrey Chapman and Patrick Ball, "The Truth of Truth Commissions: Comparative Lessons from Haiti, South Africa, and Guatemala," *Human Rights Quarterly* 23 (2001).

[29] See Naomi Roht-Arriaza, "The New Landscape of Transitional Justice," in *Transitional Justice in the Twenty-First Century: Beyond Truth versus Justice*, ed. Naomi Roht-Arriaza and Javier Marriezcurrena (Cambridge: Cambridge University Press, 2006), 1–16.

[30] Charles Villa-Vicencio, "A Different Kind of Justice: The South African Truth and Reconciliation Commission," *Contemporary Justice Review* 1 (1999): 407–28.

[31] Statement by Civil Society Organizations and concerned individuals in South Africa on the decision made by the AU to refuse cooperation with the ICC (July 13, 2009).

[32] See Charles Villa-Vicencio, "Restorative Justice: Dealing with the Past Differently," in *The Provocations of Amnesty: Memory, Justice, and Impunity*, ed. Charles Villa-Vicencio and Erik Doxtader (Claremont: David Philip Publishers, 2003) and Johnny de Lange, "The Historical Context, Legal Origins and Philosophical Foundation of the South African Truth and Reconciliation Commission," in *Looking Back, Reaching Forward: Reflections on the Truth and Reconciliation Commission of South Africa*, ed. Charles Villa-Vicencio and Wilhelm Verwoerd (Cape Town: University of Cape Town Press, 2000); Desmond Mpilo Tutu, *No Future without Forgiveness* (New York: Doubleday, 1999), 54–5; 155–7; Alex Boraine, *A Country Unmasked: Inside South Africa's Truth and Reconciliation Commission* (Oxford: Oxford University Press, 2000), 278–99; 387–400.

Restorative justice theory emerged out of a range of informal alternative justice practices, encompassing juvenile justice, alternative dispute resolution, Native American talking circles, and other indigenous justice practices in New Zealand, Canada, and a number of African countries.[33] In contrast with the secular tradition of legalism, restorative justice has been influenced by theological approaches to reconciliation.[34] In contrast with the legalistic emphasis on enforcing rules, restorative justice aspires to repair injuries or damages caused by crime and violence. This not only requires a response to the harms experienced by victims of crime, but also strategies for rehabilitating or reintegrating those who are responsible for crime by outlining ways that they can make amends. This expansive set of goals has led commentators to refer to restorative justice as a morally ambitious theory.[35] Restorative justice does not exclude punishment, and may even require it, but rejects the view that punishment ought to be the goal of justice. Instead, punishment is part of the broader process of repair, which might also encompass expressions of apology, atonement, and forgiveness.[36] In contrast with the legalistic preference for formal rules, restorative justice calls for standards of judgment that are flexible and responsive to local contexts, practices, and values. Instead of using law to mediate the emotional response to crime, restorative justice calls for victims, perpetrators, and communities to participate directly in the process of justice.

South Africa's TRC has had a remarkable influence on the theory and practice of transitional justice worldwide. "[S]ince the advent of South Africa's TRC in the 1990s," writes one commentator, "it is difficult to conjure an example of a political or post-conflict transition in which the idea of establishing a

---

[33] See Howard Zehr, *Changing Lenses: A New Focus for Crime and Justice* (Scottsdale, PA: Herald Press, 1990); John Braithwaite, *Restorative Justice and Responsive Regulation* (Oxford: Oxford University Press, 2002).

[34] See Daniel Philpott, "What Religion Brings to the Politics of Transitional Justice," *Journal of International Affairs* 61, no. 1 (2007): 93–110; Michael L. Hadley, ed., *The Spiritual Roots of Restorative Justice* (Albany, NY: State University of New York Press, 2001); Leslie Vinjamuri and Aaron P. Boesenecker, "Religion, Secularism, and Nonstate Actors in Transitional Justice," in *The New Religious Pluralism*, ed. Thomas Banchoff (Oxford: Oxford University Press, 2008).

[35] Elizabeth Kiss, "Moral Ambition within and Beyond Political Constraints: Reflections on Restorative Justice," in *Truth v. Justice: The Morality of Truth Commissions*, ed. Robert I. Rotberg and Dennis Thompson (Princeton, NJ and Oxford: Princeton University Press, 2000).

[36] Jennifer Llewellyn and Robert Howse, "Institutions for Restorative Justice: The South African Truth and Reconciliation Commission," *University of Toronto Law Journal* 49 (1999): 355–88. Villa-Vicencio, "Restorative Justice: Ambiguities and Limitations of a Theory"; Lisa LaPlante and Kimberly Theidon, "Truth with Consequences: Justice and Reparations in Post-Truth Commission Peru, *Human Rights Quarterly* 29, no. 1 (2007): 228–50.

truth commission has been overlooked."[37] The Deputy Chair of South Africa's TRC, Alex Boraine, went on to found the influential International Center for Transitional Justice, which plays an active role in consulting with leaders involved in establishing truth commissions and other transitional justice institutions. One influential edited volume on the morality of truth commissions is entirely dedicated to debates on South Africa's TRC.[38] The TRC has become a focal point for debates in political theory on the themes of forgiveness and reconciliation.[39]

South Africa's TRC has also influenced a particular way of adapting restorative justice to the context of political violence, which I refer to as "therapeutic justice." More specifically, the TRC has inspired the view that as a response to political violence, one of the most important goals associated with restorative justice is to establish a therapeutic process that aims to "heal the wounds of the past." This variant of restorative justice emphasizes the importance of addressing the trauma resulting from past abuses, which, if left unchecked, might fuel ongoing cycles of violence and mistrust. Truth commissions contribute to restorative justice, in this view, by providing new information that might foster psychological closure, opportunities for therapeutic testimony, or cathartic encounters between victims, perpetrators, and sympathetic observers. [40]

This "healing model" of transitional justice has its critics. Some reject the idea of restorative justice as intellectually incoherent and contend that a better moral defense of truth commissions rests on establishing their role in advancing deliberative democracy.[41] Others are concerned with the way

[37] Freeman, *Truth Commissions and Procedural Fairness*, 11.
[38] Rotberg and Thompson, eds., *Truth v. Justice*.
[39] See for example, Jean Bethke Elshtain, "Politics and Forgiveness," in *Burying the Past: Making Peace and Doing Justice after Civil Conflict*, ed. Nigel Biggar (Washington DC: Georgetown University Press, 2003); Andrew Schaap, *Political Reconciliation* (London and New York: Routledge, 2005); Peter Digeser, *Political Forgiveness* (Ithaca, NY: Cornell University Press, 2001); Fuyuki Kurasawa, *The Work of Global Justice: Human Rights as Practices* (Cambridge: Cambridge University Press, 2007); Mark Amstutz, "Restorative Justice, Political Forgiveness, and the Possibility of Reconciliation," in *The Politics of Past Evil: Religion, Reconciliation, and Transitional Justice*, ed. Daniel Philpott (Notre Dame, IN: Notre Dame University Press, 2006). Aletta Norval, "Memory, Identity, and the (Im)possibility of Reconciliation: The Work of the South African Truth and Reconciliation Commission," *Constellations* 5, no. 2 (2002): 250–65.
[40] Both Minow and Kiss associate restorative justice with therapeutic testimony. However, it is important to note that neither scholar *reduces* restorative justice to therapy. See Kiss, "Moral Ambition" and Minow, "The Hope for Healing: What Can Truth Commissions Do?" in *Truth v. Justice*, ed. Rotberg and Thompson.
[41] Amy Gutmann and Dennis Thompson, "The Moral Foundations of Truth Commissions," in *Truth v. Justice*, ed. Rotberg and Thompson, 22–44.

that restorative justice identifies justice with healing and therapy. "A person plagued by cancer is not at fault," write Roth and Des Forges, "Murderers ... are different." Treating them as victims of social psychosis or trauma is dangerous in their view, "because it signals to other would-be mass murderers that they risk not punishment but, at most, communal therapy sessions."[42] Even sympathetic observers, such as Minow, have noted that this therapeutic conception of justice is in tension with political responses to past abuses.[43]

Nevertheless, the therapeutic approach to transitional justice has been influential in shaping ideas about the role of truth commissions and the meaning of restorative justice as a response to political violence. Rwanda's *gacaca* courts ostensibly represent an alternative way to enact a restorative response to atrocity – one that does not center on investigating and narrating the past, but entails a participatory process of adjudication and punishment.[44] However, for a number of reasons, this approach to restorative justice has not been as influential as the therapeutic approach associated with South Africa's TRC.[45] Although the amnesty provisions associated with the TRC have not been replicated, truth commissions commonly (though not uniformly) follow South Africa's lead by framing their work in relation to therapeutic categories. Sierra Leone's Truth and Reconciliation Commission, for example, encouraged people to participate in the process with signs that read, "Revealing is Healing!"[46] Restorative justice principles were also incorporated into the design of the International Criminal Court, which provides space for victim testimony and a reparations fund.[47]

---

[42] Kenneth Roth and Alison Des Forges, "Justice or Therapy?" *Boston Review* (Summer 2002).

[43] Martha Minow, *Between Vengeance and Forgiveness: Facing History after Genocide and Mass Violence* (Boston: Beacon Press, 1998), 63.

[44] See Drumbl, *Atrocity, Punishment, and International Law*; Timothy Longman, "Justice at the Grassroots? Gacaca Trials in Rwanda," in *Transitional Justice in the Twenty-First Century: Beyond Peace versus Justice*, 206–28.

[45] Mark Drumbl argues that Rwanda's *gacaca* process has moved away from its restorative and reconciliatory goals to become something more punitive and retributive (*Atrocity, Punishment, and International Law*, 94). See also, Phil Clark, *The Gacaca Courts, Post-Genocide Justice and Reconciliation in Rwanda: Justice without Lawyers* (New York: Cambridge University Press, 2010).

[46] Rosalind Shaw, "Rethinking Truth and Reconciliation Commissions: Lessons from Sierra Leone," *United States Institute of Peace Special Report* (Washington DC: USIP, 2005). See also, Tim Kelsall, "Truth, Lies, Ritual: Preliminary Reflections on the Truth and Reconciliation Commission of Sierra Leone," *Human Rights Quarterly* 27, no. 2 (2005).

[47] Among those who participated in the negotiations leading to the Rome Statute of the International Criminal Court, writes Christopher Muttukumaru, there was a "gradual realization" that victims "not only had an interest in the prosecution of offenders but also an interest in restorative justice." See Christopher Muttukumaru, "Reparation to Victims," in *The International Criminal Court: The Making of the Rome Statute: Issues, Negotiations, Results*, ed. Roy S. Lee (The Hague: Kluwer Law International, 1999), 264.

Although legalism remains the dominant framework for promoting and evaluating transitional justice, restorative justice has emerged as a prominent alternative. The two frameworks offer distinctive ways of addressing political violence, yet they are not mutually exclusive. I refer to them as "frameworks" because they are not simply sets of policy preferences, but rather refer to a broader network of assumptions regarding the relationships among justice, politics, and memory in the aftermath of political violence. These theoretical frameworks have influenced the kinds of institutions and strategies that are promoted to judge and remember political violence. They have influenced the way that transitional justice strategies are critically evaluated. More generally, legalism and restorative justice have influenced the way that policymakers and scholars understand, analyze, and commemorate political violence.

Despite their differences, legalism and restorative justice share a basic problem: Both are derived from criminal justice models that define crime as *deviance* from common norms and practices. Yet as applied to the context of transitional justice, they are used as a basis for judging crimes of *obedience* – violent or abusive acts that have been authorized by political leaders and rationalized or justified in the name of political communities. Both frameworks are premised on the availability of consensus regarding the terms of debate on past abuses, yet are applied in contexts characterized by ongoing volatile conflict over the fundamental question of how past violence ought to be judged. Both frameworks analyze and investigate the experience of innocent victims and guilty perpetrators, yet apply this framework to the context of systematic atrocities characterized by "gray zones" of complicity and ambiguous involvement. These frameworks have been appealing as approaches to transitional justice not *in spite of* the way that they are in tension with political responses to past abuse, but precisely *because* they provide strategies for depoliticizing the process of judgment and remembrance. Addressing their limitations means taking a closer look at this logic of depoliticization.

REMEMBERING VICTIMS AND PERPETRATORS, FORGETTING POLITICS

Transitional justice institutions are commonly criticized on the grounds that they are, or that they risk becoming, politicized. Where transitional justice becomes too political, according to such critics, it amounts to little other than a "witch hunt." This was the charge that the National Party, which presided over apartheid, leveled at South Africa's TRC. This was also the message that Republican leaders in the United States broadcast in response to those who have called for an investigation of Bush Administration officials for torture and other human rights abuses. Such comments suggest that if any degree of political judgment enters into the investigation of past abuses, then the entire process will be illegitimate and invite destructive backlash.

Criminal justice frameworks provide a way to respond to such charges by depoliticizing the terms of investigation. Depoliticizing the process of judgment is seen as a basis for establishing the legitimacy of transitional justice investigations in contexts characterized by volatile conflict over the very terms of debate. Focusing on discrete individual infractions and experiences is a way to demonstrate that transitional justice investigations are independent, rather than partisan, and concerned with reestablishing the integrity of the law or alleviating the suffering of individual victims. It is also a strategy for challenging political justifications for violence. Following the lead of major human rights organizations, transitional justice institutions analyze actions that may have been widely accepted as a matter of duty and recast them as "violations," "abuses," and "atrocities." Finally, in contexts where politics has become synonymous with violent exclusion, depoliticization has been a strategy for promoting reconciliation and a common sense of justice. Yet this has also been a problematic and contradictory strategy.

One problem is that depoliticization does not *transcend* the politics of transitional justice, but rather functions to obfuscate and naturalize the way that politics operate in the process of judging the past. Depoliticization masks the particular political and social values that frame the investigation and its judgments.[48] It also naturalizes the political compromises and asymmetries that define the scope of transitional justice mandates. Critics of the human rights movement have argued that depoliticization functions to foreclose debate on the terms of global justice, while presenting the values and traditions associated with western liberalism as universal.[49] Depoliticization has also obfuscated the ways in which international justice norms are gendered.[50] In the context of transitional justice, these are particularly troubling problems. Transitional justice institutions not only define the terms of justice

---

[48] Michael Barnett and Martha Finnemore. "The Politics, Power, and Pathologies of International Organizations," *International Organization* 53, no. 4 (1999): 699–732.

[49] See Makau Mutua, "Savages, Victims, and Saviors: The Metaphor of Human Rights," *Harvard International Law Journal* 42 (2001): 201–45.

[50] See Helen Kinsella, "Gendering Grotius: Sex and Sex Difference in the Laws of War," *Political Theory* 34, no. 2 (2006): 161–91; Charli Carpenter, *Innocent Women and Children: Gender, Norms, and the Protection of Civilians* (Ashgate, 2006); Laura Sjoberg, *Gender, Justice, and the Wars in Iraq: A Feminist Reformulation of Just War Theory* (New York: Lexington, 2006); Katherine Franke, "Gendered Subjects of Transitional Justice," *Columbia Journal of Gender and Law* 15, no. 3 (2006); Fionnuala Ni Aoláin, "Political Violence and Gender During Times of Transition," *Columbia Journal of Gender and Law* 15, no. 3 (2006). See also, Christine Bell and Catherine O'Rourke, "Does Feminism Need a Theory of Transitional Justice? An Introductory Essay," *International Journal of Transitional Justice* 1, no. 1 (2007): 23–44.

for past abuses, but also frame the terms of an official process of remembrance. They function as a basis for "imagining community" in contexts characterized by violent division over the terms of debate.[51] By naturalizing the compromises, distortions, and asymmetries that frame their investigations, these institutions foreclose or limit ongoing debate regarding the terms of official memory in the process of political change.

A second, related objection is that depoliticizing transitional justice institutions has been at odds with their claim to challenge denial and learn from the past. To depoliticize is to analyze or address problems by removing them from their political and historical context.[52] Criminal trials *can* reveal a great deal about the workings of systemic injustice.[53] But this aspiration is in tension with the requirements of due process and the goal of individualizing guilt.[54]As David Kennedy observes, "speaking law to politics is not the same thing as speaking truth to power."[55] More generally, human rights legalism has analyzed and understood political violence primarily as a problem of "impunity," or the absence of judgment and punishment, regardless of the historical context and dynamics that shape abuses or atrocities. Restorative justice has been associated with a somewhat different view of the problem of political violence as fundamentally concerning the legacy of unresolved psychological injuries resulting from past abuses. In fact, both impunity and trauma *are* important problems associated with political violence, and it is not my intention to dismiss or belittle these problems. Rather, my concern is with the way that legalism and restorative justice have been employed as frameworks for analyzing and commemorating systematic political violence. By displacing attention to the political dynamics and contexts of the abuses under investigation, these frameworks undermine the critical role of transitional justice as a challenge to denial and as a basis for learning from the past.

---

[51] See Benedict Anderson, *Imagining Communities* (London: Verso, 1983); Richard A. Wilson, *The Politics of Truth and Reconciliation in South Africa: Legitimizing the Post-Apartheid State* (Cambridge: Cambridge University Press, 2001).

[52] Wendy Brown, *Regulating Aversion: Tolerance in the Age of Identity and Empire* (Princeton, NJ and Oxford: Princeton University Press, 2006).

[53] See Bass, *Stay the Hand of Vengeance*; Mark Osiel, *Mass Atrocity, Collective Memory, and the Law* (New Brunswick, NJ: Transaction Press, 1997); and Lawrence Douglas, *The Memory of Judgment: Making Law and History in the Trials of the Holocaust* (New Haven, CT and London: Yale University Press, 2001).

[54] Drumbl, *Atrocity, Punishment and International Law*; Laurel Fletcher and Harvey M. Weinstein, "Violence and Social Repair: Rethinking the Contribution of Justice to Reconciliation, *Human Rights Quarterly* 23, no. 3 (August 2002): 573–639.

[55] David Kennedy, *The Dark Sides of Virtue: Reassessing International Humanitarianism* (Princeton, NJ and Oxford: Princeton University Press, 2004).

Karl Jaspers, who remained in Germany throughout the Nazi era with his Jewish wife, Gertrude, rejected the view that all Germans should be held criminally responsible for the genocide. Yet he was frustrated with what he saw as a failure on the part of most German people to consider their responsibility for supporting the regime, or failing to effectively protest its actions. Jaspers argued that criminal guilt should be restricted to the worst offenders, but that all Germans should be pressed to examine their own moral and political guilt for the atrocities.[56] Contemporary transitional justice institutions abandon this goal to the extent that they use individual guilt in a manner that implicitly exonerates those who were actively involved or otherwise complicit in systematic abuses.[57] Although depoliticizing such investigations is usually justified as a prerequisite for justice and reconciliation, it has also functioned to limit the scope of accountability and to blunt official moral condemnations of past practices.

At the same time, relying on a victim-perpetrator framework to frame official investigations of past injustice plays into the fear that such investigations will become paralyzing and undermine the pursuit of political reconciliation or ongoing reform. By limiting official remembrance of past suffering to the experiences of those who might be characterized as passive or innocent victims, transitional justice institutions fail to acknowledge the complexities of suffering and agency, as well as the role of those who *did* take action to protest or resist oppression and political violence.[58] They put forth a morality based on obedience, deference, and internalization of shared norms, which elides the problem of their collapse or absence. At the same time, they exclude potentially powerful examples of agency, protest, refusal, and solidarity that might usefully inform a response to this problem.

A third objection is that the depoliticization of transitional justice assents to an exceedingly narrow and self-defeating vision of politics – one that is in tension with the goal of advancing democratic change. It suggests that we are incapable of making distinctions between good and bad in politics, that all forms of political judgment are equally pernicious and that the very act of taking sides in a political debate is an affront to the goal of reconciliation or to the integrity

---

[56] Karl Jaspers, *The Question of German Guilt*, trans. E.B. Ashton (New York: Dial Press, 1947). See also, Stephen L. Esquith, "Re-enacting Mass Violence." *Polity* 4 (2003): 513–34.

[57] See Fletcher and Weinstein, "Violence and Social Repair"; Drumbl, *Atrocity and Punishment in International Law*; Pablo De Greiff, "Trial and Punishment: Pardon and Oblivion: On Two Inadequate Policies for the Treatment of Former Human Rights Abusers," *Philosophy and Social Criticism* 22 (1996): 106.

[58] David Kennedy refers to this as "privileging the baby seal" in a human rights framework that sees the world as "uncivilized deviants, baby seals, and knights errant" (*The Dark Sides of Virtue*, 29).

of the judicial process. This premise is at odds with the view that democratic politics must remain open to an ongoing process of conflict and contestation.[59] As Wendy Brown observes, depoliticization tends to substitute "emotional and personal vocabularies for political ones."[60] It also sets transitional justice in tension with the pursuit of political mobilization on behalf of ongoing change to advance democratic reform or address the legacy of the past.

As strategies for depoliticizing the past, legalism and restorative justice have offered narrowly construed and largely symbolic accounts of justice. Although restorative justice theory requires measures to address and repair underlying social and political conflict, it is commonly identified with the goal of psychological adaptation and closure. And although proponents of human rights legalism are often uncompromising when it comes to opposing amnesties, they have acceded to a vision of justice that is narrowly defined as the accumulation of exemplary legal victories. In his account of Amnesty International, Stephen Hopgood reveals that in its effort to establish a stance of political impartiality, the organization moved away from grassroots organizing toward a dynamic of "largely white middle-class westerners working as experts on behalf of largely nonwhite non-Westerners."[61] Similarly, efforts to depoliticize transitional justice have been associated with the view that the process of dealing with the past is most successful, fair, and just when handled by professionals such as lawyers, psychologists, and social scientists, in accordance with evolving standards of "best practice."

This book argues that the use of legalistic and restorative frameworks to depoliticize public memory undermines the critical role of transitional justice in important ways. Transitional justice is premised on the importance of challenging denial regarding state-sponsored and other forms of political violence, yet legalism and restorative justice have both functioned as strategies for avoiding the ambiguities of the gray zone by shifting attention away from the themes of complicity in, and resistance to, political violence. The critical role of transitional justice institutions is associated with their claim to remember and learn from the past, yet legalism and restorative justice have also fostered new forms of organized forgetting and mythmaking. Both frameworks are championed as strategies for connecting the pursuit of justice with the

---

[59] On this theme, see Chantal Mouffe, "Democracy in a Multipolar World," *Millennium Journal of International Studies* 37, no. 3 (2009): 549–61; Schaap, *Political Reconciliation*; Alan Keenan, *Democracy in Question: Democratic Openness in a Time of Political Closure* (Stanford, CT: Stanford University Press, 2003).

[60] Brown, *Regulating Aversion*, 16.

[61] Stephen Hopgood, *Keepers of the Flame: Understanding Amnesty International* (Ithaca, NY and London: Cornell University Press, 2006), 98.

goal of advancing political and democratic change, yet they have been framed in ways that denigrate political compromise, contestation, and agency.

RECOVERING POLITICAL JUDGMENT

A number of scholars have developed proposals for broadening the scope of transitional justice investigations to better address systematic, politically authorized injustices. Jaspers made the case for differentiating moral, criminal, political, and what he termed "metaphysical" guilt for Nazi atrocities.[62] More recently, Mahmood Mamdani argued that South Africa's TRC ought to have examined the responsibility of *beneficiaries* – those who continue to reap benefits from the legacy of apartheid.[63] Mark Drumbl suggests that in the aftermath of atrocity, collective responsibility ought to be assessed through civil remedies, which have a broader reach than criminal guilt.[64] Audrey Chapman and Patrick Ball have argued that the problem is methodological. Instead of relying on the legal framework for analyzing individual guilt, truth commissions should make use of social science methodology to establish the causes and dynamics of systemic violence.[65] Such proposals offer creative ways to widen the scope of transitional justice investigations in order to provide a critical and political response to systematic injustice. However, they sidestep an important problem, which is the way that the victim-perpetrator framework has been defended as a basis for depoliticizing transitional justice investigations.

To move beyond the confines of this framework, I suggest, it will be important to recover, defend, and evaluate the role of political judgment in transitional justice. The theme of political judgment has received little sustained attention in contemporary debates on transitional justice. What is striking about this omission is that many of the thinkers that influenced contemporary human rights legalism and restorative justice, particularly those writing in response to the challenges of judging Nazism and apartheid, defended the role of political judgment in efforts to reckon with massive atrocities and systemic injustice. For example, Judith Shklar, who is considered perhaps the most important theorist of legalism, defended the Nuremberg tribunal on the

---

[62] Jaspers, *The Question of German Guilt.*
[63] Mahmood Mamdani, "Reconciliation without Justice," *Southern Review* 10, no. 6 (1996): 22–5.
[64] Drumbl, *Atrocity, Punishment, and International Law,* 196.
[65] Audrey Chapman and Patrick Ball, "Levels of Truth: Macro-Truth and the TRC," in *Truth and Reconciliation in South Africa: Did the TRC Deliver?,* ed. Audrey R. Chapman and Hugo Van der Merwe (Philadelphia: University of Pennsylvania Press, 2008).

grounds that it had subordinated the imperatives of legalism to a creative and flexible process of political judgment.[66] Hannah Arendt, who is frequently cited as an inspiration for scholarship on international criminal justice and forgiveness, developed a thorough critique of depoliticization and argued that political judgment should be a central response to twentieth-century atrocities.[67] Kader Asmal, who is credited with originating the idea for a South African TRC, argued that the primary goal of the truth commission should be to develop a political judgment of apartheid.[68] Even South African thinkers who defended the narrow investigative framework of the TRC, such as Charles Villa-Vicencio and Desmond Tutu, nevertheless made the case for incorporating political judgment into the restorative justice framework.

These writings on political judgment have been neglected as a result of the individualistic focus of transitional justice theory and policy. This book examines them in order to recover a different set of lessons that might be drawn from the examples of Nuremberg and the South African TRC regarding the role of political judgment in the aftermath of political violence. It also seeks to recover the concept of political judgment from the prevailing conventional wisdom that characterizes it as intrinsically divisive or antithetical to the pursuit of justice.

In so doing, one goal of this book is to argue that political judgment is essential to the critical role of transitional justice and, more generally, to the process of developing moral responses to systematic injustice. First, transitional justice institutions must make judgments, whether implicit or explicit, about the political systems, institutions, or values that authorize systematic violence and abuse. Second, transitional justice institutions make judgments in the absence of agreed upon rules and standards. They may invoke international or local norms, yet they do so in a context of radical disagreement over the meaning and application of these standards. They do not simply render judgment on past events by invoking a set of standards or laws, but also aspire to make their judgments politically meaningful in contexts where such standards have been hollow, completely disregarded, or malevolent. Finally, transitional justice institutions seek to judge in dynamic contexts, where the goal is not to reinforce existing rules or even to affirm tentative pacts and negotiations, but rather to address past injustices as part of an ongoing

---

[66] Shklar, *Legalism*, 156–68.

[67] Hannah Arendt, *Lectures on Kant's Political Philosophy Lectures on Kant's Political Philosophy*, ed. Ronald Beiner (Chicago: University of Chicago Press, 1982), 1–3.

[68] Kader Asmal, Louise Asmal, and Ronald Suresh Roberts. *Reconciliation through Truth: A Reckoning of Apartheid's Criminal Governance* (Cape Town: David Philips Publishers, 1996).

process of change.[69] Political judgment is important, as Leslie Thiele writes, because "there are no rules to determine where, when, and how new rules should be invented and old rules bent or broken."[70] Understood in this way, political judgment is a crucial dimension of praxis, the process of connecting theory to action.

The book develops this argument by addressing the charge that the criteria commonly used for evaluating political judgment are essentially at odds with the goals associated with transitional justice. Many scholars of political judgment begin with the basic premise that politics is tragically and inescapably violent. This idea is on display in the logic employed by the Athenian delegation to Melos in Thucydides' *Peloponnesian War*: "the strong do what they have the power to do and the weak accept what they have to accept."[71] International relations realists have cited the grisly fate of the Melians, who refuse to "look the facts in the face" and submit to the superior power of the Athenian empire, as a failure of political judgment.[72] The idea that political judgment requires a tragic sensibility and a willingness to compromise moral principles runs through the classics of realist theory from Machiavelli's *The Prince* to Weber's "Politics as a Vocation" and Morgenthau's ethic of "political realism."[73] José Zalaquett, a Chilean truth commissioner widely cited in the literature on transitional justice, invoked this approach to political judgment by citing Weber's "ethic of responsibility" as a way to justify the narrow parameters of Chile's initial transitional justice program.[74] Others have argued that transitional justice requires strategies designed to appease potential "spoilers" who have an incentive to derail a democratic transition or negotiated settlement.[75] The trouble with this approach is that it tends to identify good political judgment with a posture of resignation and acceptance with regard to prevailing divisions and dynamics of power.

---

[69] Ruti Teitel has argued that in the context of political transition, law "is caught between the past and the future, between backward-looking and forward-looking, between retrospective and prospective" (*Transitional Justice*, 6).

[70] Leslie Paul Thiele, *The Heart of Judgment: Practical Wisdom, Neuroscience, and Narrative* (New York: Cambridge University Press. 2006), 4

[71] Thucydides, *The History of the Peloponnesian War: Revised Edition*, ed. Rex Warner, trans. M.I. Finley (New York: Penguin Classics, 1954), 402.

[72] For an alternative interpretation of Thucydides, see Richard Ned Lebow, *The Tragic Vision of Politics: Ethics, Interests, and Orders* (New York: Cambridge University Press, 2003), 65–167.

[73] See Michael Joseph Smith, *Realist Thought from Weber to Kissinger* (Baton Rouge: Louisiana State University Press, 1986).

[74] José Zalaquett, "Balancing Ethical Imperatives and Political Constraints: The Dilemma of New Democracies Confronting Past Human Rights Violations," *Hastings Law Journal* 43 (1992): 1425–38.

[75] Snyder and Vinjamuri, "Trials and Errors."

Another influential approach posits that political judgments ought to be guided by the shared traditions and experiences of political communities. For Aristotle, *phronesis*, or practical wisdom, was a central human virtue that enables people to make judgments in the dynamic realm of the polis. In contrast with theoretical wisdom, Aristotelian *phronesis* "is concerned with human affairs and with matters about which deliberation is possible."[76] Because it is concerned with action, *phronesis* deals with particulars rather than universals. Aristotle argued that this kind of judgment could not be attained through philosophical contemplation, but rather through experience and "good sense," which he characterized as "the quality which makes us say of a person that he has the sense to forgive others."[77] Thus, according to Ronald Beiner, Aristotelian judgment is connected to understanding and "fellow feeling" in a political community.[78] Similarly, in Roman humanism, *sensus communis* is the basis of political judgment.[79] This understanding of political judgment may be discerned in prominent accounts of restorative justice. For example, John Braithwaite has argued that restorative justice must be guided by the shared norms or traditions of a community.[80] From this perspective, it is a mistake to presume that political judgment is antithetical to collective moral aspirations. Yet a critical moral response to systematic, politically authorized injustice cannot rely on community tradition, past shared experience, or conventional wisdom and must instead examine how prevailing notions of "common sense" might have been implicated in the abuses under investigation.

I draw on Arendt's unfinished writings on this theme to pursue an alternative way to think critically about the role of political judgment in transitional justice. Arendt was influenced by Aristotelian thought but moved away from the view that political judgment ought to be guided by community traditions and practices. Instead, she developed a basis for critically evaluating political judgment by drawing on Kant's idea of a kind of impartiality based on "enlarged mentality," which is achieved through an effort to take diverse perspectives into account without presuming to transcend a partial, subjective position. One reason that Arendt's account of political judgment is useful for debates on transitional justice is that it outlines a basis for attempting to bridge seemingly intractable divisions, yet without appealing to prepolitical or apolitical criteria.

[76] Aristotle, *Nichomachean Ethics*, trans. Martin Ostwald (New York: MacMillan, 1962), 1141b 10–15.
[77] Aristotle, *Nichomachean Ethics*, 1143a.20.
[78] Ronald Beiner, *Political Judgment* (London: Metheune & Co., 1983), 79.
[79] Beiner, *Political Judgment*, 21.
[80] John Braithwaite, *Crime, Shame, and Reintegration* (Cambridge: Cambridge University Press, 1989).

Arendt's discussion of political judgment is also useful because it exposes tensions between two distinctive stances or activities associated with good political judgment. Her writings on the theme of political judgment remained unfinished at the time of her death and scholars continue to disagree over the direction she would, or should, have taken with them had she lived. Arendt sometimes seems to suggest that political judgment entails active engagement in politics through dialogue and persuasion. In others, she identifies political judgment with the "spectator" or historian, whose capacity to imagine and account for alternative perspectives depends on the achievement of some kind of distance from the violent passions of past events. As efforts to reckon with systematic injustice, transitional justice projects require both forms of political judgment. They are mutually reinforcing, but they are also in tension with one another. That is, the parameters of their historical investigations are informed by political persuasion, deliberation, and compromise. However, if they are to serve as a critical response to systematic atrocities and injustices, transitional justice institutions must also strive for the critical distance of the historian, whose reflections on past events expose the limitations of political compromise and challenge the parameters of prevailing "common sense." Instead of regarding this as problem to be resolved (in debates on Arendt or in debates on transitional justice), I suggest that the tension between them is essential to the critical role of transitional justice.

This approach to political judgment does not accommodate avoidance or denial, but rather insists upon potentially unsettling historical investigation and reflection. Paradoxically, transitional justice institutions are championed as a basis for reckoning with historical wrongs, yet their investigations are treated as a kind of welcome by-product of their role in achieving partial remedies for systematic abuses. Proponents of legalism have argued that by prosecuting individuals, courts can persuasively establish historical records of past violence. Proponents of restorative justice have tended to frame the role of transitional justice investigations in relation to therapeutic categories. In these arguments, the role of historical reflection and remembrance is bound up in, and limited by, the pursuit of politically feasible remedies for past injustices. In contrast, I suggest that the critical role of transitional justice requires a process of historical reflection that is somewhat detached from the project of remedy – one that might thereby shed light on the *limitations* of transitional remedies and compromises.

Good political judgment, as Arendt characterized it, must be constructive and imaginative as well as critical. If transitional justice is to be a basis for imagining the possibility of political community or reconciliation after atrocity, it should not be limited to addressing the experiences of victims and perpetrators, but should also investigate the experiences of those who engaged in acts of resistance against systematic atrocities. The primary threat that Arendt associated with "holes of oblivion" was in the effort to erase traces of struggle, to make protest and dissent appear futile in the face of overwhelming state-sponsored repression. Contemporary transitional justice institutions are championed as tools in what Milan Kundera referred to as the "struggle of memory against forgetting,"[81] yet these institutions have made no space for the memory of resistance.[82] A common fear is that stories of resistance are invariably conveyed in Manichean terms, as a struggle of good against evil, and that recalling them will undermine the pursuit of dialogue and persuasion across lines of division. Although investigations that examine the theme of resistance may be unsettling, I suggest that they also illuminate possibilities for solidarity and innovation that are neglected in the effort to depoliticize transitional justice investigations.

The argument developed here makes three primary contributions to the theoretical literature on transitional justice. First, the argument challenges prominent approaches to defining and evaluating what it means to "do justice" in debates on transitional justice and human rights. Scholars engaged in theoretical and empirical research on these themes generally characterize human rights advocacy as idealistic and legalistic. This book does not take issue with a basic aspiration of legalism, which is to establish law as a basis for constraining abuses of power. Nor does it aim to provide an exhaustive critique of legalism as an ideology.[83] Instead, the book exposes the contradictions and limitations inherent in a particularly influential variant of legalism – human rights legalism. It challenges the claim that legalistic strategies delineate the realm of law or justice from the biases, compromises, and conflicts of politics. And it argues that as a response to systematic political violence, legalistic strategies may be obfuscating or critical depending on the quality of political judgment that informs them. Recognizing this does not mean that we ought to reject war crimes tribunals or abandon the project of international criminal justice, but that we should acknowledge and critically evaluate the role of political

---

[81] Milan Kundera, *The Book of Laughter and Forgetting* (New York: Harper Perennial, 1999).

[82] Robert Meister addresses this theme in "Ways of Winning: The Costs of Moral Victory in Transitional Regimes," in *Modernity and the Problem of Evil*, ed. Alan D. Schrift (Bloomington, IN: Indiana University Press, 2005).

[83] For more general studies of legalism in other contexts, see Wendy Brown and Janet Halley, eds., *Left Legalism/Left Critique* (Durham, NC and London: Duke University Press, 2002); McEvoy, "Beyond Legalism"; Robert Kagan, *Adversarial Legalism: The American War of Law* (Cambridge, MA: Harvard University Press, 2003); Ruti Teitel, "Humanity's Law: A Rule of Law for a New Global Politics." *Cornell International Law Journal* 35 (2002): 355–87.

judgment in their operation. It also reveals the limitations of legalism as a basis for evaluating alternative approaches to justice, framing moral action, and guiding historical reflection beyond the confines of the criminal trial.

Restorative justice has been characterized as a kind of large-scale therapy session and associated with a return to local or traditional approaches to resolving conflict. As a result, it has been too easy for critics to dismiss restorative justice as a retreat from accountability and the framework has not been taken seriously as a theoretical alternative to legalism. The debate on restorative justice has oversimplified the contributions of thinkers who influenced South Africa's TRC, and neglected their efforts to reflect on the TRC's limitations and disappointments. This book takes the discourse of transitional justice seriously. However, in this work I consider how thinkers and leaders who influenced that discourse went on to reflect on it critically, as scholars and as theorists. Building on these reflections and on restorative justice theory, I develop an alternative approach to conceptualizing restorative justice as a response to political violence – one that requires political judgment and responsibility, rather than a therapeutic "talking cure." I suggest that this approach to restorative justice offers an important response to the limitations of legalism. In developing this argument, the book also addresses ongoing debates regarding the ways that local actors work with the human rights framework, as well as emerging research on the influence of religious activists in developing international approaches ethics and justice.[84] In the South African context, local human rights leaders and religious activists did not just adapt international norms to address local dilemmas and problems, but also developed an innovative theoretical critique of human rights legalism.

Second, the argument bridges a persistent divide in scholarship on transitional justice. Human rights advocates, along with many prominent human rights scholars, have seen transitional justice as an essentially critical response to abuses of power. Transitional justice investigations may be imperfectly designed or implemented, in this view, but their fundamental function is to challenge denial, to investigate and address the extent of past violence.[85]

---

[84] See, for example, Shareen Hertel, *Unexpected Power: Conflict and Change Among Transnational Activists* (Ithaca, NY: Cornell University Press, 2006); Sally Engle Merry, *Human Rights and Gender Violence: Translating International Law into Local Context* (Chicago: University of Chicago Press, 2006); Cecelia Lynch, "Acting on Belief: Christian Perspectives on Suffering and Violence," *Ethics and International Affairs* 14 (2000).

[85] See for example, Roht-Arriaza and Mariezcurrena, eds., *Transitional Justice in the Twenty-First Century*; Eric Stover and Harvey M. Weinstein, eds., *My Neighbor, My Enemy: Justice and Community in the Aftermath of Atrocity* (Cambridge: Cambridge University Press, 2004); Victor Peskin, *International Trials in Rwanda and the Balkans: Virtual Trials and the Struggle for State Cooperation* (New York: Cambridge University Press, 2009); Kathryn Sikkink and Carrie

Commentators from a range of backgrounds and theoretical orientations have contested this view by arguing that transitional justice discourse and institutions primarily function to manage prevailing dynamics of power, cultivate consent for compromise, or establish new legitimating mythologies.[86] This book demonstrates that both perspectives are, to some extent, valid. Depoliticization is a powerful legitimating strategy that often masks the extent to which transitional justice institutions and practices are influenced by dynamics of power and inequality. However, these institutions also open up new possibilities for advancing critical, transformative responses to systematic injustice and brutality. Efforts to pursue such an agenda cannot rely on the technical acumen of professional policy makers, but also require political judgment.

Third, the book addresses ongoing debates on the relationship between the politics of memory and change. Transitional justice institutions and practices have long been challenged on the grounds that to insist on investigating or commemorating past atrocities and injustices is a self-defeating or ultimately paralyzing activity. The German *Historikerstreit* centered on the claim made by some historians that collective identity should not be weighed down by an oppressive obligation to remember the shameful deeds of previous generations.[87] In this view, common among conservatives, countries should be free to selectively emphasize heroic episodes from their histories as a basis for establishing unity, patriotism, and pride, without facing continual pressure to integrate past atrocities into their collective identity. Former Argentine President Carlos Menem argued that too much attention to human rights abuses would damage the cause of reconciliation.[88] Fears regarding the burden of memory are not only expressed by apologists or conservatives, but also

Booth Walling, "The Impact of Human Rights Trials in Latin America," *Journal of Peace Research* 44, no. 4 (2007), 427–45.

[86] Samuel Huntington, *The Third Wave: Democratization in the Late 20th Century* (Norman, OK: University of Oklahoma Press, 1991); Snyder and Vinjamuri, "Trials and Errors"; Wilson, *The Politics of Truth and Reconciliation in South Africa*; Robert Meister, "Human Rights and the Politics of Victimhood," *Ethics and International Affairs* 16, no. 2 (2002): 91–108. Ruti Teitel has argued that transitional justice entails a process of negotiation between critical and conservative responses to past wrongs. See, *Transitional Justice*, 213–28; "Transitional Justice Genealogy," *Harvard Human Rights Journal* 16 (2003): 69–94.

[87] See Charles Maier, *The Unmasterable Past: History, Holocaust, and German National Identity* (Cambridge, MA: Harvard University Press, 1988); Jurgen Habermas, *A Berlin Republic: Writings on Germany* (Lincoln, NE: University of Nebraska Press, 1997).

[88] See, Luis Roniger and Mario Sznajder, *The Legacy of Human Rights Violations in the Southern Cone: Argentina, Chile, and Uruguay* (Oxford: Oxford University Press, 1999), 78, 163.

by liberals, who observe that the idea of a community that bears an obligation or debt to the past is in tension with the idea of a rights-based political
community with porous boundaries and the capacity to alter its identity over
time.[89] Others have expressed the fear that an obsessive focus on past injury is
symptomatic of, and functions to reinforce, a declining faith in the possibility
of collective action for a better future.[90]

This book rejects the idea that transitional justice insists upon *too much*
memory, too much attention to past wrongs, along with the view that an obligation to remember past wrongs will undermine the goal of political change.
At the same time, the book suggests that the *frameworks* that animate transitional justice institutions and practices *have* undermined this goal. By limiting the process of reckoning with past wrongs to the experiences of victims
and perpetrators, they frame official remembrance in ways that illuminate
helpless suffering and criminal guilt, while relegating stories of complicity,
resistance, and refusal to the shadows. The distinction between victims and
perpetrators is fundamental to our sense of justice. Yet to limit our practices of
remembrance and remedy to these categories is to radically curtail our commitment to acknowledge and learn from past injustices.

PLAN OF THE BOOK

The second and third chapters of the book examine influential theoretical articulations of human rights legalism and restorative justice in historical context against the backdrop of events that have defined the contours
of contemporary theory and practice. Specifically, these chapters examine
how human rights legalism and restorative justice have functioned to depoliticize transitional justice in response to volatile conflict over the terms of
investigations.

Chapter 2 examines variation and change in legalistic approaches to transitional justice from Nuremberg to the present. The analysis builds on a
neglected distinction at the center of Shklar's seminal book, *Legalism*. Shklar
was deeply critical of what she viewed as academic, or ideological, legalism,
which advanced a messianic view that law could transcend and overcome
politics. However, Nuremberg represented to her an alternative approach to
legalism that was creative, flexible, and explicitly political. The chapter argues

[89] See William James Booth, "Communities of Memory: On Identity, Memory and Debt," *American Political Science Review* 93 (1999).
[90] John Torpey, "Introduction: Politics and the Past," in *Politics and the Past: On Repairing Historical Injustices*, ed. John Torpey (Lanham, MD: Rowman and Littlefield, 2003).

that the contemporary human rights movement has incorporated *both* forms of legalism, the creative and the messianic, yet the two are starkly at odds with one another. As a result, human rights legalism is increasingly cited as a basis for political intervention and change, yet also functions to obfuscate the politics driving systematic abuse and atrocity.

Chapter 3 examines how South Africa's restorative approach to justice took shape against the backdrop of the transitional period, from the negotiations to end apartheid through the writing of the TRC's final report. It argues that the TRC's restorative approach to justice was influenced by two distinctive challenges to human rights legalism. One challenge was articulated by human rights lawyers associated with the African National Congress (ANC), who rejected human rights legalism as an inadequate response to systemic injustices and saw the TRC as a potential basis for political judgment and ongoing reform. The TRC's theoretical framework was also informed by South African leaders from various "healing" professions, including religious leaders, medical doctors, psychologists, and therapists, who developed the case for an alternative approach to justice centered on "healing the wounds of the past." In the text of the *TRC Report*, this "healing" framework became a basis for depoliticizing the TRC's assessment of apartheid-era violence. This undermined the TRC's critical response to apartheid and has led proponents and critics alike to overlook the significance of South Africa's theoretical challenges to human rights legalism.

Together, these chapters demonstrate how the logic of depoliticization undermines the role of transitional justice as a response to systemic political violence. They demonstrate that this logic of depoliticization is not a *legacy* of, but rather a *departure* from the ideas that animated the Nuremberg Trials and the South African TRC. These chapters also locate an alternative theoretical tradition that has defended the role of political judgment in transitional justice and examines how such thinkers have faced persistent criticism from those that identify political judgment with resignation, moral compromise, or the uncritical adoption of community values.

Chapter 4 develops the argument that Hannah Arendt's writings on the theme of political judgment as "enlarged mentality" provide a way to move beyond this impasse. Although Arendt has influenced contemporary legalism and restorative justice, she was deeply critical of depoliticization in the human rights movement. The first section of the chapter examines this critique, which traces depoliticization to a pervasive sense of despair in the possibility of meaningful political engagement. The chapter then considers how Arendt's writings on political judgment address this problem. It examines two prominent ways of interpreting Arendt's theory of political judgment: one that identifies political judgment with action and deliberation, and another that identifies political judgment with critical distance and detached reflection. The chapter demonstrates how these distinct approaches illuminate claims regarding the role of political judgment that have been implicit, yet underdeveloped, in debates on transitional justice. It argues that the two are mutually reinforcing, but in tension with one another and that both are vital to the critical role of transitional justice. A concluding section develops this argument and its implications by reconsidering Aeschylus's *Oresteian Trilogy* as a drama of transitional justice.

Chapter 5 builds on this argument by developing a conceptual distinction between restorative justice and therapeutic justice as responses to political violence. In contrast with therapeutic justice, restorative justice requires political judgment and political responsibility for addressing the consequences of crime and violence. The problem is that restorative justice is based on the premise that community practices and values ought to guide the process of political judgment. Yet judging political violence requires a critical response to the ways that communities are implicated in, and constructed by, political violence. I locate three distinctive responses to this problem in the reflections of Desmond Tutu, Charles Villa-Vicencio, and Mahmood Mamdani, as they considered the limitations and disappointments associated with the TRC. Tutu and Villa-Vicencio offer distinctive theoretical approaches to restorative justice, yet both associate the framework with an approach to political judgment that is grounded in active persuasion, compromise, and transformative dialogue. In contrast, Mamdani argues that restorative justice requires a critical and historical approach to political judgment – one that exposes denial and examines the legacy of the past in the present. Building on the argument developed in Chapter 4, I suggest that restorative justice requires both forms of political judgment and consider how truth commissions might better mediate the tensions between them.

Chapter 6 considers how transitional justice institutions might move beyond the victim-perpetrator framework to investigate the theme of resistance. The chapter examines three ways of investigating resistance and the unique concerns that are raised by each approach. One possibility, which Arendt proposed in her analysis of the Eichmann trial, is to examine the failure to resist, or to refuse compliance with, systems and institutions that are responsible for committing atrocities. A second possibility, articulated by Kader Asmal, is that truth commissions could investigate and commemorate political resistance, rather than restricting their investigations to experiences of passive suffering and guilt. A third approach, found in the arguments presented by both Arendt and Asmal, is to investigate examples of what might be referred to as *privileged* resistance – acts of resistance by individuals who broke ranks with their own communities to protest atrocities that were committed in their name. Each of these approaches to examining resistance is revealing and unsettling in ways that are potentially at odds with the project of political reconciliation. Yet investigating resistance also illuminates possibilities for political community, agency, and solidarity that are obscured by the victim-perpetrator framework of contemporary transitional justice and human rights institutions. Returning to Primo Levi's essay, "The Gray Zone," I argue that transitional justice investigations might contribute to these goals by acknowledging the shades of gray that emerge in stories of resistance as well as the failure to resist systematic political violence and atrocity.

Chapter 7 concludes the volume by integrating the analysis and discussing its implications for recent debates on the dilemmas of judging systematic, politically authorized forms of violence.

2

Human Rights Legalism and the Legacy of Nuremberg

In the summer of 2001, Slobodan Milosevic was delivered to the International Criminal Tribunal for the Former Yugoslavia (ICTY) to face charges of crimes against humanity. The extradition of Milosevic to The Hague followed a dramatic series of events that had occurred that spring. The former president of Yugoslavia was arrested by Serb forces on charges of corruption and abuse of power in early April after a long series of negotiations at his home, where he had allegedly "waved a gun, threatened to kill himself, his wife and daughter, and showed evidence of violent mood swings."[1] Milosevic had resigned from office after a popular uprising the previous October but continued to live in the official presidential residence and to act as leader of the socialist party. He surrendered only after having been assured that he would get a fair trial and that his arrest was not a pretext for transfer to The Hague. A few months later, however, the Serbian government handed him over to the international tribunal.

Human rights advocates hailed the extradition of Milosevic as a "great triumph for the victims of war crimes in the former Yugoslavia" and as evidence that "no leader accused of crimes against humanity is beyond the reach of international justice."[2] The ICTY was the first international criminal tribunal to be established since the Nuremberg Trials and widely viewed as a model, or at least a major precedent, for the International Criminal Court. To many commentators and scholars observing the excitement generated by the ICTY in the 1990s, it appeared that the Cold War had merely been a long interruption of what would otherwise have been the natural progression

[1]   Steven Erlanger and Carlotta Gall, "The Milosevic Surrender: The Overview; Milosevic Arrest Came with Pledge for a Fair Trial." *The New York Times*, April 2, 2001.
[2]   Human Rights Watch, "Milosevic Arrest Breaks Ground in International Justice" (June 28, 2001).

of international law and institutions following the Second World War. A great deal of scholarship that emerged at this time characterized the court as emblematic of the contemporary legacy of Nuremberg.[3] The ICTY was associated with a lofty set of goals. It would not only serve as a major precedent in the development of international justice, according to proponents, but also further the process of postwar reconciliation. Indeed, the official website of the tribunal declared that the indictment of Milosevic, "paves the way for the reconciliation process within the war-torn societies of the former Yugoslavia."[4]

Milosevic insisted on representing himself and, aware that a timetable for completion was in place, he soon perfected the art of stalling. On some days, he would not attend, citing ill health. On other days, he would use the trial as a platform to opine on Serb nationalism. When I attended the trial in the summer of 2003, I was told that Judge May had taken charge of things by installing a button that would shut off Milosevic's microphone if the defendant engaged in acts of contempt. Given that he was representing himself, Milosevic was also allowed to cross-examine those who came to testify as victims of the atrocities he was accused of committing. Both Milosevic and Judge May were dead before the trial could be completed.

One day I spoke with a young man in the audience who was carefully observing the trial. It turned out that he had survived the Srebrenica massacres by serving as a translator for the Dutch peacekeepers and was now working as a journalist covering the trial. It angered him to see Milosevic questioning victims. He felt that the trial was strangely sanitized and had done little to address the problem of denial in the population. It also bothered him that lower-level perpetrators were still at large and that so many people refused to acknowledge the Srebrenica killings. Around the same time, a number of scholarly studies were published that would echo many of these concerns. Surveys would suggest that the ICTY had done little, if anything, to change people's perceptions of wartime atrocities.[5] One study argued that the ICTY had contributed to a nationalist backlash in Croatia

3   Belinda Cooper ed., *War Crimes: The Legacy of Nuremberg* (New York: TV Books, 1999); Thomas Buergenthal, "The Normative and Institutional Evolution of Human Rights," *Human Rights Quarterly* 19 (1999): 703–23.
4   International Criminal Tribunal for the former Yugoslavia, "Bringing Justice to the Former Yugoslavia: the Tribunal's Core Achievements." Available: http://www.un.org/icty/cases-e/factsheets/achieve-e.htm
5   Eric Stover and Harvey M. Weinstein, "Introduction: Conflict, Justice, and Reclamation," in *My Neighbor, My Enemy: Justice and Community in the Aftermath of Mass Atrocity*, ed. Eric Stover and Harvey M. Weinstein (New York: Cambridge University Press, 2004): 1–26.

that actually strengthened the political position of those implicated in committing atrocities.[6]

This chapter argues that the disappointments associated with the ICTY and other efforts to prosecute war crimes can be better understood by examining the limitations and contradictions of human rights legalism as a response to systematic political violence. It takes Judith Shklar's analysis of the Nuremberg Trials as a starting point for critically examining human rights legalism. Contemporary scholars generally follow Shklar in defining legalism as "the ethical attitude that holds moral conduct to be a matter of rule-following."[7] Recent scholarship in transitional justice also follows Shklar in identifying the Nuremberg Trials as a major exemplar of legalism. Yet although Shklar viewed Nuremberg as a "great legalistic act," she also observed that the trials triggered a moral crisis for those with a commitment to legalism.[8] The first section of the chapter takes a closer look at this apparent puzzle. It argues that Shklar presented two visions of legalism, which she took to have quite different moral and political implications. Nuremberg, in her view, exemplified the possibility of legalism as a creative response to the collapse of political authority, which was valuable when guided by good political judgment. Shklar contrasted this practical approach to legalism with what she characterized as the ideological legalism of academic legal scholarship, which, in her view, threatened to undermine the accomplishments of strategic legalism with a rigid and messianic conception of international law.

Building on this analytic distinction, the chapter examines the work of scholars and human rights advocates that have been influential in shaping the theoretical premises of human rights legalism in the decades following the Nuremberg Trials. The second section examines the legalism of Amnesty International, which pioneered human rights advocacy in the Cold War era. The following section examines the theoretical case for a "duty to prosecute," which was developed by prominent human rights lawyers in the aftermath of Argentina's aborted efforts to prosecute human rights abuses committed during the "dirty war." Next, I look at how human rights legalism was articulated as a basis for expanding international criminal justice and promoting national reconciliation in the post–Cold War era. In each case, I focus on the writings of scholars that have been particularly influential in shaping the theoretical premises guiding contemporary transitional justice advocacy and institutions.

[6] Victor Peskin and Mieczyslaw P. Boduszynski, "*International Justice and Domestic Politics: Post-Tudjman Croatia and the International Criminal Tribunal for the Former Yugoslavia*," *Europe-Asia Studies* 55, 7 (2003): 1117–42.
[7] Shklar, *Legalism*, 1.
[8] Shklar, *Legalism*, 155.

The chapter argues that contemporary human rights legalism is better under-stood as a departure from, rather than a continuation of, the legalism that ani-mated the Nuremberg Trials. The contemporary human rights movement utilizes legalism creatively, in the sense that Shklar understood Nuremberg to have been legalistic, as a policy designed to promote explicitly political goals, including democratic change and domestic reconciliation. However, the human rights movement has also imported ideas that Shklar associated with ideological legalism, including an ahistorical, apolitical conception of international law that rejects or disavows the role of political judgment. This has generated a conflict-ing set of aspirations for war crimes trials. Criminal prosecution has been cham-pioned as a strategy for judging and understanding systematic political violence. However, war crimes trials have also been promoted and designed as a basis for constructing community by obfuscating and avoiding the problem of "the gray zone" – widespread and varied forms of complicity in systematic political vio-lence. Human rights legalism has championed war crimes trials as a basis for transcending political conflict and rejected amnesty as an illegitimate form of compromise, but accepted compromise in other forms, such as the narrowing of investigative mandates. Although proponents of legalism may insist that there can be "no peace without justice," they have accepted an increasingly narrow and largely symbolic definition of what it means to "do justice" after atrocity.

THE CREATIVE LEGALISM OF NUREMBERG

The charter of International Military Tribunal was developed in a series of negotiations between representatives of the United States, Britain, France, and the Soviet Union, who ran the tribunal jointly. Officials from these countries arrived with very different agendas for the trials. One of the Soviet representa-tives, Andrei Vishinsky, had presided over Stalin's show trials, and another del-egate, I.T. Nitichencko, argued that the goal of a trial would not be to establish guilt but only to present evidence against the accused and deliver sentences.[9] The delegates also had to negotiate the legal structure of the tribunal, given the differences between the Anglo-American and the Continental legal systems.[10]

---

[9] Bass, *Stay the Hand of Vengeance*, 200.
[10] Telford Taylor, *The Anatomy of the Nuremberg Trials* (New York: Knopf, 1992), 64. In the adver-sarial Anglo-American system, evidence is presented in an open court by lawyers, whereas in the Continental, "inquisitorial" system, evidence is gathered by a magistrate and witnesses are usually questioned by judges rather than by opposing counsel. Telford Taylor characterizes the discrepancy between the two legal systems as the "most intractable problem" faced by the delegates in drafting the IMT Charter and reports that Nitichencko had to ask, "What is meant in English by 'cross examine'?"

The American delegates to Nuremberg were primarily concerned with prosecuting the Nazi regime for aggressive war.[11] Today, however, the trials are remembered for their contributions to the elaboration of human rights and humanitarian law. The International Military Tribunal at Nuremberg was the first to successfully prosecute leaders for "Crimes against Humanity" as a distinct type of war crime that encompassed abuses committed by leaders against their own citizens.[12] As a result, Nuremberg came to stand for the principle that a state's treatment of its own citizens should be seen as a matter for international oversight.[13] Codified in the aftermath of the trials, The Nuremberg Principles eliminated the "act of state" as a defense under international law, as well as the defense of "due obedience" for acts committed on orders from above. Nuremberg would also have a profound influence on how human rights organizations would come to understand what constitutes a just response to political violence and war crimes.[14]

At the time, the Nuremberg Trials were highly controversial. George Kennan, who crafted America's Cold War containment policy, rejected what he referred to as a "legalistic-moralistic approach to international problems" and advocated summary execution for Nazi leaders instead. Hans Morgenthau also favored summary execution.[15] The realist tradition in international relations has generally rejected the pursuit of international justice and characterized international legal institutions as mechanisms that merely reflect or manage the balance of power. From this perspective, the trials were simply "victor's justice."

The Nuremberg Trials were not only criticized by realists, but also by those who saw Nuremberg as a betrayal of *legalism*. The Nuremberg Trials punished Nazi officials for atrocities that had been legal at the time of their commission. Critics observed that this was a violation of *nullen crimen sine lege, nulla poena sine lege*, or "no crime without law, no punishment without law." This general principle is applied in different ways depending on the legal context, for example in the prohibition of *ex post facto* laws and in limitations on the use of analogy in interpreting criminal law.[16] H.L.A. Hart

---

[11] Bass, *Stay the Hand of Vengeance*, 173; Shklar, *Legalism*, 170.

[12] In 1915, the Allies formally accused the Ottoman empire of crimes against humanity following the Armenian genocide. However, this charge did not result in successful prosecutions. See Bass, *Stay the Hand of Vengeance*, 106–7.

[13] Teitel, "Nuremberg and Its Legacy," 44.

[14] Teitel, "Nuremberg and Its Legacy," 45.

[15] Bass, *Stay the Hand of Vengeance*, 10. For a critique of the realist assessment of the interwar period, see Cecelia Lynch, *Beyond Appeasement: Interpreting Interwar Peace Movements in World Politics* (Ithaca, NY: Cornell University Press, 1999).

[16] See Hans Kelsen, "Will the Judgment in the Nuremberg Trial Constitute a Precedent in International Law?" *The International Law Quarterly* 1, no. 4 (1947): 153–71.

addressed this theme in response to a 1949 case in which a German court convicted a woman for denouncing her husband to the Nazi authorities. Although her acts were legal at the time, the court argued that they violated the "sound conscience and sense of justice of human beings."[17] Hart rejected this logic and defended legal positivism, arguing that prior written laws, even if immoral, should be recognized until they are replaced.

This kind of argument exemplified what Shklar took to be the defining puzzle of legalism: *"legalism as an ideology is too inflexible to recognize the enormous potentialities of legalism as a creative policy."*[18] What does she mean by this? It turns out that Shklar has in mind not only two distinctive ways of applying legalism to political conflict, but also two quite different ways of understanding and defining legalism. The main difference between the two has to do with how they define the place of politics in the pursuit of justice.

The ideology of legalism, according to Shklar, is based on two central premises. The first is the view that justice is not simply one of many virtues, but rather the "pinnacle of goodness, the epitome of morality."[19] Justice is defined narrowly as fairness, impartiality, and "a disposition to give each man his due." Those committed to legalism may engage in bitter debates over the source and content of rules, but share a basic commitment to impartial rule-following. Shklar dismisses the debate between positivists, such as Hart, and natural law theorists, such as Lon Fuller, as merely a "family quarrel among legalists."[20] A second major premise of ideological legalism has been the view that "[l]aw aims at justice, while politics looks only to expediency. The former is neutral and objective, the latter the uncontrolled child of competing interests and ideologies."[21] This view is animated by the premise that law is distinct from, and superior to, politics as a mechanism for adjudicating conflict.

Shklar rejected the assertion that legalism was politically neutral and argued that the ideology of legalism could be associated with a distinctive set of political preferences and tendencies. Shklar saw legalism as an inherently conservative ideology, one that prefers order and stability to change. The "rule of law," she wrote, aims to promote the stability of expectations by relying on what "appears already to have been established and accepted."[22]

---

[17] H. L. A. Hart, "Positivism and the Separation of Law and Morals," *Harvard Law Review* 71, no. 4 (1958), 619.

[18] Shklar, *Legalism*, 112.

[19] Shklar, *Legalism*, 113.

[20] Shklar, *Legalism*, 106.

[21] Shklar, *Legalism*, 111.

[22] Shklar, *Legalism*, 10.

Formalism also tends to support an "inherent preference for authority."[23] Drawing on the work of Weber and Tocqueville on the "aristocratic habits" of legal culture, Shklar argued that the intrinsically conservative dimensions of legalistic ideology are reinforced by conservatism in legal culture.

It might seem strange that Shklar would identify legalism with conservative politics in a work that was published in 1964, an era that saw legal battles waged and won in the name of fundamental political and social change. Stuart Scheingold addresses the less obvious tensions between the legalistic and political dimensions of the American Civil Rights movement in his book, *The Politics of Rights*. In that context, Scheingold develops a discussion of how legal reasoning can reinforce conservative political tendencies. He observes that resistance to change is built into the legal process, because judges are under pressure to take precedent seriously and to make changes in the "halting kind of way that tends to mask change with the appearance of stability."[24] Scheingold also observes that the formalization of new rules can complicate debates on policy and political mobilization.[25] Judges are tied up in procedural absolutes and bound to enforce obligations with minimal attention to the consequences.[26] The logic they employ is in tension with even very basic strategies to advance political goals such as assessing and reassessing tactics or examining trade-offs among conflicting aspirations.

To the extent that legalism defines justice in relation to the impartial execution of existing laws, it provides no basis for questioning the morality of the law. "It cannot be repeated often enough," writes Shklar, "that procedurally 'correct' repression is perfectly compatible with legalism."[27] Justice Robert Jackson, chief prosecutor at Nuremberg, made a similar statement in a 1945 report, in which he warned that the "common sense of justice" should not be "obscured or complicated by sterile legalisms developed in the age of imperialism to make war respectable."[28] Legalism can mask state-sponsored abuse and repression by focusing critical attention on the adoption of laws and policies rather than practice.

---

[23] Shklar, *Legalism*, 17.

[24] Stuart Scheingold, *The Politics of Rights: Lawyers, Public Policy, and Political Change* (New Haven, CT: Yale University Press, 1974), 107

[25] Scheingold, *The Politics of Rights*, 110.

[26] Scheingold, *The Politics of Rights*, 111

[27] Shklar, *Legalism*, 17.

[28] Robert H. Jackson, "Report to the President from Justice Robert H. Jackson, Chief Counsel for the United States in the Prosecution of Axis War Criminals," *Department of State Bulletin* (June 10, 1945) 1071.

Shklar also saw legalism as antipolitical – a stance that should not be confused with politically neutral or objective. She observed that "politics" had become a dirty word, a "word of scorn" in the works of prominent legal scholars.[29] She thought that this hostility to politics was particularly prominent among scholars of international law. To the extent that proponents of legalism view politics with contempt, she argued, they will also tend to reject negotiation and persuasion as a basis for change. To the extent that such a posture undermines political change, the antipolitical strain of legalism would also have conservative implications. In her assessment of international legal scholarship, Shklar was particularly critical of what she saw as a growing faith in the power of international law to overcome political conflict altogether. "The idea that all international problems will dissolve with the establishment of an international court," wrote Shklar, "is an invitation to political indolence. It allows one to make no alterations in domestic political action and thought ... to try no new approaches and yet appear to be working for peace."[30]

This hostility to politics is reinforced by the epistemology of Western legalism, including "a preference for case by case treatment of all social issues, the structuring of all possible human relations into the form of claims and counterclaims."[31] The reliance on adversarial categories functions to reify and intensify conflict, while reinforcing the hostility to politics that Shklar associates with ideological legalism. It also means that legalism is limited as a framework for analyzing the causes of systematic atrocity and political violence. The court's narrow focus on establishing individual responsibility is in tension with the historian's effort to understand general patterns of social behavior.[32]

Legalism thus elevates the law and "rule of law" as the primary responses to conflict and injustice, yet provides no basis for understanding how laws become politically meaningful or legitimate. In the writings of the most influential legal scholars of her day, such as Roscoe Pound, Shklar discerned an underlying "faith in progress as a law of history,"[33] as well as the view that law has its own history that naturally evolves from a "primitive" state to maturity, without regard to social and political context.[34] Shklar viewed the embrace of legalism in the post–Second World War era as part of a larger process of

29 Shklar, *Legalism*, 122.
30 Shklar, *Legalism*, 134.
31 Shklar, *Legalism*, 10.
32 Shklar, *Legalism*, 196.
33 Shklar, *Legalism*, 139.
34 Shklar, *Legalism*, 138.

claiming a mythical, "self-congratulatory view of the Western past" in an era of decolonization – an effort to revise the history of the Western conquest by promoting "rule of law" as the defining contribution of the West.[35]

Although Shklar was deeply critical of ideological legalism, she did not reject legalism per se. Instead, she argued that legalism has "enormous creative potentialities" that can be particularly useful in the aftermath of systematic political violence, in the context of a political vacuum. Shklar thought legalism at Nuremberg was successful for three reasons. First, the Nuremberg Trial functioned politically as an alternative to vengeance: "It replaced private, uncontrolled vengeance with a measured process of fixing guilt in each case."[36] Mass acts of vengeful retribution were indeed common in a number of European countries following the end of the Second World War (though it is not clear that high-level trials helped dampen this trend).[37] Second, the trial "gave the elite a demonstration of the meaning and value of legalistic politics."[38] They did so through a process that was flawed, but one that still offered "a decent model of a trial."[39] Third, the trial rendered the history of the Nazi regime in a way that "the political elite could not shrug off," by offering a "great legalistic drama," that established evidence in painstaking detail.

What, then, distinguishes the "creative legalism" of Nuremberg from the manipulative legalism of a show trial, or from crude "victor's justice"? Shklar addresses this question in two ways. First, she proposes that law should not be thought of as a "discrete entity," but rather as "part of a social continuum."[40] Instead of thinking about legalism as either present or absent, then, we might think about legalism as a matter of degree.[41] Although the Nuremberg Trials were not in keeping with the requirements of legalistic ideology, they did contain a significant *degree* of legalism. Most notably, the trials adhered to basic standards of due process.[42] Each defendant was provided with a German defense lawyer. Although the trials had a political aim, the outcome of individual investigations was not determined in advance. Two of the defendants were acquitted altogether and several defendants were acquitted of at least some of the original charges against them. The acquittals demonstrated that the trials

[35] Shklar, *Legalism*, 22.
[36] Shklar, *Legalism*, 158.
[37] See Luc Huyse, "Justice in Transition: On the Choices Successor Elites Make in Dealing with the Past," *Law and Social Inquiry* 20, no. 1 (1995): 51–79.
[38] Shklar, *Legalism*, 169.
[39] Shklar, *Legalism*, 169.
[40] Shklar, *Legalism*, 3.
[41] Shklar, *Legalism*, 156.
[42] Shklar, *Legalism*, 168.

were not simply a spectacle with predetermined results, but rather involved what Otto Kirchheimer referred to as an "element of irreducible risk."[43]

Second, Shklar insists that promoting and evaluating strategic approaches to legalism means rejecting the traditional contempt for politics that has been associated with legalism and engaging in political judgment. The notorious "Vishinskyian" show trials did not result simply from the use of law for political ends, she argues, but rather from the use of the legal form to support totalitarian domination. Instead of asking whether or not law is political, Shklar proposes, we should ask, "what sort of politics can law maintain and reflect?"[44] She eschews the view, shared by legalists and realists alike, that good political judgment is devoid of moral content or intrinsically at odds with legal judgment. Instead, she evaluates political judgment at Nuremberg by analyzing the relationship between the political role of the court and its moral or legal claims. Her analysis of Nuremberg as a political judgment, then, focuses on the role of the court in persuading an audience to accept its findings and in establishing a historical judgment of the Nazi regime. This approach is evident in Shklar's response to the tu quoque charge that was leveled at the Nuremberg Tribunal. "If the trial is to be justified in terms of what it could contribute to German political behavior, not in terms of legal analogies," she reasons, "it is obvious that the Germans could learn nothing worthwhile from men who were superior to the Nazis only in having gotten away with it."[45] She addresses this concern by arguing that although the Allied forces committed their own massacres, they did not engage in genocide. From the standpoint of ideological legalism, the newly defined charge of "crimes against humanity" was one of the most problematic elements of the trial. Evaluating it from a strategic standpoint, Shklar argues that it was the most *legitimate* of the charges.

Shklar characterizes Nuremberg as a triumphant example of the power of creative legalism – an approach to legalism that is modified and guided by political judgment. However, her analysis is not a ringing endorsement of strategic legalism as a response to political violence and mass atrocity in all contexts. Perhaps the most important insights to be gleaned from her commentary concern the *limitations* of legalism. Nuremberg was politically effective, in her view, because of the strong legalistic tradition in Germany. In the absence of such a tradition, she suggests, legalism might prove to be ineffective or even counterproductive. Shklar observes that the adversarial

[43] Otto Kirchheimer, *Political Justice: The Use of Legal Procedure for Political Ends* (Princeton, NJ: Princeton University Press, 1961), 339.
[44] Shklar, *Legalism*, 144.
[45] Shklar, *Legalism*, 161.

structure of the criminal trial may facilitate a powerful and persuasive public drama. However, she warns that adversarial legalism can also reify or intensify lines of conflict, and so undermine constructive debate and mobilization. With its emphasis on rule-following and procedural impartiality, legalism also has built-in conservative tendencies that may be in tension with the goal of advancing political and social change. Like contemporary legalists, Shklar observes that the process of establishing individual guilt in a court may be an effective way to prevent people from "taking matters into their own hands" with reprisal killings. However, she also warns that this same emphasis on individual guilt may obfuscate systemic patterns of violence.

According to conventional wisdom, the human rights movement has built on the "legacy of Nuremberg," and contemporary war crimes tribunals are driven by the same idealism and legalism that is said to have animated the Nuremberg Trials. In the sections to follow, I complicate this view. Contemporary proponents of international criminal justice have adopted many elements of the strategic approach to legalism that Shklar saw on display at Nuremberg. In contrast with legalistic critics of the Nuremberg Trials, contemporary human rights organizations have endorsed legalism as a strategy for democratic change, and are willing to modify legalism in order to further desired political goals. In this sense, human rights legalism is not quite as idealistic as commentators have suggested. However, contemporary human rights legalism has *also* adopted basic premises that Shklar associated with legalistic ideology, including an ahistorical, apolitical conception of international law and, most notably, a tendency to reject or disavow the role of political judgment as a response to systematic violence and atrocities.

AMNESTY INTERNATIONAL AND HUMAN RIGHTS LEGALISM IN THE COLD WAR ERA

In the period following the Second World War, the human rights movement was associated with specific political goals and movements for radical social and political change. The major conventions collectively known as the "International Bill of Human Rights" are premised on the model of a liberal democratic (or social democratic) welfare state.[46] The development of human rights contributed to, and was furthered by, the struggle against colonialism.[47]

---

[46] Jack Donnelly, "Human Rights and Asian Values: A Defense of 'Western' Universalism," in *The East Asian Challenge for Human Rights*, ed. Joanne R. Bauer and Daniel A. Bell. (Cambridge: Cambridge University Press 1999), 68.

[47] Paul Gordon Lauren, *The Evolution of International Human Rights: Visions Seen* (Philadelphia: University of Pennsylvania Press, 1998), 204–40.

Even before the Universal Declaration of Human Rights was drafted in 1948, W.E.B. Du Bois had submitted a petition to the United Nations Commission on Human Rights on behalf of the National Association for the Advancement of Colored People, which hoped that the petition would inspire "submerged and underprivileged groups" around the world "to carry their cases directly to the world body in the hope of redress."[48]

As Cold War conflict intensified, the organizations that came to shape the identity of the human rights movement turned to legalism as a strategy for establishing moral authority and generating consensus in protesting specific forms of state-sponsored violence.[49] This strategy was developed by Amnesty International, which became the pioneering organization of the contemporary human rights movement. A British lawyer named Peter Benenson founded Amnesty International in 1961. Initially focused on the plight of "prisoners of conscience," Amnesty widened the scope of its activism over time to address a wide array of abuses covered by the major human rights covenants. Amnesty International was the first human rights organization to gain wide international recognition, and served as a training ground for human rights activists around the world.[50] It is still widely viewed as the most influential human rights organization.[51] The organization developed a strategy of amassing detailed information about abuses and the individuals who were targeted for abuse in a given country. The group would then seek to generate widespread attention to specific cases and urge its membership to petition their own governments to lobby for change.

In some respects, Amnesty's activism resembles the strategic approach to legalism that Shklar saw on display at Nuremberg. Amnesty International and other prominent organizations, such as Human Rights Watch, aim to exert pressure on state leaders by "naming and shaming" those responsible for violations of international human rights law. Amnesty pioneered the strategy of focusing on individual cases and victims as a way to dramatize the problem of human rights abuses and mobilize grassroots support for

---

[48] Lauren, *The Evolution of International Human Rights*, 227.
[49] Bronwyn Leebaw, "The Politics of Impartial Activism: Humanitarianism and Human Rights," *Perspectives on Politics Perspectives* 5, no. 2 (2007): 223–38.
[50] Margaret Keck and Kathryn Sikkink, *Activists Beyond Borders: Advocacy Networks in International Politics* (Ithaca, NY: Cornell University Press, 1998), 88
[51] Keck and Sikkink, *Activists Beyond Borders*; Ann Marie Clark, *Diplomacy of Conscience: Amnesty International and Changing Human Rights Norms* (Princeton, NJ and Oxford: Princeton University Press, 2001); James Ron, Howard Ramos, and Kathleen Rodgers, "Transnational Information Politics: NGO Human Rights Reporting 1986–2000," *International Studies Quarterly* 49 (2005): 557–87.

their campaigns. Amnesty International also used legalism strategically to generate consensus in an era of Cold War polarization, by framing confrontational and provocative human rights activism as politically impartial. The organization developed a set of rules designed to guarantee that its reporting would be characterized as the dispassionate and impartial analysis of legal experts. The "rule of threes," established that Amnesty would scrutinize cases from the "first," "second," and "third" worlds in order to demonstrate independence from Cold War politics. The organization also developed a rule that prevented members from working on behalf of fellow citizens, which was designed not only to protect members, but also to enhance their claim to legal impartiality.[52] These strategies have been a basis for Amnesty International and other human rights groups to establish their role as critical authorities in evaluating abuses of power, and to mobilize a common commitment to confronting such abuses among people with diverse values.

At the same time, Amnesty International and other human rights organizations that became prominent in the Cold War era, adopted certain assumptions associated with what Shklar referred to as "ideological legalism." Instead of evaluating the role of legalism as a strategy in relation to political goals, Amnesty would use evolving legal standards as the measure of political achievement. When human rights norms clash with traditions, practices, or political ideologies, these conflicts are reformulated in the texts of human rights reports as problems of enforcement of, and compliance with, the law. As legal enforcement and the expansion of legal norms became a central focus of the human rights movement, ideal conceptions of international justice were closely identified with procedural impartiality. Like Amnesty, many of the most prominent international human rights organizations, including Human Rights Watch, Physicians for Human Rights, Fédération Internationale des Ligues des Droits de l'Homme (FIDH), Global Rights, Rights International, and Human Rights First, have made the prosecution of human rights violations and the dissemination of human rights reports the major focus of their work. Although Amnesty International works to generate grassroots support, the "rule of threes" meant that the organization would cultivate professionals trained to develop expertise on far away peoples and places, while delegitimizing expertise gained through experience.[53] Amnesty and other prominent human rights organizations would focus narrowly on the kinds of abuses that

---

52 Clark, *Diplomacy of Conscience*, 13.
53 Stephen Hopgood, *Keepers of the Flame: Understanding Amnesty International* (Ithaca, NY and London: Cornell University Press, 2006).

were amenable to legal strategies – emphasizing violations of "physical integrity" over economic and social injustices. [54]

Stephen Hopgood's extended study of Amnesty International details ongoing conflict between members committed to the purity of the mandate ("keepers of the flame") and those who have pushed the organization toward a more political approach to human rights work ("reformers"). Although Hopgood does not address the theme of legalism in his study, the group that he refers to as "keepers of the flame" arguably seek to preserve elements of ideological legalism within the organization, including the emphasis on procedural impartiality, a commitment to articulating a clear distinction between politics and law, and a narrow focus on issues that are amenable to legal remedies. In contrast, the "reformers" call for an approach to human rights that would acknowledge the limits of legalism and develop more explicitly political strategies for addressing political violence, as well as racism, homophobia, sexual violence, and economic injustices. "Keepers of the flame" within Amnesty reject this turn because it moves the organization in a more explicitly political direction. As activists became involved in lobbying efforts to support human rights prosecutions and international criminal justice, they would further develop the case for strategic legalism, as well as the claims that Shklar associated with ideological legalism.

ARGENTINA'S TRANSITION AND THE "DUTY TO PROSECUTE"

Aryeh Neier has written that, "if a day were to be chosen to mark the beginning of the modern global struggle for accountability for crimes committed by states, it would be December 10, 1983."[55] This was the day that Raul Alfonsín was inaugurated as the first democratically elected president of Argentina after more than seven years of military dictatorship. Once Alfonsín was in office, Congress approved a package of bills that repealed the military amnesty, imposed penalties for the crime of torture, and ratified international instruments dealing with human rights. He began to work immediately on his campaign promise to prosecute leaders of the prior regime for human rights abuses. This would be the first major effort by a successor regime to prosecute human rights violations committed under a prior regime. Alfonsín also

---

[54] See for example, Kenneth Roth, "Defending Economic, Social and Cultural Rights: Practical Issues Faced by an International Human Rights Organization," *Human Rights Quarterly* 26, no. 1 (2004): 63–73.

[55] Aryeh Neier, *War Crimes: Brutality, Genocide, Terror, and the Struggle for Justice* (New York: Random House, 1998), 35.

created a truth commission, the Comisión Nacional Para la Desaparicion de Personas (CONADEP) to investigate past abuses.[56] This dramatic sequence of events would become a focal point for emerging debates on transitional and international justice.

Alfonsín had decided that the military courts could maintain preliminary jurisdiction, but if they did not complete trials within six months, the federal court of appeals could take over the cases.[57] When the military court failed to assume responsibility for the prosecutions, the Federal Court of Appeals of Buenos Aires assumed jurisdiction and conducted trials for members of the Juntas and of the Buenos Aires regional commanders. These highly publicized and dramatic trials generated demand on the part of human rights groups for more trials.[58] Organized groups including *Las Madres de la Plaza Mayo*, the *Centro de Estudios Legales y Sociales* (CELS) and *Asamblea Permanente de Derechos Humanos* flooded the courts with charges. Between February and August of 1984, nearly 2,000 were filed.[59]

A public opinion poll found that 92 percent of Argentines supported the junta trials while they were ongoing.[60] Nevertheless, the Alfonsín administration had an interest in finding a way to limit the scope of human rights prosecutions for two reasons. First, the administration was concerned with the question of how to balance the demand for extensive prosecutions against the threat that the military establishment could present. The situation in Argentina, where the military still retained a degree of power and political support, was very different from the context of the Nuremberg Trials, which occurred after an unconditional surrender and were implemented by occupying powers. Second, even aside from the potential for military backlash, it would have been impossible to prosecute everyone who could be declared guilty of human rights violations, given the extensive involvement in abuses throughout the military establishment.[61] Given that Argentina's judiciary was itself implicated in the abuses, such prosecutions would also have to be accompanied by significant judicial reform.

---

[56] Carlos S. Nino, "The Duty to Punish Past Abuses of Human Rights Put into Context: The Case of Argentina," *Yale Law Journal* 100 (1991): 2619–25.

[57] Nino, "The Duty to Punish," 2625.

[58] See David Pion-Berlin, *Through Corridors of Power: Institutions and Civil-Military Relations in Argentina* (University Park, PA: Pennsylvania State University Press, 1997), 89; Alison Brysk, *The Politics of Human Rights in Argentina: Protest, Change, and Democratization* (Palo Alto, CA: Stanford University Press, 1994), 89–105.

[59] Pion-Berlin, *Through Corridors of Power*, 89.

[60] Keck and Sikkink, *Activists Beyond Borders*, 109.

[61] Nino, "The Duty to Punish"; Jaime Malamud-Goti, "Transitional Governments in the Breach: Why Punish State Criminals?" *Human Rights Quarterly* 12 (1990): 1–16.

Alfonsín's strategy for limiting the scope of the human rights prosecutions was to recommend a "revocable" presumption that those who committed crimes under orders had mistakenly relied on the legitimacy of the orders received. However, Congress overrode these efforts, insisting that the principle would not apply in cases of "abhorrent or atrocious" acts. This left hundreds of additional officers open to prosecution.[62] As time passed, the military opposition to prosecution grew. The government responded to military unrest by enacting what is known as the "full stop law," which established a sixty-day limit for indicting men for involvement in human rights abuses. As the courts worked to process the 450 indictments that followed the deadline announcement, the military response became more threatening. Alfonsín subsequently proposed a law that would allow for the defense of "due obedience," which would mean that no officers beneath the rank of colonel would be criminally prosecuted.[63] With the passage of this law, Alfonsín's support declined dramatically and his own human rights group attacked him. When Alfonsín's successor, Carlos Menem, took office, he granted pardons to approximately 280 members of the security forces still awaiting trial, including senior generals and other high-ranking officials. Menem argued that prosecuting past abuses would undermine the goal of national reconciliation. "Argentina will not be possible," he said, "if we continue tearing open old wounds."[64] This set of events was at the center of debates that took place at a series of influential conferences held in the 1980s and early 1990s to explore the dilemmas of transitional justice in comparative context. [65]

Jaime Malamud-Goti, an advisor to Alfonsín, who supported the decision not to try lower-level officers, argued that the application of criminal justice in the context of political transition is "largely a matter of political judgment."[66] Carlos Nino, also an advisor to Alfonsín, observed that the operation of criminal law can do little to further the development of a just order if it is "not accompanied by a process of argumentation based on common ground."[67] He opposed Alfonsín's decision to narrow the scope of prosecution through the presumption of due obedience not because the decision compromised moral

[62] Nino, "The Duty to Punish," 2626.
[63] Nino, "The Duty to Punish," 2629; Malamud-Goti, "Transitional Governments in the Breach," 5.
[64] Roniger and Sznajder, "The Politics of Memory and Oblivion," (1998), *History and Memory* 10, no. 1 (1998):148.
[65] Paige Arthur, "How 'Transitions' Shaped Human Rights: A Conceptual History of Transitional Justice," *Human Rights Quarterly* 31, no. 2 (2009): 321–67.
[66] Malamud-Goti, "Transitional Governments in the Breach," 5.
[67] Nino, "The Duty to Punish," 2633.

or legal principles, but because he believed that such concessions would contribute to escalating demands on the part of the military.[68]

Chilean human rights activist, José Zalaquett, also defended the role
of political judgment in establishing just responses for political violence.
Zalaquett had been part of the Allende government before it was overthrown
in 1973. He had been arrested several times and eventually exiled during the
Pinochet era. During his exile, Zalaquett worked for Amnesty International
and would go on to serve as a member of Chile's Truth and Reconciliation
Commission.[69] He has been described as extraordinarily influential in the
human rights movement – an inspiration to his generation of activists.[70]
Zalaquett maintained that the lesson of Argentina is that the "Nuremberg
model" did not work, and was generally not adequate in a context where perpetrators continued to wield power.[71] Zalaquett developed this argument by
drawing on Weber's distinction between the "ethic of absolute ends" and the
"ethic of responsibility." Prosecution might support the abstract demands of
justice, he argued, yet it is not *responsible* where it will endanger the authority
and legitimacy of a democratizing government. Thus, Zalaquett rejected the
idea that decisions regarding the process of judging political violence could be
guided by formal legal criteria or evolving international standards, and argued
that each country would require a different approach.

Zalaquett's defense of an "ethic of responsibility" was not merely a rationale
for compromise. Instead, he championed truth commissions as an alternative
strategy for challenging denial and condemning political violence. Zalaquett
argued that truth commissions might actually be a superior mechanism for
persuading people to accept accountability for political violence and injustice and for shedding light on the historical causes and consequences of past
wrongs.[72] He also argued that truth commissions could provide a limited kind
of remedy to victims, to the extent that they established a basis for documenting and officially acknowledging their experiences of abuse.

Against this view, several other influential human rights lawyers, including
Juan Méndez, Aryeh Neier, and Diane Orentlicher, responded to the events
in Argentina by making the case for a formal "duty to prosecute" human rights
abuses committed under a prior regime. Orentlicher, who was then serving as
General Counsel for the International League of Human Rights, developed

---

[68] Owen Fiss, "The Death of a Public Intellectual," *The Yale Law Journal* 104, no. 5 (1995): 1187–200.

[69] Arthur, "How 'Transitions' Shaped Human Rights," 349.

[70] Keck and Sikkink, *Activists Beyond Borders*, 91.

[71] Zalaquett, "Balancing Ethical Imperatives and Political Constraints," 1425, 1428.

[72] Zalaquett, "Balancing Ethical Imperatives and Political Constraints," 1429–30.

this argument in an extraordinarily influential article.[73] The Argentine prosecutions would not have been so destabilizing, argued Orentlicher, had they
been more limited in scope. Citing the six-month deadline that Greece
imposed on transitional prosecutions as an example, Orentlicher proposed a
"bounded program of exemplary punishment."[74] Such a program would only
encompass "notorious crimes that were emblematic of past violations."[75] In
other words, the duty to prosecute should encompass primarily the "big fish"
and leave lower-level operatives alone. It might be easier to prosecute those
with less power and less visibility. As the U.S. public grappled with the torture
and humiliation committed at Abu Ghraib prison, the Bush administration
quickly adopted the position that the abuses were committed by a handful of
"bad apples" who did not represent the U.S. military in any significant way.
This is precisely what Orentlicher warned against in outlining her case for
exemplary prosecutions. At the same time, she argues that lower-level operatives should not be pardoned or excused on the grounds that they were "just
following orders."

In some respects, this approach to legalism is similar to the strategic legalism
that Shklar saw on display at Nuremberg. Like Shklar, Orentlicher claims that
legalistic policies can aid in consolidating democratic reform. Her "bounded
program" echoes Shklar's claim that legalism may be understood as a matter
of degree. Also like Shklar, Orentlicher's defense of legalism is premised on the
message that is conveyed by trials, along with the lessons that they might teach
about the history of atrocities. She argues that criminal punishment can prevent
future political repression by "laying bare the truth about violations of the past
and condemning them" by demonstrating that "no sector is above the law," and
by affirming "the supremacy of publicly accountable civilian institutions." [76]

However, Orentlicher's case for the "duty to prosecute" is closer to the
ideological legalism that was the target of Shklar's critique. Her primary goal
is to establish that positive international law has evolved to require an affir-
mative duty to prosecute especially "atrocious crimes." The idea that human
rights covenants had expanded the *basis* for prosecuting violations of human
rights had already been established.[77] However, these covenants had not
previously been recognized as establishing an *obligation* to do so. Orentlicher

---

[73] Diane Orentlicher, "Settling Accounts: The Duty to Prosecute Human Rights Violations of a
   Prior Regime." *Yale Law Review* 100 (1991): 2539–615.
[74] Orentlicher, "Settling Accounts," 2601.
[75] Orentlicher, "Settling Accounts," 2599.
[76] Orentlicher, "Settling Accounts," 2542, 2544.
[77] Orentlicher focuses on systematic patterns of torture, disappearance, and "extra-legal execution," as well as genocide.

painstakingly established the case for such an obligation by analyzing evolving doctrine and commentary since the Nuremberg Trials. This international "duty to prosecute" would override any domestic laws or amnesties that authorized or granted impunity for human rights abuses. This set of arguments had a significant impact on the development of international criminal justice norms and practices in the 1990s. In 1997, Louis Joinet submitted a report to the UN Commission on Human Rights, which outlined a set of principles to guide efforts to combat impunity. The Joinet Principles affirmed that victims of human rights violations have a "right to know," a "right to justice" (defined as prosecution), and a "right to reparations."[78]

Although Orentlicher recognized that international law ought to be applied in ways that are sensitive to political and historical context, her analysis suggested that the political causes of systematic atrocities are largely irrelevant. "Societies scourged by lawlessness need look no farther than their own pasts to discover the costs of impunity," she writes, "[t]heir history provides sobering cause to believe, with William Pitt, that tyranny begins where law ends."[79] Her support for symbolic prosecution as a response to political violence is reinforced, then, by an understanding of political violence as essentially caused by "lawlessness," rather than any specific political program or system. To the extent that Shklar thought Nuremberg illuminated history and challenged denial, this was because the trials shed light on how the political system operated. Shklar and Jackson both warned that the individual focus of trials could serve to detract from this goal. Orentlicher invoked Jackson's argument that those on the dock should serve as "living symbols." However, whereas Jackson saw individual defendants as symbols of the institutions and ideas that defined the Nazi regime, Orentlicher argued that the role of individual prosecutions is to insist on a clear hierarchical distinction between law and politics.[80] In her view, individual prosecutions do not symbolize the judgment of specific political movements or ideas, but rather the abstract principle that "no one is above the law." In contrast with Shklar's view that the effectiveness of the Nuremberg Trials was related to the legalistic history of German political culture, then, Orentlicher explicitly rejected Zalaquett's assertion that the role of legalistic strategies might vary in relation to political or cultural context. The "duty to prosecute" would only be effective, in her view, if imposed as a standard obligation under international law.

[78] U.N. Economic and Social Council. Commission on Human Rights, *The Administration of Justice and the Human Rights of Detainees: Question of the Impunity of Perpetrators of Human Rights Violations*, October 2, 1997 (E/CN.4/Sub.2/1997/20/Rev.1).
[79] Oretlicher, "Settling Accounts," 2542.
[80] Orentlicher, "Settling Accounts," 2550.

As articulated in Diane Orentlicher's defense of a "duty to prosecute," human rights legalism is intensely strategic, but also ideological. Human rights organizations have drawn on this set of arguments to move beyond "naming and shaming" as a strategy for exerting pressure on repressive leaders. At the same time, the "duty to prosecute" associates criminal prosecution with an ambitious set of political aspirations. The argument suggests that human rights prosecutions not only serve to alleviate human rights abuses, but also facilitate democratization following periods of authoritarian rule. Nevertheless, Orentlicher's case for a "duty to prosecute" rejects Zalaquett's claim that political judgment ought to guide or modify the role of legal responses to state-sponsored violence. The case for a "duty to prosecute" associates the pursuit of justice with the subordination of political conflict to legal adjudication, and dismisses political judgment as a form of resignation.

RECONCILING WITH THE LAW

International criminal law and institutions developed dramatically in the decade following the end of the Cold War. In 1993, the United Nations Security Council established the ICTY and shortly thereafter established a similar tribunal in response to the genocide in Rwanda (ICTR). These were the first international criminal tribunals since the Nuremberg Trials. In 1998, the Rome Treaty for the International Criminal Court was approved by the United Nations General Assembly. By 2002, the ICC statute had received the requisite number of ratifications to enter into force. The mandates of these institutions represent the incorporation of principles associated with human rights law, which deals with the relations between state and citizen, into the laws of war, which traditionally encompassed only the relations among states.[81] These institutions also expanded the scope of international criminal justice. The Nuremberg Tribunal had restricted the scope of its jurisdiction over "Crimes Against Humanity" by requiring a "nexus" to international conflict.

---

[81] The list of crimes against humanity that would be prosecuted at these tribunals expands the list at Nuremberg to include abuses covered under human rights law, such as torture and rape. U.N. Security Council, *Statute of the International Tribunal for the Prosecution of Persons Responsible for Serious Violations of International Humanitarian Law Committed in the Territory of the Former Yugoslavia Since 1991* (May 25, 1993), Article 5; Annex to S/Res/955; U.N. Security Council, *Statute of the International Criminal Tribunal for the Prosecution of Persons Responsible for Genocide and Other Serious Violations of International Humanitarian Law Committed in the Territory of Rwanda and Rwandan Citizens Responsible for Genocide and Other Such Violations Committed in the Territory of Neighboring States between January 1 1994 and December 31 1994*, November 8, 1994, Art. 3; *Rome Statute of the International Criminal Court* (U.N. Doc. A/CONF.183/9*), 1998, Art. 7.

The creation of the Rwandan tribunal established a precedent for prosecuting crimes against humanity that were not committed in the context of an international armed conflict.[82]

These developments were accompanied by significant shifts in the terms of debate on transitional justice. First, whereas transitional justice had previously been studied in comparative context, as a problem of dilemmas confronted by successor regimes, it was increasingly seen as a matter of international concern and a target for increased international involvement.[83] Second, "reconciliation" was no longer viewed as a code word for illegitimate compromise and denial, but instead came to signify the legitimate aspiration for enduring peace in the aftermath of divisive conflict and systematic violence. Following Zalaquett's lead, other high-profile leaders with moral authority – most notably Nelson Mandela – now embraced the term. Once primarily associated with the goal of advancing democratic reform, transitional justice was now increasingly viewed as a basis for advancing lasting political reconciliation and even conflict resolution.

In this context, a new variant of human rights legalism emerged. Proponents of the "duty to prosecute" had defended legalism as a basis for democratic change. They had acknowledged that prosecution might be destabilizing and offered strategies for minimizing instability while also justifying prosecution as a basis for long-term change. In contrast, ICTY and ICTR were justified on the grounds that international prosecution would facilitate national reconciliation. In a 1994 speech, Madeleine Albright went so far as to argue that the ICTY should be seen as *"essential to* – not an obstacle to – national reconciliation."[84]

Payam Akhavan, who served as the first legal advisor to the ICTY prosecutor, outlined a set of arguments that would become prominent in advocacy for international criminal tribunals. Akhavan builds on Albright's assertion that international criminal prosecution facilitates reconciliation by establishing a shared truth about the past. This does not mean that we should expect war crimes trials to establish exhaustive history lessons. Rather, Akhavan suggests that "through the exercise of prosecutorial discretion," international tribunals may use their limited resources for "constructing the optimal truth."[85] More specifically, the "optimal" truth that should be constructed, according

---

[82] Teitel refers to these developments as representing a "paradigm shift" in the international legal system ("Humanity's Law," 365).

[83] Roht Arriaza, "The New Landscape of Transitional Justice."

[84] Madeleine Albright, "Bosnia in Light of the Holocaust: War Crimes Tribunals," *State Department Dispatch*, April 18, 1994.

[85] Payam Akhavan, "Justice in the Hague, Peace in the Former Yugoslavia? A Commentary on the United Nations War Crimes Tribunal," *Human Rights Quarterly* 20, no. 4 (1998), 774.

to Akhavan, is that individuals, rather than groups, are responsible for atrocities. In the case of the former Yugoslavia, what is decisive in Akhavan's view
is that the killings were orchestrated by elites and were not, as some initially argued, the product of "primordial" resentments or "ancient hatreds."
Ahkavan takes instrumentalist accounts of ethnic violence from the social
sciences as a useful basis for developing a moral response to violence. The
general population is not, in his view, culpable for atrocities and might better
be understood as having been "swept up in the frenzy." Whether or not this
is morally or legally plausible, Akhavan views it as a politically useful "slice of
truth" that can be constructed in the context of international prosecutions,
one that can serve as the basis for national reconciliation.[86]

Whereas individual guilt at Nuremberg and Argentina was to represent the broader array of those who could not be prosecuted due to lack of
resources, the argument that individual guilt *generates* reconciliation rests on
the premise that the bulk of those who participated or were complicit with
the atrocities either are not responsible or should not be held responsible for
acts committed under the sway of elite manipulation. In making the case for
this approach to constructing shared truth, Akhavan cites Renan's famous
claim that "the essence of a nation is that all individuals share a great many
things in common and also that they have forgotten some things."[87] Implicit
in Akhavan's argument is the suggestion that legalism contributes to reconciliation, not by facilitating acknowledgment, but by fostering a kind of social
forgetting.[88]

Ahkavan suggests that if elites were successful in manipulating the masses
through propaganda, then the international criminal tribunal can undo this
manipulation by revealing how it functioned. "If ethnic hatred and violence is
the product of a campaign of indoctrination and misinformation," he argues,
"it is equally possible to engage in a campaign of truth and justice by which
the role of individual leaders in fomenting war is exposed."[89] In this manner,
Akhavan continues, "respect for humanitarian principles and peaceful multi-
ethnic coexistence can be internalized." As Akhavan observes, this logic was
prominent in official statements regarding the purpose of ICTY. The first

[86] Akhavan, "Justice in the Hague," 765.
[87] Akhavan, "Justice in the Hague," 774; Ernst Renan, "What Is a Nation?" trans. Martin Thom,
    in *Nation and Narration*, ed. Homi K. Bhabha (London: Routledge, 1990).
[88] As Laurel E. Fletcher and Harvey M. Weinstein put it, "to extent that the logic of "individual-
    izing guilt" is successful, it offers individuals "the opportunity to rationalize or deny their own
    responsibility for crimes committed in their name" ("Violence and Social Repair: Rethinking
    the Contribution of Justice to Reconciliation," *Human Rights Quarterly* 24, no. 3 [2002]: 573–
    639). See also, Drumbl, *Atrocity, Punishment, and International Law*, 147.
[89] Akhavan, "Justice in the Hague," 758.

President of the tribunal, Antonio Cassesse argued that, "if responsibility for the appalling crimes … is not attributed to individuals, then whole ethnic and religious groups will be held accountable for these crimes and branded as criminal."[90] Former director of Human Rights Watch, Areyh Neier similarly stated that "[b]y trying and punishing those directly responsible, the burden of blame would not be carried indiscriminately by members of an entire ethnic group. Culpability would not be passed down from generation to generation."[91]

Akhavan's case for establishing international criminal justice institutions as a basis for promoting national reconciliation is premised on a strategic modification of legalism whereby judges and prosecutors deliberately construct "truths" that are deemed politically useful. He argues that prosecutors ought to strategically select defendants in order to optimize the potential for reconciliation. Like Orentlicher, Akhavan favors prosecuting the "big fish" because he takes this to be the best way to establish a politically useful narrative regarding elite responsibility. However, Akhavan also acknowledges that international courts may not be able to secure the arrest of major leaders. For this reason, the ICTY began by prosecuting lower-level soldiers, Dusan Tadic and Drazen Erdemovic. Akhavan endorses this strategy as a way to protect the image of a "court in action."[92]

At the same time, Akhavan's case for international prosecution as a basis for national reconciliation incorporates the epistemological framework that Shklar identified among the academic legalists of her day, characterized by the tendency to view social and political phenomena through the lens of individual cases, and to analyze them in relation to legal priorities. Akhavan contends that war crimes prosecutions not only contribute to peace by individualizing guilt, but also by putting an end to "cultures of impunity."[93] This argument resonates with Orentlicher's analysis of impunity and the positions advanced by a number of influential human rights activists and scholars. In a discussion of violence in Haiti, for example, Kenneth Roth writes that "impunity emboldened reactionary forces to resume killing each time a

---

[90] Antonio Cassesse, "Is There a Need for International Criminal Justice?" Distinguished Lecture at the Summer Session of the Academy of European Law, European University Institute in Florence, July 7, 1997.

[91] Aryeh Neier, "Rethinking Truth, Justice and Guilt after Bosnia and Rwanda" in *Human Rights in Political Transitions: Gettysburg to Bosnia*, ed. Carla Hesse and Robert Post (New York: Zone Books, 1999), 45.

[92] Akhavan, "Justice in the Hague," 781.

[93] Payam Akhavan, "Justice and Reconciliation in the Great Lakes Region of Africa: The Contribution of the International Criminal Tribunal for Rwanda," *Duke Journal of Comparative and International Law* 7 (1997): 325–48.

supposedly reformist regime took power."[94] These claims regarding the "culture of impunity" suggest that although political violence might *initially* result from organized elite manipulation for instrumental reasons, it will persist in a more spontaneous manner in the absence of criminal prosecution. The idea that prosecution can contribute to deterrence by addressing the problem of impunity for state-sponsored violence makes sense intuitively. The argument becomes more problematic, however, when the focus on impunity per se supercedes attention to the political and social context in which atrocities occur.

Akhavan stresses that international criminal tribunals need not prosecute everyone involved in order to combat a culture of impunity. Rather, his argument suggests that the symbolic assertion of criminal accountability, through the prosecution of elites, is sufficient to address the "culture of impunity."[95] If atrocity is a product of lawlessness, then the answer is not negotiation, persuasion, or protest, but rather the symbolic assertion of law. To the extent that human rights legalism characterizes impunity as the fundamental cause of atrocity, regardless of context, this suggests that prosecution is the most important and urgent priority, regardless of factors that may circumscribe or undermine the effectiveness of criminal courts.

Akhavan's argument also incorporates the mistrust of politics and messianic view of international law that Shklar identified as hallmarks of ideological legalism.[96] He invokes Jackson's idea that individuals prosecuted for systematic atrocities will be "living symbols" of political ideas and institutions. However, in contrast with Jackson, Akhavan argues that courts should focus on individual cases and experiences as a way to avoid potentially controversial political judgments. For example, he argues that courts can transcend conflicting interpretations of the past by reinforcing the "elementary truths that snipers should not murder helpless civilians in cold blood … that the pain of a bereaved mother or an orphaned child transcends ethnic affiliation."[97] By shifting attention to these "elementary truths," Akhavan argues, international criminal courts may effectively challenge and even undo the manipulation associated with political violence, regardless of how defendants are viewed by the local population.

---

[94]   Kenneth Roth, "Human Rights in the Haitian Transition to Democracy," in *Human Rights in Political Transition from Gettysburg to Bosnia*, ed. Carla Hesse and Robert Post (New York: Zone, 1999), 126.

[95]   Akhavan, "Justice in the Hague."

[96]   See also Ruti Teitel, "Bringing the Messiah Through the Law," in *Human Rights in Political Transitions: Gettysburg to Bosnia*, ed. Carla Hesse and Robert Post (New York: Zone Books, 1999), 177–94.

[97]   Akhavan, "Justice in the Hague," 772.

The utopian rhetoric that characterized human rights legalism in the 1990s would eventually give way to a more modest and nuanced set of claims. One reason for this, as discussed in the introduction to this chapter, is the general recognition that international justice cannot transcend local conflict. ICTY, ICTR, and the ICC have all depended on the cooperation of local authorities, and where that cooperation is not forthcoming, the courts rely on pressure from the United States or Europe to secure compliance.[98] The ICTR has thus far refused to indict members of the Rwandan Patriotic Front, which was led by the current President Paul Kagame. The ICC became involved in talks with Acholi leaders who feared that indictments would derail peace talks. Local leaders have utilized the work of international courts as a means to their own political ends, which may have little to do with the pursuit of justice.[99] A new generation of "hybrid" ad hoc tribunals has been developed as a way of navigating the relationship between local politics and international standards.

Even scholars who once fiercely defended an international "duty to prosecute" have now qualified their positions. Diane Orentlicher has called for a greater appreciation of the contribution of nonjudicial mechanisms, especially truth commissions, in addressing political violence. As President of the International Center for Transitional Justice, Juan Méndez similarly argued that accountability for past abuses can only be realized over time, through a variety of mechanisms.[100] Orentlicher has also qualified her position on amnesties, arguing that although they are invalid under international law, victims ought to be able to "stay the hand of prosecution" if they believe that doing so is in their own best interests.[101]

In addressing the disappointments of international legal institutions, it will also be important to take a closer look at the limitations and contradictions of contemporary human rights legalism. Proponents of human rights legalism have insisted upon criminal prosecution as a basis for establishing accountability in the aftermath of state-sponsored violence and challenging various forms of denial. However, the legalistic focus on individual guilt has also been utilized strategically as a way foster reconciliation by encouraging people

---

[98] See Victor Peskin, *International Justice in Rwanda and the Former Yugoslavia: Virtual Justice and the Struggle for State Cooperation* (New York: Cambridge University Press, 2008).

[99] Jelena Subotic, *Hijacked Justice: Dealing with the Past in the Balkans* (Ithaca, NY: Cornell University Press, 2009).

[100] Juan Méndez, Presentation at the Second Public Hearing of the Office of the Prosecutor at the International Criminal Court, New York, October 19, 2006.

[101] Diane Orentlicher, "Settling Accounts Revisited: Reconciling Global Norms with Local Agency," *The International Journal of Transitional Justice* 1 (2007): 10–22.

to "forget" the problem of widespread complicity. International war crimes tribunals have been championed as a way to establish historical records of systematic violence, yet they have also been appealing as the basis for an epistemological framework designed to avoid the political and historical context of atrocities. Human rights legalism is premised on the view that a "duty to prosecute" overrides other political and moral considerations that arise in the context of political transitions, yet has promoted a narrow vision of justice that amounts to what is a largely symbolic assertion of law in response to only the most extreme forms of physical violence.

CONCLUSION

Contemporary advocacy on behalf of international criminal justice is widely viewed as an effort to build on the legacy of the Nuremberg Trials. In debates on transitional justice, human rights legalism has generally been portrayed as idealistic and uncompromising. To critics, proponents of legalism appear stubbornly averse to any form of pragmatism. Legalism has also been defended on the grounds that there can be no peace without justice, no reconciliation without a serious effort to confront denial. A closer look at approaches to human rights legalism that became influential in the aftermath of the Second World War reveals a more complicated picture.

I have argued that contemporary human rights legalism is better understood as a departure from Nuremberg. At Nuremberg, legalism was creatively and strategically modified in response to the challenge of judging Nazi war criminals. The tribunal established a basis for justice that was flawed, but still powerful, by utilizing legalism to temper the influence of political judgment without displacing it altogether. Like Nuremberg, contemporary human rights legalism is strategic, creative, and political. In contemporary debates on transitional justice, international criminal law has been championed as a strategy for achieving ambitious political goals, including democratization and political reconciliation in the aftermath of massive atrocities. Proponents of international criminal justice have looked for ways to modify and moderate legalism, so as to avoid interfering with these political aspirations. However, human rights legalism has also incorporated ideas that Shklar associated with ideological or academic legalism, including a tendency to analyze conflict in relation to individual cases, a tendency to denigrate political judgment, and an understanding of justice as defined by procedural impartiality.

Shklar's analysis of the Nuremberg Trials identifies some of the ways in which the assumptions associated with ideological legalism serve to undermine the aspirations of strategic legalism. To the extent that legalism denigrates political judgment, it is at odds with the goal of utilizing legalism to judge politically authorized violence and to advance an ongoing process of political change. To the extent that legalism analyzes political violence through the lens of individual cases, it is limited as a basis for evaluating the systemic causes and consequences of state-sponsored violence. Shklar was particularly concerned with the myth that law is distinct from, and superior to, politics. She viewed this as doubly obfuscating in the sense that it blurs both the political foundations and the moral limitations of law.

Shklar, Zalaquett, and Nino all took issue with the basic assumptions animating what Shklar referred to as "academic" legalism, but they did not reject legalism altogether. Instead, each of these thinkers argued that as a response to systematic atrocities and political violence, legalism is informed by political judgment. For such scholars, political judgment could not be reduced to mere capitulation and did not signify the abandonment of justice. Rather, it meant recognizing that the process of defining just responses to systematic political violence is inherently political. This challenge to ideological legalism was limited in two important ways. First, although they rejected the narrow view that would equate political judgment with mere compromise or resignation, these thinkers did not address the question of what ought to guide political judgment in a context characterized by seemingly intractable divisions and pervasive despair in the possibility of meaningful political engagement. Second, Shklar, Nino, and Zalaquett all challenged the legalistic tendency to equate justice with impartial rule-following, but they also accepted the basic premise that just responses to mass atrocity ideally take the form of the criminal trial. South Africa's Truth and Reconciliation Commission would challenge this idea and articulate an alternative way to conceptualize justice in the aftermath of political violence.

3

A Different Kind of Justice: South Africa's Alternative to Legalism

Eugene de Kock was known as "Prime Evil" for the deeds he had committed as commander of Vlakplaas, an infamous South African counterinsurgency unit. As an assassin for the apartheid state, de Kock had orchestrated a series of brutal murders and cross-border raids. In 1997, de Kock appeared before South Africa's Truth and Reconciliation Commission to give testimony concerning his role in the assassination of three black policemen. He explained how he had arranged to have explosives planted in the car that was taken by the policemen to pursue a false mission that he had devised for them. The three widows of his victims sat in the audience as de Kock relayed, in intimate detail, the steps that he had taken to organize the murder of their husbands. After the hearing, de Kock surprised TRC officials by requesting a meeting with the widows, stating that he wished to apologize to them privately. Recalling the incident, truth commissioner Pumla Godobo-Madikizela writes that she was not sure how the widows would respond to the request, or how such a meeting would proceed. "Would the widows be willing to see de Kock?" she wondered, "What would he say? 'I'm sorry I killed your husbands?'"[1] Two of the women, Pearl Faku and Doreen Mgoduka, agreed to the meeting with de Kock. According to Godobo-Madikizela, they were both deeply moved by the apology. "I would like to hold him by the hand," said Mrs. Faku in her debriefing with Godobo-Madikizela, "and show him that there is a future, and that he can still change."[2]

On display in de Kock's appearance before the TRC was nearly everything that observers found most promising and most problematic about the idea of restorative justice. Godobo-Madikizela saw de Kock's encounters with the

---

[1]   Pumla Godobo-Madikizela, *A Human Being Died That Night: A South African Story of Forgiveness* (Boston and New York: Houghton Mifflin Company, 2003), 14.

[2]   Godobo-Madikizela, *A Human Being Died That Night*, 15.

widows as evidence of the possibility that even the most brutal and calculating murderers can change when given the chance to atone for what they have done. She also saw the opportunity to forgive as potentially (though not invariably) empowering for victims. De Kock's testimony implicated a number of his colleagues and superiors, leading many of them to come forward with confessions in exchange for amnesty. Thus, it was cited as evidence that the process had contributed to a greater understanding of, and accountability for, apartheid-era violence. Others saw de Kock's confession as a cynical maneuver and were unconvinced by his expressions of remorse.[3] For critics of the TRC, de Kock's story represented the way that the process had shifted attention away from the systemic injustices and institutionalized racism of apartheid to focus on a small number of individuals who had committed the most extreme brutalities. This perspective reinforced the view that South Africa's appeal to restorative justice was merely a way to legitimate transitional compromises with a compromised version of history.[4]

What proponents and critics of the TRC have in common is a tendency to identify South Africa's restorative approach to justice with the kinds of individual encounters that Godobo-Madikizela describes in her report on de Kock, and with a therapeutic notion of truth as a basis for "healing past wounds." This assessment radically oversimplifies the debate on restorative justice in South Africa and overlooks the theoretical critique of legalism that animated the development of South Africa's TRC.

This chapter examines how the TRC's theoretical framework took shape over the course of the transition.[5] It argues that South Africa's restorative approach to transitional justice was informed by two distinctive critical responses to human rights legalism. In the early stages of developing the TRC, human rights lawyers associated with the African National Congress articulated a multipronged critique of human rights legalism that centered on the limitations of legalism as a response to racism and economic injustices. The first section of the chapter examines this argument and how it developed against the backdrop of the negotiations to end apartheid. In this context, ANC lawyers argued that advancing political reconciliation and justice after apartheid would require political judgment and ongoing political reform. They

---

3 For analysis of the South African media's response to the de Kock hearings, see Leigh Payne, *Settling Accounts: Neither Truth nor Reconciliation in Confessions of State Violence* (Durham, NC and London: Duke University Press, 2008), 251–78.

4 Wilson, *The Politics of Truth and Reconciliation in South Africa*.

5 This chapter builds on and develops ideas presented in Bronwyn Leebaw, "Legitimation or Judgment? South Africa's Restorative Approach to Transitional Justice," *Polity* 34, no. 1 (2003): 23–51.

envisioned the TRC as a basis for furthering these goals through investigations that would expose the injustices of apartheid and its legacy, while also promoting ongoing dialogue across political and social divides.

The TRC's restorative approach was also profoundly influenced by South African leaders from various "healing" professions, including religious leaders, as well as medical doctors, psychologists, and therapists, who participated in a series of conferences designed to develop the theoretical framework of the TRC. The second section of the chapter examines how such participants developed South Africa's TRC as an alternative to legalism that would "heal the wounds of the past" and argues that the idea of a "healing truth" functioned to elide ongoing conflict over the extent to which the TRC would address the systemic injustices of apartheid.

In the text of the *TRC Report*, restorative justice became the basis for depoliticizing the work of the TRC. The third section of the chapter examines this development, focusing on how it informed the dominant analysis presented in the *TRC Report*. In this context, restorative justice was invoked as a basis for transcending political conflict over the process of judging the past. However, the effort to depoliticize the TRC's investigations functioned to legitimate transitional compromises and a process that would largely avoid, rather than examine, the historical and political context of apartheid.

THE CASE FOR POLITICAL JUDGMENT

South Africa's TRC was formally established by the Promotion of National Unity and Reconciliation Act of 1995 (TRC Act). Its basic mandate was to "provide for the investigation and establishment of as complete a picture as possible of the nature, causes, and extent of gross violations of human rights" committed in the country between 1960 and 1994.[6] A Committee on Amnesty would grant amnesties on an individual basis to those who made "full disclosure of all the relevant facts relating to acts associated with a political objective" committed during the time frame covered by the commission. A Committee on Human Rights Violations was established to give victims "an opportunity to relate the violations they suffered," and a Committee on Reparation and Rehabilitation was given the task of making recommendations aimed at preventing human rights violations in the future. "Gross violations of human rights," were defined as the violation of human rights through the "killing, abduction, torture, or severe ill-treatment" of any person, or "any attempt,

---

[6] No. 34 of 1995: Promotion of National Unity and Reconciliation Act, 1995 (July 26, 1995).

conspiracy, incitement, instigation, command or procurement to commit" such an act.

The provisions of the TRC Act were informed by a series of compromises that occurred during the negotiations to end apartheid. In 1990, President F.W. de Klerk announced the "unbanning" of the ANC, the South African Communist Party (SACP), and the Pan African Congress (PAC). Negotiations soon intensified, and the fate of exiles and political prisoners became a pressing problem. The process of releasing prisoners began in 1990 in accordance with the "Norgaard principles" that had been developed for use in the UN settlement of the Namibian conflict.[7] The Norgaard principles became the basis for the TRC's "political objective" requirement for amnesty. They provided amnesty for those charged with political crimes and specified terms for evaluating the relationship between the political objective and action taken.[8]

Meanwhile, the South African security forces began to pressure de Klerk to provide unconditional amnesty. After the first round of multiparty negotiations (CODESA) broke down, Joe Slovo, Secretary General of the South African Communist Party, whose wife, Ruth First, had been assassinated by state officials, articulated support for an "amnesty in which those seeking to benefit will disclose in full those activities for which they require an amnesty," as a compromise in exchange for democratic change.[9] Other key figures, including Boutros Boutros Ghali and Archbishop Desmond Tutu, echoed his support for this selective form of amnesty.[10] The National Party continued to lobby for an unconditional amnesty. The NP eventually agreed to the requirement of "full disclosure" in exchange for amnesty, only on the condition that it would also apply to members of the liberation movements.[11] Amnesty provisions were formalized in the 1993 Interim Constitution that called for the people of South Africa to "transcend the divisions and strife of the past" and stated that "there is a need for understanding but not for vengeance, a need for reparation but not for retaliation, a need for *ubuntu*, but not for victimization."[12] *Ubuntu* is derived from the bantu word, *umuntu*,

7   On the history of the amnesty provisions, see Erik Doxtader, "Easy to Forget or Never (Again) Hard to Remember? History, Memory, and the 'Publicity' of Amnesty," in *The Provocations of Amnesty: Memory, Justice, and Impunity*, ed. Charles Villa-Vicencio and Erik Doxtader (Trenton, NJ: Africa World Press, 2003), 121–55.

8   Truth and Reconciliation Commission of South Africa, *TRC Report* vol. 1, 51.

9   Joe Slovo, "Negotiations: What Room for Compromise?" *African Communist* (1992): 36–40.

10 Lynn Berat and Yossi Shain, "Retribution or Truth-Telling in South Africa?: Legacies of the Transitional Phase," *Law and Social Inquiry* 20 (1995): 177.

11 George Bizos, interview by author, Johannesburg, March 30, 1999.

12 Interim Constitution of South Africa Act (no. 200 of 1993).

meaning, "the person." It is sometimes referred to as "humaneness," or "the art of being human."[13]

During this period, a group of lawyers, mostly associated with the ANC, articulated a theoretical critique of legalism that informed the development of the TRC. Kader Asmal is widely credited with developing the official ANC position on transitional justice during the negotiations period.[14] Asmal described himself as someone who had once campaigned vigorously for a "South African equivalent of the Nuremberg Trials," but was transformed by the experience of the negotiated transition.[15] Albie Sachs was deeply influential in developing the initial framework of the TRC. Sachs had been placed in solitary confinement under the apartheid regime for his work with the liberation movement, and later went into exile in Mozambique. In 1988, he lost an arm to a car bomb placed by South African security agents. He would go on to become a member of South Africa's Constitutional Court (the equivalent of the U.S. Supreme Court). George Bizos, who had served as a lawyer for Nelson Mandela, helped draft the amnesty provisions and presented them before parliament. Johnny De Lange and Willie Hofmyer became ANC representatives on the Justice Portfolio Committee in parliament, which drafted the TRC legislation.

These were individuals who had a deep respect for human rights and international law and had been engaged in utilizing legal strategies as part of the struggle against apartheid. Sachs and Asmal had also produced significant scholarly work on these themes. It was this very familiarity with the relationship between law and politics that informed their skepticism regarding the claims made by proponents of human rights legalism. The multipronged critique of legalism that they developed would have an important influence on the TRC's theoretical claims. ANC lawyers did not articulate a theoretical defense of political judgment. However, they concurred with Shklar and Zalaquett in arguing that the practice of transitional justice ought to be responsive to local political contexts and ought to encompass explicitly political as well as moral goals. They also went further than Shklar and Zalaquett in rejecting the legalistic view that criminal prosecution represents the ideal form of justice.

According to Bizos, doubts regarding the value of the "Nuremberg model" for the South African transition were voiced as early as 1988 among ANC

---

[13] Tutu, *No Future without Forgiveness.*

[14] Alex Boraine, *A Country Unmasked: Inside South Africa's Truth and Reconciliation Commission* (Oxford: Oxford University Press, 2000), 12.

[15] Kader Asmal, Louise Asmal, and Ronald Suresh Roberts, *Reconciliation through Truth: A Reckoning of Apartheid's Criminal Governance* (Cape Town: David Philip Publishers, 1996), 3.

leadership.[16] To some extent, these doubts echoed those expressed by leaders in Latin America. South African leaders feared that the country lacked the institutional and social foundations to support a program of retroactive prosecution. Given the scale of the violence, the refusal of the majority of the whites to recognize apartheid as an unjust system, and the fragility of the new regime, transitional criminal prosecutions would be socially divisive and potentially destabilizing.[17] As Asmal observed, international law is built on the practice of states and not on "narrow legalisms," adding that "[n]o rule of international law requires the pursuit of perpetrators regardless of the risk of reducing the body politic to ashes."[18] South African leaders followed Zalaquett and Nino in rejecting the human rights argument for a "duty to prosecute" under international law.

Like Shklar, ANC lawyers argued that human rights legalism had conservative political implications that would undermine the pursuit of political and social change in the aftermath of apartheid's profound injustices. This argument was informed by their experience with the legalization of apartheid following the 1948 electoral victory of the Nationalists.[19] State partition was a major declared aim of the apartheid government, and a series of legislative acts legalized the removal of political and economic power from the black population. The apartheid government also developed a program to resettle black people from the white areas of the country to these rural homelands, namely those considered "surplus" to the needs of the white farming community. Forced removals resulted in a large number of deaths, perhaps numbering in the millions.[20] Group Areas Acts created racially homogeneous and physically separated white urban areas with peri-urban townships for African, Indian, and "colored" population groups. The "influx control" program, designed to meet the need for cheap labor, while keeping blacks from residing in white urban centers, prohibited blacks from being present in South African cities for more than seventy-two hours and strictly enforced "pass laws" to ensure compliance.[21]

Human rights lawyers sometimes achieved small victories in the apartheid-era court system, but the judiciary was generally dedicated to upholding the

[16] George Bizos, *No One to Blame? In Pursuit of Justice in South Africa* (Claremont: David Phillip, 1998), 229–30.

[17] "They said, just use a criminal justice model. This would put us at each other's throats forever" (Johnny De Lange, interview, Cape Town, March 4, 1999).

[18] Asmal et al., *Reconciliation through Truth*, 20.

[19] Robert Price, *The Apartheid State in Crisis: Political Transformation in South Africa 1975–1990* (New York: Oxford University Press, 1991), 13.

[20] Chapman and Ball, "Levels of Truth," 149.

[21] Price, *The Apartheid State in Crisis*, 20.

system of apartheid. In this context, the apartheid regime "fetishized and brandished legality as a tool of domination and control."[22] In townships and rural areas, various forms of informal justice were relied on as alternatives to the state system, and in the 1980s, informal "people's courts" became an explicitly political and oppositional form of justice.[23] Against this backdrop, ANC lawyers tended to view the ostensible impartiality of formal legality as generally biased in favor of the powerful. In a 1999 interview, Willie Hofmyer stressed that he had rarely seen a successful criminal prosecution and observed that victims were often disoriented in the courtroom, which made it easier for skilled defense lawyers to manipulate their testimony.[24] Bizos made similar comments regarding his own experience as a lawyer.[25] Asmal rejected the very idea that a "bright line" could divide law and politics as a "reactionary falsehood."[26]

Shklar argued that Nuremberg's greatest contribution was in the historical records established through the trials, yet she also observed that individual trials are limited as a basis for examining the causes and consequences of systematic political violence. Kader Asmal took this argument further, questioning the success of Nuremberg as a vehicle for confronting the Nazi past. Ordinary Germans "remained wholly outside the Nuremberg process," he wrote, "they could too easily escape self-probing by simply parroting the world's demonization of the few in the dock."[27] Asmal, along with coauthors Louise Asmal and Ronald Suresh Roberts, criticized the Nuremberg trials for downplaying Nazi atrocities against the Jews, which did not fit easily into existing categories of international law. Nuremberg, he argued, had placed history on "the altar of prosecutorial expediency."[28] ANC leaders also argued that criminal investigations can obfuscate the problem of complicity in systematic crimes because such investigations are narrowly focused on establishing individual guilt. Moreover, the rigorous burden of proof in a judicial proceeding may mean that many leaders who are responsible for past abuses

---

[22] Mahmood Mamdani, "Amnesty or Impunity? A Preliminary Critique of the Report of the Truth and Reconciliation Commission of South Africa (TRC)," *Diacritics* 32, no. 3–4 (2002): 33–58.

[23] Wilfried Scharf and Baba Ngcokoto, "Images of Punishment in the People's Courts of Cape Town 1985–1987: From Prefigurative Justice to Populist Violence," in *Political Violence and the Struggle in South Africa*, ed. N. Chubani Manganyi and Andre du Toit, 341–71 (London: McMillan, 1990); John Hund and Malebo Kotu-Rammopo, "Justice in a South African Township: The Sociology of *Makglotla*," *The Comparative and International Law Journal of South Africa* 16 (1983): 179–209.

[24] Interview by author, Cape Town, March 6, 1999.

[25] Interview by author, Johannesburg, March 30, 1999.

[26] Asmal et al., *Reconciliation through Truth?* 21.

[27] Asmal et al., *Reconciliation through Truth?* 19.

[28] Asmal et al., *Reconciliation through Truth?* 19.

are deemed "not guilty." This problem is exacerbated where investigations are in the hands of an unreformed judiciary. The narrow scope of judicial fact finding is compounded by the high costs of trials, which limit the number that can be held.

The trial of Magnus Malan exemplified this set of problems for many in South Africa. Malan refused to apply for amnesty from the TRC and was charged with killing thirteen family members of an ANC operative as part of a conspiracy to foment a civil war between the ANC and the Inkhata Freedom Party. The charge also alleged that Malan had been involved in sponsoring a covert unit to launch attacks on the ANC. Despite the efforts of a specialized investigative unit, consisting of more than thirty detectives and six civilian analysts, Malan was eventually found "not guilty." Because Malan had been a state employee, it fell to the new state to bear the financial burden of his legal defense, which eventually exceeded 12 million Rand.[29]

ANC lawyers also argued that criminal proceedings undermine the goal of understanding systematic political violence by radically circumscribing the voice of victims. "Court records," writes Sachs, "are notoriously arid as sources of information. Outside of the microscopic events under inquiry, you learn very little."[30] Criminal trials are not only limited as a basis for understanding the causes of systemic violence, but also largely exclude consideration of the *consequences* of crime.

In Shklar's view, legalism was bound up in an evolutionary mythology of "the West," characterized by the notion that the identity of Western nations centered on a tradition of "rule of law." She argued further that legalism would be far less effective where it was not integrated into the political and cultural identity of a country or people. In the context of the 1994 transition, South African leaders incorporated a vast array of human rights provisions into their constitution and committed to investigating past human rights violations. However, they also argued that South Africa should strive to integrate evolving standards of international human rights law with local traditions, practices, and philosophies of justice. Reflecting on their role in reconstructing the judicial system of Mozambique, Albie Sachs and his coauthor, Gita Welch, insisted that "Western" law and "customary" law need not represent stark dichotomous choices.[31] In his opinion for *S. v. Makwanyane and Another*,

---

[29] *TRC Report* vol. 1, 123.

[30] Albie Sachs, "Fourth DT Lakdawala Memorial Lecture" (presented at the Institute of Social Sciences Nehru Memorial Museum and Library Auditorium, New Delhi, India, December 18, 1998).

[31] Albie Sachs and Gita Welch, *Liberating the Law: Creating Popular Justice in Mozambique* (London: Zed Books, 1990), 124.

a landmark Constitutional Court case that invalidated the death penalty, Sachs wrote that although the Court could not provide redress for the injustices of the past, it could, "restore dignity to ideas and values that have long been suppressed or marginalized."[32] Sachs added that in so doing, the Court should strive to integrate "regard to public international and foreign case law" with "all the dimensions of the evolution of South African law, including traditional African jurisprudence."

In *S. v. Makwanyane and Another* (1995), the South African Constitutional Court invoked the constitutional principle of *ubuntu* in holding the death penalty unconstitutional. Judge Madala argued that *ubuntu* entails recognizing the humanity of the perpetrator of even the most heinous offenses. The judges interpreted *ubuntu* as connoting values of community, interdependence, reciprocity, and, in the words of Judge Madala, a "balancing of the interests of society against those of the individual."[33] It was this aspect of *ubuntu* that was invoked in *Azanian Peoples Organization (AZAPO) and Others v. President of the Republic of South Africa and Others* (1996); the Court used the principle of *ubuntu* to uphold the state's right to grant amnesty, as against the constitutional right to have complaints settled by a court of law.[34] It is important to note that this use of *ubuntu* did not represent a return to traditional African approaches to justice, but rather a creative appropriation of *ubuntu* to navigate competing political and moral claims in the context of the transition.[35]

ANC lawyers also questioned the legalistic tendency to define justice as individual criminal prosecution. First, they observed that criminal prosecution is not designed to provide redress to victims of crime. Some have argued that victims may experience a sense of "closure" or relief through the process of official retribution. However, this has not been a primary rationale for punishment, and efforts to promote this goal through prosecution are generally in tension with the basic due process provisions championed by legalists. This critique of prosecution has also been a central component of restorative justice theory. For ANC lawyers, this limitation was particularly problematic in the use of legalism as a response to the economic injustices and racial inequalities that were the legacies of apartheid. As Johnny De Lange put it, "it would be

---

[32] Constitutional Court of South Africa, *S. v. Makwanyane and Another* (6) BCLR 665 (1995), paragraph 365

[33] Constitutional Court of South Africa, *S. v. Makwanyane and Another* (6) BCLR 665 (1995), paragraph 751.

[34] Constitutional Court of South Africa, *Azanian Peoples Organization (AZAPO) and Others v. President of the Republic of South Africa* (8) BCLR 1015 (1998).

[35] See Wilson, *The Politics of Truth and Reconciliation in South Africa*, 11.

essential to broaden our perception of justice beyond punishment ... We had to look at the fate of victims and the whole political and social framework."[36] Instead of conceptualizing transitional justice as the criminal prosecution of a handful of leaders, they argued for a wider vision of justice that would encompass the ongoing pursuit of political and social change.

Although the category "gross violations of human rights" would later be interpreted narrowly as encompassing only acts that were illegal under apartheid, Asmal maintained that by including "severe ill-treatment" in the definition of "gross violations," the *TRC Act* provided grounds to investigate more routine dimensions of life under apartheid, such as forced removals and other abuses that were lawful under apartheid.[37] He also argued that the mandate to investigate the "causes, nature, and extent" of human rights violations would place "crucial questions of moral and political responsibility on the agenda of the Truth and Reconciliation Commission."[38] Essential in addressing such questions would be an effort to examine "the more diffuse patterns of conduct and of expectation, the innumerable forms of subtle and explicit homage that apartheid's privileged paid to the system."[39]

In making the case for a truth commission that would investigate systematic injustices, ANC lawyers were influenced by the impact of a commission of inquiry led by Justice Richard Goldstone (Commission of Inquiry regarding the Prevention of Public Violence and Intimidation) from 1992 through 1995. Goldstone's reports, which were initially cautious, grew increasingly critical of the government. By 1994, the Goldstone Commission confirmed the involvement of senior South African police officers in a network of criminal activity and established a *prima facie* case that a "third force" was operating within the military-security establishment to try to destabilize South Africa by fomenting paramilitary violence in order to halt the transition to democracy. The political impact of the Goldstone Commission demonstrated the potential of independent commissions of inquiry as a basis for challenging denial. The ANC lawyers were also influenced by their experience with truth commissions that the ANC had developed to examine its own internal abuses.[40]

[36] Johnny de Lange, "The Historical Context, Legal Origins, and Philosophical Foundation of the South African Truth and Reconciliation Commission," in *Looking Back, Reaching Forward: Reflections on the Truth and Reconciliation Commission of South Africa*, ed. Charles Villa-Vicencio and Wilhelm Verwoerd, 2–13 (Cape Town: University of Cape Town Press, 2000), 24.

[37] Kader Asmal, "Truth, Reconciliation, and Justice: The South African Experience in Perspective," *The Modern Law Review* 63, no. 1 (2000): 1–24.

[38] Asmal et al., *Reconciliation through Truth?* 25.

[39] Asmal et al., *Reconciliation through Truth?* 145.

[40] Hayner, *Unspeakable Truths*, 60.

The idea that the TRC would be responsible for making political judgments was not seen as inconsistent with its mandate to scrutinize the actions of the ANC and other liberation movements.

The TRC would improve on this kind of commission by examining the *consequences* of apartheid through the accumulation of testimony from victims. The TRC would not be an "austere institution making highly formalized findings," as Sachs put it, but rather an "intensely human and personalized body ... there to hear what people had been through."[41] By providing space for victims to explain their stories in their own words, the TRC would contribute to transforming *knowledge* or basic awareness of the details of past violence into *acknowledgment* of its emotional and social significance.[42] At the same time, the TRC would provide a basis for reparations to those identified as victims through the process.

In its early stages of development, the TRC was conceptually linked to a redistributive economic program, known as the Reconstruction and Development Program (this program was ultimately abandoned, and the country adopted a more neoliberal economic program, known as GEAR). It was hoped that by investigating the underlying causes and consequences of apartheid-era violence, the TRC would generate a sense of political responsibility for longer-term social and political change. Thus, the ANC lawyers did not envision the TRC simply as a basis for *ratifying* the compromises of the transition, but also as a way to expose the limitations of provisional compromises in order to pursue an ongoing process of change. Although they made the case for political compromise as a basis for reconciliation, they did not equate the two. Asmal defined reconciliation as a process of "facing ... unwelcome truths in order to harmonise incommensurable world views so that inevitable and continuing conflicts and differences stand within a single universe of comprehensibility." He argued further that this would require "moral and political restitution."[43]

Despite the Orwellian sound of the title, "truth commission," ANC lawyers characterized the work of the TRC as a process of ongoing political persuasion and dialogue. Asmal maintained that commentary on general complicity in apartheid-era injustices should be anecdotal and suggestive rather than exhaustive. He added that such commentary should not demonize those who were supporters of apartheid, but rather aim to "coax them towards us through

---

[41] Sachs, "Fourth DT Lakdawala Lecture."

[42] Albie Sachs, "His Name Was Henry," in *After the TRC: Reflections on Truth and Reconciliation in South Africa*, ed. Wilmot James and Linda Van De Vijver (Claremont: David Philip Publishers, 2000), 97.

[43] Asmal et al., *Reconciliation through Truth?* 46

public acknowledgement of what they have rigorously overlooked.'[44] In making the case for a TRC that would engage in explicit political judgment, Asmal also acknowledged that a truth commission should not seek to resolve all conflicts over how to interpret past violence, but should rather strive to place them "within a single universe of comprehensibility."[45] Albie Sachs similarly argued that in contrast with a legalistic approach to fact finding, a truth commission could usefully confront the history of apartheid-era violence in a way that would encourage, rather than resolve, political debate. Sachs claimed that the strength of South Africa's TRC was precisely that it was not "a case of people coming in as prosecutors and saying: we stand for the state, we are going to examine and get the truth out of you," but rather "based essentially on dialogue, on hearing all the different viewpoints" as part of a process of understanding divisions of the past.[46]

The critique of legalism that was articulated by ANC lawyers during the context of the negotiations would influence the development of South Africa's restorative justice framework in important ways. ANC lawyers did not have a uniform perspective on the TRC. For example, Asmal would go on to challenge the TRC's narrow investigative framework, whereas Sachs would vigorously defend it. However, they offered a common critique of human rights legalism. They argued that the truth commission would not simply be a lesser alternative to prosecution, but a basis for establishing justice in a broader sense than that implied by criminal trials. They called for an approach that would foster dialogue and reconciliation, and one that would shift from individual punishment to a broader conception of repair. These thinkers, particularly Kader Asmal, characterized political judgment as intrinsic to the role of the TRC's critical response to apartheid. Most importantly, they argued that the TRC could improve upon criminal trials by investigating, judging, and remembering apartheid as a political system, rather than limiting the scope of analysis to individual guilt.

HEALING PAST WOUNDS

ANC lawyers had envisioned the TRC as a basis for judging the apartheid system as well as human rights abuses committed by liberation groups. However, representatives of the National Party and the Democratic Party contested plans to condemn the prior political order and fought for a more

---

[44] Asmal et al., *Reconciliation through Truth?* 211.
[45] Asmal et al., *Reconciliation through Truth?* 46.
[46] Sachs, "Fourth DT Lakdawala Lecture."

narrowly defined investigation. During the 1995 parliamentary debates, the National Party, which had designed and presided over institutionalized apartheid, condemned the TRC as a "witch hunt." Danie Schutte, representing the National Party, stated in parliament that, "[i]f there is any suggestion that a distinction is to be made between persons who fought for or against the previous government, it can only be perceived as being discriminatory."[47] Democratic Party representative Dene Smuts voiced her fear that the TRC would produce a revisionist official history, based on "moral relativism."[48] General Constand Viljoen suggested that the TRC should analyze "the fight against Communist expansionism" in assessing the philosophy of apartheid.[49]

When Minister of Justice Dullah Omar introduced the TRC legislation to parliament in May 1995, he acknowledged the priorities of the ANC (his own party) by recalling that apartheid had been recognized as a crime against humanity, and that South Africa had obligations to those who demanded that justice be done. He then acknowledged the fears of those affiliated with the former state, reaffirming that the TRC would follow the constitutional principles that called for "understanding, but not for vengeance … for reparation but not for retaliation."[50] Weighing these competing political concerns, Omar stated that the goal of the commission would be to "heal the wounds of the past."

The idea that the TRC would "heal past wounds" was developed as members of what might be referred to as "healing professions" became involved with the truth commission. Shortly after South Africa's political transition, the Institute for the Study of Democratic Alternatives in South Africa (IDASA) sponsored two conferences, respectively entitled, "Dealing with the Past," and "Truth and Reconciliation," which provided a forum for an emerging network of human rights advocates and leaders involved in transitional justice to discuss the theoretical framework of South Africa's TRC.[51] Those present at the IDASA conferences included Juan Méndez, Aryeh Neier, and José Zalaquett, as well as leaders and scholars from Eastern Europe, such as Joachim Gauck and Adam Michnik. South African representatives to the conference not only

---

47 Hansards, Parliamentary Debate, May 17, 1995, 1375.
48 Hansards, Parliamentary Debate, May 17, 1995, 1386.
49 Brian Stuart, "Truth Probe 'Could Name Ministers'" *Citizen*, February 25, 1995.
50 Hansards, Parliamentary Debate, May 17, 1995, 1342.
51 The papers presented at these conferences were published in two volumes: Alex Boraine, Janet Levy, and Ronel Scheffer, eds., *Dealing with the Past* (Cape Town: IDASA, 1994), and Alex Boraine and Janet Levy, eds., *The Healing of a Nation?* (Cape Town: Justice in Transition, 1995).

included legal scholars, such as Asmal and Sachs, but also religious leaders.[52] Alex Boraine had been the President of the Methodist Church of Southern Africa before founding IDASA. When truth commissioners were selected the following year, the group of seventeen not only included a number of lawyers, but also two reverends, Khoza Mgojo and Bongani Finca, as well as Archbishop Desmond Tutu, who was selected to chair the truth commission. In addition, the group included two medical doctors, Fazel Randera and Wendy Orr, and a psychiatric nurse, Glenda Wildschut. Alex Boraine was selected as the Deputy Chair of the Commission.

The idea that the TRC would "heal past wounds" became the basis for the claim that it was a form of restorative justice. This idea did not reflect a singular vision, but provided a framework that would be interpreted in radically different ways by the conflicting parties. It was also informed by three ways of conceptualizing "healing" with distinctive implications for the future of the truth commission: psychological healing, physical healing, and redemptive healing.

Psychological Healing

Reflecting on his work as a truth commissioner in Chile, José Zalaquett described witnessing the "cathartic power" of truth-seeking. He observed that many families seemed to find psychological relief in the process. At the second IDASA conference, Zalaquett suggested that by taking testimony, investigating, and acknowledging past abuses, truth commissions might help address the trauma suffered by victims and survivors.[53] Zalaquett's presentation had a powerful impact on South Africans present at the conference.[54] South African leaders would develop his ideas further in articulating a therapeutic role for truth commissions.

This broad assertion that truth commissions advance a psychological healing process has been associated with at least four separate claims. First, truth commissions aspire to provide *information* to those who have suffered from past abuse and may be searching for some kind of explanation or evidence that

---

[52] Boraine, A *Country Unmasked*, 17.

[53] Alex Boraine and Janet Levy, eds. *The Healing of a Nation?* (Cape Town: Justice in Transition, 1995), 49–55.

[54] Of Zalaquett's speech on the Chilean experience with a Truth and Reconciliation Commission, Antjie Krog wrote, "[i]t takes Chilean philosopher and activist José Zalaquett … precisely seven and a half minutes to convert me to the idea," *Country of My Skull*, 23. Boraine also describes Zalaquett's contribution as extremely influential (A *Country Unmasked*, 43). See also, Amy Ross, "The Politics of Truth in Transition: Latin American Influences on the South African Truth and Reconciliation Commission," *Politique Africaine* 92 (2003): 18–38.

will establish once and for all what happened. This aspiration has emerged in response to the unique agony confronted by those whose loved ones have been "disappeared." Without decisive evidence regarding the fate of the disappeared, survivors may be tormented by the thought that there might still be something that can be done to rescue their loved ones and find it impossible to move forward with their lives. It is hoped that by uncovering information on individual cases, truth commissions will help such individuals attain some kind of closure.[55]

Second, it is hoped that by allowing victims the chance to give *testimony*, to have their stories heard and acknowledged by a sympathetic audience, truth commissions may foster a cathartic healing process. Thomas Buergenthal, who served as commissioner for the United Nations Truth Commission for El Salvador, observed that many of the people who came to the Commission reported that they had never previously spoken of the abuses that they had suffered during the war. "One could not listen to them," Buergenthal recalled, "without recognizing that the mere act of telling what had happened was a healing emotional release, and that they were more interested in recounting their story and being heard than in retribution."[56] Others suggest that witnessing perpetrator confessions and having the opportunity to forgive perpetrators may facilitate psychological healing in victims of violence.[57]

This set of claims was challenged from early on by South African psychologists and therapists involved in the process, as well as scholarly commentators.[58] Observing that the therapeutic process is predicated on the availability of long-term care and support, many questioned the idea that a single appearance before a truth commission would be therapeutic for participants. Critics also warned that testifying before a truth commission could "re-traumatize" participants.[59] Others questioned the assumption that victims would benefit from the discovery of new information about their losses. "I never really

---

[55] Zalaquett, "Balancing Ethical Imperatives and Political Constraints," 1433; Alex Boraine, "Truth and Reconciliation in South Africa: The Third Way," in *Truth v. Justice: The Morality of Truth Commissions*, ed. Amy Gutmann and Dennis Thompson (Princeton, NJ: Princeton University Press), 154.

[56] Quoted in Martha Minow, *Between Vengeance and Forgiveness: Facing History after Genocide and Mass Violence* (Boston: Beacon Press, 1998), 68.

[57] Godobo-Madikizela, *A Human Being Died That Night*, 86, 95.

[58] Minow, *Between Vengeance and Forgiveness*, 73. For a more recent evaluation of the psychological impact of truth commissions, see David Mendeloff, "Trauma and Vengeance: Assessing the Psychological and Emotional Effects of Post-Conflict Justice" *Human Rights Quarterly* 31, no. 3 (2009): 592–623.

[59] See for example, Trudy de Ridder, "The Trauma of Testifying," *Track Two: Constructive Approaches to Community and Political Conflict* 6, no. 3–4 (1997); Minow, *Between Vengeance and Forgiveness*, 73.

wanted to find out who sent or planted the bomb," said Marius Schoon, who lost his wife and young daughter to a letter bomb that was sent to his home in exile.[60] When the TRC identified the man responsible for the bomb, Schoon said that all he had gained was a more specific target for his anger. "Now it's personal," he said, "There's a good chance that I might actually shoot him." Ultimately, however, the TRC was not very effective in providing individual victims with new information.[61]

Third, truth commissions aim to provide opportunities to understand and address underlying psychological *motivations* of those who participate in violence and abuse. The South African TRC argued further that the process of confession would be cathartic for perpetrators, providing an opportunity to "obtain relief from the burden of guilt or an anxiety that they might have been living with for years."[62] Finally, it is often implied that truth commissions will have a cathartic impact on the *audience* that witnesses the spectacle of violence, pain, and remorse that truth commissions place on display.[63]

The idea that truth commissions address political violence by furthering a kind of large-scale therapeutic process became popular at a time when the idea of "therapeutic justice" was assuming a prominent role in international organizations. This is not to be confused with the movement for "therapeutic jurisprudence" among some legal scholars in the United States, which seeks to provide psychological counseling to defendants as part of the criminal justice process. Rather, "international therapeutic justice" has been characterized as a broad paradigm that recasts injustice as psychological injury and exclusion by emphasizing individual frustration and aggression over broader social and material concerns.[64] Vanessa Pupavac has traced the rise of therapeutic justice from the emergence of social psychology in the interwar years to more recent tendency to characterize post–Cold War era conflicts as "cycles of trauma."[65]

South African leaders developed this set of ideas to articulate how truth commissions, in contrast with trials, might address the needs of victims and

[60] Quoted in Hayner, *Unspeakable Truths*, 142.
[61] Timothy Sizwe Phakathi and Hugo Van der Merwe, "The Impact of the TRC's Amnesty Process on Survivors of Human Rights Violations," in *Truth and Reconciliation in South Africa: Did the TRC Deliver?*, 132–4; Chapman and Van der Merwe, *Truth and Reconciliation in South Africa: Did the TRC Deliver?*, 250–1.
[62] *TRC Report* vol. 1, 130.
[63] Teresa Godwin Phelps, *Shattered Voices: Language, Violence, and the Work of Truth Commissions* (Philadelphia: University of Pennsylvania Press, 2004).
[64] Vanessa Pupavac, "International Therapeutic Peace and Justice in Bosnia," *Social and Legal Studies* 3, no. 3 (2004), 379.
[65] See also, John Torpey, "Politics and the Past," in *Politics and the Past*, ed. John Torpey (New York: Rowman & Littlefield, 2003); Minow, *Between Vengeance and Forgiveness*, 22.

contribute to the reintegration of perpetrators. The idea of justice as therapy had important political implications. It suggested that the goal of the TRC would be to advance adaptation and closure. Thus, it was at odds with the aspiration of the ANC lawyers to utilize the truth commission as a basis for an ongoing process of remembrance and change. Moreover, as discussed below, the focus on therapeutic justice would lead the TRC to locate the causes of conflict in the idea of a dysfunctional culture or society, shifting attention away from the political and social dimensions of apartheid-era violence.[66]

Physical Healing

South African leaders also likened the TRC investigations to a process of "cleansing" unhealed bodily wounds. For example, Mamphele Rampele, a medical doctor, anthropologist, and long-time liberation struggle activist, gave a speech at one IDASA conference that compared the violent legacy of South Africa's past to "an abscess," which "cannot heal properly unless it is thoroughly incised and cleaned out."[67] In this view, the short-term "pain" of the investigation process would be unpleasant, but necessary as a basis for a long-term "healing" process. Boraine echoes this sentiment in his reflections on the TRC's victim hearings. He quotes an opinion piece by Phylicia Oppelt, who stated bluntly that the TRC "with its quest for truth, has not healed my wounds. It has opened ones I never knew I had."[68] In response, Boraine suggests that the purpose of the TRC was not to "perpetuate the myth of the so-called rainbow nation where everyone claims to love one another," but rather "to reveal the serious divide that does exist" on the grounds that "the acknowledgment of this divide is the first step towards bridging it."

In making this claim, Boraine argued that the long-term process of reconciliation in South Africa would have to entail a commitment to alleviate the racialized economic inequalities that are the legacy of apartheid. In this view, South Africa's healing model would build upon Asmal's conception of reconciliation as a process of "confronting unwelcome truths" in order to identify and narrow sources of division. In these comments, the analogy to "cleansing" is invoked to justify a broad response to the systemic abuses of apartheid. In contrast with assertions regarding psychological healing, these comments invoke the analogy to healing as part of a direct rebuke to those who sought

---

[66] Pupavac, "International Therapeutic Peace and Justice."
[67] Boraine, *The Healing a Nation?* 34.
[68] Boraine, *A Country Unmasked*, 343.

to narrow the scope of the TRC's investigations. The rhetorical function of the analogy is to make the case for challenging denial regarding the injustices of apartheid even if such a process is divisive and destabilizing. Importantly, in this formulation, the "truth" telling process is not actually responsible for healing. Rather, it is characterized as a necessary and unpleasant *preliminary* to any process of justice or reconciliation.

Yet likening the TRC to a process of "cleansing wounds" was open to a very different interpretation that would become prominent in the text of the *TRC Report*. The analogy implied that all South Africans should be understood as victims. It also implied that the main focus of the TRC should be on physical wounds rather than economic injustices and racism. This logic was in direct conflict with the goal of analyzing the systematic exploitation and exclusion of the majority to the benefit of the white minority.

Redemptive Healing

In 1985, South Africa's Institute for Contextual Theology published a document, known as the *Kairos Document*, which challenged dominant theological conceptions of reconciliation.[69] Contextual Theology was inspired by the teachings of the Second Vatican and had been influenced by Black Theology. The declared methodology of Contextual Theology was to begin with experience rather than doctrine and "do theology from within the context of real life in the world."[70] *Kairos* reprimanded South African theologians for invoking reconciliation in such a way as to quell the demand for social and political change. This, according to *Kairos*, was a "false reconciliation." Reconciliation would only be meaningful and "genuine" when accompanied by justice. Importantly, the document specified that justice, in South Africa, could not be reduced to individual guilt, but would instead require a radical change in social structure. Thus, *Kairos* called for social analysis and the development of political strategy to supplant the uncritical application of abstract theological principles. Charles Villa-Vicencio, who directed the writing of the *TRC Report*, was an original signatory of the *Kairos* document.[71] Frank Chikane, who was present at the conferences that contributed to the theoretical framing

---

[69] *The Kairos Document: Challenge to the Church: A Theological Comment on the Political Crisis in South Africa* (Grand Rapids, MI: Eerdemans, 1985).

[70] Tristan Anne Borer, *Challenging the State: Churches as Political Actors in South Africa 1980–1994* (Notre Dame, IN: University of Notre Dame Press, 1998), 100.

[71] Charles Villa-Vicencio discusses *kairos* and his approach to contextual theology in his book, *A Theology of Reconstruction: Nation-Building and Human Rights* (New York: Cambridge University Press, 1992), 281.

of the TRC legislation, and Bongani Finca, who served as a TRC commissioner, were also original signatories.[72]

The idea of redemptive healing put forth by religious leaders associated with the TRC seems to depart from the *Kairos* commitment to radical social change. Tutu, Boraine, and Godobo-Madikizela characterized the TRC's contribution to healing as a process of confession, atonement, and forgiveness. Theology reminded me," writes Tutu, "that however diabolical the act, it did not turn the perpetrator into a demon ... Theology told us they were children of God with the capacity to repent, to be able to change."[73] In Tutu's view, this Christian ideal of redemption was also supported by the concept of *ubuntu*. "In the spirit of *ubuntu*," he writes, "the central concern is the healing of breaches ... a seeking to rehabilitate both the victim and the perpetrator." I examine Tutu's theory of *ubuntu* in greater detail in Chapter 5. Tutu took this argument a step further by basing the possibility of redemption not only in the capacity for repentance and transformation, but also on the idea that those who commit injustices are also victims of those same injustices. In Tutu's view, "[e]ven the supporters of apartheid were victims of the vicious system which they implemented."[74] A truth commission could aid in healing perpetrators, then, by providing them with the opportunity and the space to repent, atone, and make restitution for their acts.

Godobo-Madikizela and Boraine drew upon Hannah Arendt's *The Human Condition* in making the case for the political relevance of forgiveness.[75] Arendt argues that vengeance will inevitably fail to put an end to the consequences of action and instead binds people to an endless process of action and reaction. In contrast, forgiveness "does not merely re-act, but acts anew" and therefore frees "both the one who forgives and the one who is forgiven from the consequences of action."[76] However, Arendt writes that forgiveness is only possible with regard to "trespasses." Godobo-Madikizela rejected this qualification and argued that forgiveness should be understood as a particularly important political response to massive atrocities and "gross evil."[77]

---

[72] However, Desmond Tutu did not sign the document. Borer, *Challenging the State*, 121.

[73] Tutu, *No Future without Forgiveness*, 83.

[74] Tutu, *No Future without Forgiveness*, 103.

[75] Boraine, *A Country Unmasked*, 440–1; Godobo-Madikizela, *A Human Being Died that Night*, 124–6.

[76] Hannah Arendt, *The Human Condition* (Chicago and London: University of Chicago Press, 1958), 240–1.

[77] Godobo-Madikizela, *A Human Being Died that Night*, 124. Godobo-Madikizela expands this argument in her essay, "Radical Forgiveness: Transforming Traumatic Memory beyond Hannah Arendt," in *Justice and Reconciliation in Post-Apartheid South Africa*, ed. Francois du Bois and Antjie du Bois-Pedain (Cambridge: Cambridge University Press, 2008).

These arguments could be interpreted as implying a move away from the vision of reconciliation associated with the *Kairos* document, as well as the goals that the ANC lawyers had associated with the TRC. Tutu called for unconditional forgiveness, regardless of whether or not an apology had been granted. The TRC did not require perpetrators to apologize or express remorse for their deeds in exchange for amnesty. Indeed, many of those who appeared before the TRC to confess to wrongdoing gave testimony that rationalized and justified their actions. This made logical sense, given that in order to secure amnesty, applicants had to establish a convincing political objective for their actions.

However, Tutu and Boraine explicitly rejected this interpretation of the TRC's role. Although Tutu did make the case for unconditional forgiveness, he rejected unconditional reconciliation. Tutu, Boraine, and Godobo-Madikizela all specified that reconciliation would require acknowledgment and remorse in the form of political responsibility and commitment to political change. Godobo-Madikizela wrote that the "healing of victims – will come about only if the issues of economic justice and the myriad problems that post-apartheid South Africa faces are addressed."[78] Both Tutu and Boraine expressed the hope that if the TRC could challenge denial regarding apartheid-era violence, it could pave the way for public apologies by political leaders. Apologies would not suffice, however, unless they were accompanied by restitution. As Boraine put it, "A sure and certain test for reconciliation is whether it is accompanied by ... economic justice."[79]

As they began their work with the TRC, Tutu and Villa-Vicencio developed this set of ideas into a defense of restorative justice as an alternative to legalism. Instead of identifying justice with punishment, individual guilt, and formal legal procedures, the TRC would identify justice with a process of "healing past wounds." The idea of a "healing truth" did not represent the vision of religious leaders alone. Nor did it represent the diffusion of an international model of "therapeutic justice." Rather, it encompassed a range of claims articulated by "healers" who became associated with the TRC in its early years of operation. The focus on "healing past wounds" was also appealing as a way to elide ongoing political conflict over the extent to which the TRC would examine and condemn apartheid as a system or simply legitimate transitional compromises, whether it would "close the book"

[78] Godobo-Madikizela, *A Human Being Died That Night*, 126.
[79] Boraine, *A Country Unmasked*, 377.

on the past or advance an ongoing process of remembrance and political change.

A "NATION OF VICTIMS"

The TRC took 21,519 statements from victims. From this pool, it selected about 2,000 to testify in public hearings. The commission recommended that those who were identified as victims of "gross human rights violations" by the TRC should receive payments of approximately R120,000 per person over the course of six years, along with a range of educational and health services. However, the TRC was not funded to provide the reparations, and the government decided to grant only R30,000 in a single lump sum. Approximately 7,116 people applied for amnesty from the TRC. The majority of these applications were rejected on the grounds that they did not successfully identify a "political objective"; only 1,167 amnesties were granted.[80]

The information compiled from these statements and hearings is presented in the text of the *TRC Report*. The report presented the findings, analysis, and recommendations of the Commission and elaborated on the theoretical framework that animated its work. The analysis presented in *TRC Report* reflects two conflicting approaches to thinking about restorative justice. One approach is to use restorative justice as a basis for depoliticizing investigations of past abuse. This approach functions as a way to imagine a national community by focusing on shared suffering, while shifting attention away from potentially divisive political judgments. This interpretation of restorative justice dominates the *TRC Report* and has shaped international perceptions of the TRC as a model for other truth commissions. This approach to defining restorative justice did not challenge, but rather reinforced the central problem that the ANC lawyers had associated with human rights legalism. Most importantly, it meant that injustices that were legalized by the apartheid state would go unchallenged and largely unexamined by the TRC. However, the ANC's aspirations for the truth commission are not entirely abandoned by the *TRC Report*. Instead, they appear in the form of a muted internal critique of the report's analysis and in the tentative outline of an alternative way of thinking about restorative justice – one that does not abandon, but rather requires, political judgment.

[80] Jeremy Sarkin, "An Evaluation of the TRC's Amnesty Process," in *Truth and Reconciliation in South Africa: Did the TRC Deliver?*, 94. The TRC compiled information on 300 cases to hand over to South Africa's National Prosecuting Authority. A 2005 amendment to the NPA's prosecution policy effectively granted potential defendants a second chance for amnesty. This policy is currently being challenged on the grounds that it is unconstitutional.

A Humanitarian Ethic

A defining principle of restorative justice is that crime should be defined as "injury to persons" rather than violations of law. Like legalism, however, restorative justice characterizes crime as a discrete deviation from shared norms. The idea of a justice that "restores" relationships is premised on a preexisting social harmony. The *TRC Report* applies restorative justice to the South African context by narrowing the definition of past crimes, or injustices, addressed by the commission to encompass only those acts of violence that were *in excess* of what was legal under apartheid. Thus, the TRC did not investigate brutalities associated with the pass law system, forced removals, and other institutionalized injustices that could have been classified as "severe ill-treatment" under the terms of the TRC legislation. It justified this decision by using humanitarian law to define "gross human rights violations."[81]

Humanitarian law, which is centuries older than human rights law, was developed and codified largely as a result of efforts by the International Committee for the Red Cross (ICRC). The ICRC was, and continues to be, animated by a medical ethic, and its central goals are to bring aid to victims of conflict and disaster, without regard to the historical and political causes of conflict. Humanitarian law evolved as a pragmatic response to suffering caused by war and political violence. It draws a fundamental distinction between *jus in bello* (justice in war) and *jus ad bellum* (justice of war). This distinction became the basis for setting aside endlessly controversial questions regarding cause of conflict in order to direct international humanitarian law to the task of regulating what kinds of violence would be acceptable in conflict. In advancing the principle of *jus in bello*, humanitarian laws aim to minimize "unnecessary suffering" by insisting and elaborating on two very basic principles. The first principle is that certain categories of people, including civilians, prisoners of war, and the wounded, are considered "hors de combat" and should not be targeted in war time.[82] The second major principle is that parties seek to avoid unnecessary suffering by striving for proportionality between military means and ends.[83] Thus, although

---

[81] *TRC Report* vol. 1, 58–77.

[82] For an analysis of the gendered implications of this distinction, see Helen Kinsella, "Gendering Grotius: Sex and Sex Difference in the Laws of War," *Political Theory* 34, no. 2 (2006): 161–91.

[83] On the differences between humanitarian and human rights law, as well as the changing relationship between the two bodies of law, see Theodor Meron, "The Humanization of Humanitarian Law," *The American Journal of International Law*, 94, no. 2 (2000), 239–78; Teitel, "Humanity's Law," 356–87; Bronwyn Leebaw, "The Politics of Impartial Activism," *Perspectives on Politics* 5 (2007): 223–39.

humanitarian law restricts the ways in which state leaders may engage in the use of force, it has traditionally avoided judging internal political practices.

The TRC used humanitarian law as a way to navigate the competing demands of the National Party and the ANC regarding the shape of the investigations. *The TRC Report* states unequivocally that apartheid itself was a "crime against humanity" and that "those who fought against the system of apartheid were clearly fighting for a just cause, while those who sought to uphold and sustain apartheid cannot be morally equated with those who sought to remove and oppose it."[84] The report then turns to *jus in bello* analysis, arguing that although their cause was just, liberation groups were nevertheless "under an obligation to employ just means in the conduct of this fight."[85] This analysis precedes the report's discussion of "gross violations of human rights" and clarifies that although the TRC would condemn apartheid as a system, the primary focus of investigations would be *jus in bello* violations committed by all parties to the conflict. In keeping with the medical ethic of the ICRC, the report states that this type of analysis "contributes to national unity and reconciliation by treating individual victims with equal respect, regardless of whether the harm was caused by an official of the state or the liberation movements."[86]

Humanitarian law served to validate a narrow interpretation of the TRC's mandate, which would shift the focus of its investigations to a set of actions that were committed by all parties to the conflict. The *TRC Report* associates its reliance on humanitarian law with restorative justice by arguing that restorative justice called for a "humanitarian ethic."[87] The report identifies the humanitarian focus on the suffering of victims with the restorative justice emphasis on addressing the needs of victims rather than restoring the integrity of the law.

Although this move was championed as a way to establish the impartiality of the TRC as a critical response to political divisions, it is better understood as the legitimation of compromise. The use of humanitarian law was in direct conflict with the aspiration to evaluate and condemn the systemic injustices of apartheid. Humanitarian law avoids judging internal politics and cause of war in order to advance the pragmatic goal of minimizing "unnecessary suffering." Although the *TRC Report* does condemn apartheid, the decision to focus on violence committed by all parties functioned to soften and even to contradict this judgment.

---

[84]   *TRC Report* vol. 1, 67.
[85]   *TRC Report* vol. 1, 69.
[86]   *TRC Report* vol. 1, 70.
[87]   *TRC Report* vol. 1, 127.

This is evident, for example, in the TRC's eventual response to controversy surrounding the testimony of F.W. de Klerk. De Klerk shared the Nobel Peace Prize with Nelson Mandela in 1993 for his efforts to move the National Party toward negotiations and political change. However, as Deputy Chair of the TRC, Boraine requested that de Klerk apply for amnesty. Boraine's request was in keeping with his interpretation of the TRC as having a mandate to investigate complicity in apartheid as a system. In his statement to de Klerk, he drew on Asmal's interpretation of "severe ill-treatment" under the terms of the TRC Act: "17 million people were prosecuted under the pass laws ... more than three million were forcibly removed ... As accepting political and moral responsibility for that ... it would have been helpful ... if you had taken the step of applying for amnesty."[88] De Klerk responded by stating, "only those who are involved in crimes should, in my mind, use the amnesty procedure," invoking the view that the definition of "gross violations of human rights" should be restricted to acts that were excessive and illegal within the framework of apartheid legislation.

The matter did not end there. The National Party launched legal proceedings against the TRC, claiming that Alex Boraine and Desmond Tutu were incapable of impartiality and should be forced to resign from their posts. Boraine consulted Nelson Mandela on how to respond to the charges and recalls Mandela's blunt response to the controversy: "When people and organizations attack you unfairly, don't be a sissy," urged the President, "fight back!"[89] However, Boraine, in consultation with Desmond Tutu, eventually decided that they should apologize publicly to the National Party, which agreed in response to withdraw the demand for their resignation.

The TRC aimed to examine the historical context of apartheid-era violence as a basis for challenging denial and developing a deeper historical understanding of contemporary political divisions. However, it relied on a logic associated with humanitarianism, which deliberately avoids historical context in order to treat all victims equally. Although the TRC was designed to examine the broader social and structural consequences of apartheid, the depoliticized focus on suffering victims became a basis for imagining a national community with shared wounds – a "nation of victims."[90] The *TRC Report* would shift attention away from the divisions and inequalities that resulted from apartheid in order to focus on common experiences of violence. As Tutu put

---

[88] Boraine, *A Country Unmasked*, 161.
[89] Boraine, *A Country Unmasked*, 164.
[90] *TRC Report* vol. 1, 124.

it in his forward to the report, "Our country is soaked in the blood of her children of all races and of all political persuasions."[91]

In keeping with this logic, the TRC investigations were structured in such a way as to highlight similarities and shared experiences among victims, as divorced from historical context. Of the 21,000 victims that gave statements to the TRC, 1,800 would be chosen to appear for public hearings. The commission made special appeals for whites to come forward and held several hearings focusing on issues relevant to the white community.[92] One outcome of the effort to represent victims from all sides of the conflict was that whites were approximately four times as likely to be selected to appear in hearings as blacks.[93] The decision to emphasize "common wounds" suffered by victims on all sides of the conflict was also a decision to deemphasize the long-term goal of remedying the injustice of apartheid.

The focus on humanitarian law was consistent with the restorative claim that justice requires attention to the needs of victims rather than to the guilt of perpetrators. Humanitarianism is animated by a medical ethic that centers on providing a response to suffering even where this is in tension with legal accountability. Humanitarian law provided a way to apply the restorative justice framework to the context of systemic abuse by redefining crime as a deviation from basic shared norms governing conflict, rather than the apartheid system. This shifted the focus of analysis to common suffering. However, it was a departure from the critique of legalism that ANC lawyers had articulated in the early stages of developing the TRC. This framework would respect the legality of institutionalized apartheid and it was directly at odds with the goal of investigating the historical context of South Africa's violence.

A *"Human Rights Violation Syndrome"*

Questioning at the amnesty hearings differed fundamentally from that of a criminal trial because guilt was no longer at issue. The central questions that would define the fate of the applicant concerned the objective and motivation for the violence, and whether the applicant satisfied the requirement of "full disclosure." Establishing the "political objective" often involved open-ended questions to the applicant who would then explain in depth how he or she became associated with political violence. The questioning

---

[91] *TRC Report* vol. 1, 1.

[92] *TRC Report* vol. 1, 169.

[93] Audrey R. Chapman and Patrick Ball, "The Truth of Truth Commissions: Comparative Lessons from Haiti, South Africa, and Guatemala," *Human Rights Quarterly* 23 (2001): 39.

also aimed to generate a picture of how political leaders had encouraged and supported abuses. Thus, testimony before the Amnesty Committee would dwell at length on the nature and impact of propaganda and socialization. Jean Pierre Du Plessis explained that his father "believed that the White race was an exalted race on the earth ... all the other races were mud races ... sub-races, and didn't really have a right to exist." Was his father convincing? The commissioners wanted to know. Du Plessis responded, "[m]y father is probably the most logical person I know." Du Plessis also discussed his experience in the South African Defense Force, where he was instructed that the struggle to protect apartheid was a fight against the "Communist monster," an enemy that "had to be destroyed at all costs."[94]

Although the TRC originally aimed to condemn such propaganda, this goal was opposed by members of the National Party, who argued that the TRC had to take an "even-handed" approach in responding to testimony from amnesty applicants. In summarizing the significance of perpetrator testimony, the TRC sought to avoid such conflicts by depoliticizing its analysis. It did so by invoking categories and goals associated with its restorative framework. Like human rights legalism, the restorative framework presented in the TRC's final report offers an implicit theory of political violence that would be perceived as impartial and conducive to an apolitical remedy. Where proponents of human rights legalism have suggested that the central cause of political violence is impunity or lawlessness, the TRC Report characterizes political violence as a psychological imbalance or form of mental illness. This is evident in the section of the TRC Report entitled, "Causes, Motives and Perspectives of Perpetrators." The discussion analyzes the motivations of all perpetrators in similar terms, characterizing South Africa's "culture of gross human rights violations" as a "syndrome," with identifiable symptoms. Quoting Itzhak Fried, the chapter begins by suggesting that just as a cough and fever are known symptoms of pneumonia, so too can "emerging obsessive ideology, hyperarousal, diminished affective reactivity, and group dependent aggression ... signify a situation which needs immediate political, social and scientific attention."[95]

The chapter proceeds by analyzing the behavior of the state forces and the liberation groups alike in relation to this psychological profile, beginning with the ANC. In passing, the report notes that "the violence of the powerful and the powerless is not equivalent," but leaves the meaning of this unstated. Following nearly twenty pages of psychological analysis, the report states that psychological

[94] TRC Amnesty Hearings (July 1996).
[95] TRC Report vol. 5, 259–60.

explanations are secondary to political explanations for the violence. It then proceeds to discuss the political context. In so doing, the report begins with the
Cold War, citing uncritically the view that the state was bound to fight the ANC
to stop the Marxist-communist threat in the country. It is not until twenty-three
pages into the chapter that racism is even mentioned as a factor.[96]

The role of the commission, as stated in the chapter, is that of "the onlooker,
the outsider, the observer, the recorder, the evaluator, the scientist ..." This
chapter presents the ANC statement that it was fighting a just war against systematic dispossession and racial oppression, and the National Party's conten-
tion that it was fighting primarily a Cold War struggle, as though these were
two equally legitimate perspectives on the conflict. The message here is that
the most important priority in addressing past abuse is not institutional and
political reform, but individual therapy.

The *TRC Report* also identifies restorative justice with a therapeutic
response to trauma experienced by victims of apartheid-era violence.[97] The
report argues that restorative justice is particularly important in South Africa
because of the way that the prior order "traumatized the human spirit."[98] In
discussing the terminology of victimhood, the *TRC Report* identifies the status of "victim" closely with the experience of trauma.[99] These passages identify the primary legacy of apartheid as "trauma" and identify restorative justice
with the goal of alleviating trauma through a process that enables people to
adapt to the legacy of past injustices. This conception of restorative justice was
thus at odds with the earlier aspiration to use the TRC as a basis for ongoing
remembrance and political change.

The identification of restorative justice with therapy was also in tension
with the idea that the TRC would counter dehumanization by sponsoring
democratic dialogue across lines of political division. Many of those who had
fought with the liberation movements, for example, did not appreciate being
labeled as victims in need of healing and instead viewed themselves as fighters who had received their injuries as part of the struggle. The *TRC Report*
acknowledged that the widespread refusal of ANC supporters to come to the
commission was a factor that "severely constrained" its ability to provide a
"complete" picture of the past.[100] Many of those who did appear found that the

---

[96] *TRC Report* vol. 5, 282.

[97] *TRC Report* vol. 1, 128.

[98] *TRC Report* vol. 1, 126.

[99] Vol. 1, 59.

[100] *TRC Report* vol. 5, 199; Martha Minow, "The Hope for Healing: What Can Truth Commissions Do?" in *Truth v. Justice: the Morality of Truth Commissions*, ed. Robert I. Rotberg and
Dennis Thompson (Princeton, NJ: Princeton University Press, 2000), 235–60.

TRC interpreted their testimonies as stories of victimization while downplaying their political views and activities.[101]

Throughout much of the *TRC Report*, restorative justice is invoked as a way of depoliticizing the commission's analysis of past violence. Restorative justice implied the existence of a preexisting social harmony, ruptured by "gross human rights violations," rather than centuries of white supremacy and dispossession. It was applied in the *TRC Report* to justify a narrow investigation that would focus on the "shared wounds" of victims on all sides of the conflict and to identify the goal of justice with a process of therapeutic healing. Depoliticizing the TRC's investigations was seen as a basis for transcending political conflict over the process of judging the past and establishing the TRC as a critical, independent voice. Instead, it functioned to shift attention away from the question of political responsibility for the poverty and economic exploitation in South Africa.[102] It served to legitimate the political compromises that shaped the commission's narrow interpretation of the TRC's mandate, and to justify a turn away from analyzing the historical reality of apartheid and the myriad forms of injury it inflicted overwhelmingly on the black population.

An Internal Critique

Many of the criticisms leveled at South Africa's TRC can be found in the text of the commission's own report. Among them, I suggest, is an internal critique of the theory of restorative justice that dominates the report as well as the beginnings of an alternative approach. In contrast with the bulk of the report, which uses categories of healing and repair to depoliticize the TRC's investigations, this alternative approach makes the case for incorporating political judgment into restorative justice.

Most notably, the section of the *TRC Report* that outlines the commission's contributions to restorative justice also invokes restorative principles as a critical lens through which to examine the limitations of the TRC, and for acknowledging the compromises that shaped its work. In a section entitled, "Restorative justice: victims," the report specifies that, "[t]he provision of reparations to the (relatively) few victims of gross human rights violations who appeared before the Commission cannot be allowed to prejudice apartheid's

---

[101] Fiona C. Ross, *Bearing Witness: Women and the Truth and Reconciliation Commission in South Africa* (London: Pluto Press, 2003), 164.

[102] See Emilios Christoulidis and Scott Veitch, "Reconciliation as Surrender: Configurations of Responsibility and Memory," in *Justice and Reconciliation in Post-Apartheid South Africa.*

many other victims."[103] The report then argues that "the need for social and institutional reparations is an important part of restorative justice," and acknowledges that due to its own limited powers and its overly individualistic focus, the TRC process had largely failed to contribute to this goal.[104] "It is not enough merely to identify a few high-profile 'criminals' as those responsible for the atrocities of the past," states the *TRC Report*, adding that "[t]he need for political accountability by the leaders and voters of the nation ... have (both by design and default) not been given sufficient emphasis by the Commission."[105] In contrast with the idea of justice as therapy, which permeates other sections of the report, this discussion does not call for adaptive "closure," but rather challenges readers to "keep the memories alive, not only of gross violations of human rights, but of everyday life under apartheid."[106]

In contrast with the bulk of the *TRC Report*, which focuses on individual experiences with "gross human rights violations," the entire fourth volume is devoted to the TRC's institutional hearings. These hearings focused on the political parties, business and labor, the faith community, the legal system, the health sector, prisons, and compulsory military service. These investigations did not focus on individual acts, but rather on how apartheid operated as a system. This volume takes a critical view of justifications and denials for the political ideology and institutions associated with apartheid. The chapter on the institutional responsibility of the legal community states that the organized legal profession "connived in the legislative and executive pursuit of injustice" by supporting the National Party's bid for legal legitimacy.[107] The volume also censures the media for a policy of appeasing the state and failing to maintain its independence.[108] It implicates several faith communities, notably the Dutch Reformed Church, and argues that the military chaplaincy explicitly gave legitimacy to abuses and functioned to filter out dissent within the military.[109] The volume argues that business in general and the mining industry in particular were instrumental in designing apartheid policies, and states that the "brutal suppression of striking workers, racist practices and meager wages [are] central to understanding the origins and nature of apartheid."[110] The section of the report dealing with the

---

[103] *TRC Report* vol. 1, 129.
[104] *TRC Report* vol. 1, 132.
[105] *TRC Report* vol. 1, 132.
[106] *TRC Report* vol. 1, 133.
[107] *TRC Report* vol. 4, 101.
[108] *TRC Report* vol. 4, 188.
[109] *TRC Report* vol. 4, 71.
[110] *TRC Report* vol. 4, 34.

institutional hearings analyzes complicity in the injustice of apartheid as a system and calls for political responsibility and ongoing political reform as the major responses to that injustice.

The TRC hosted several public discussions throughout the life of the commission, at which numerous critics addressed the shortcomings of the process. In this way, the commission acknowledged its own limitations as a basis for resolving past conflicts and promoting reconciliation, while signaling the view that progress in this direction would require a broader acceptance of political responsibility. For example, as a participant in a public dialogue sponsored by the TRC, scholar Mahmood Mamdani had argued that the TRC's focus on "gross violations of human rights" would distort the history of apartheid, and suggested that it would be politically and morally important to analyze the guilt of apartheid's *beneficiaries*. This argument is accurately paraphrased in volume one of the *TRC Report* and presented as a warning regarding the limitations of the commission.[111] Volume 4 returns to Mamdani's argument, citing his focus on the beneficiaries of the apartheid system in response to members of the business community who had denied direct involvement in "gross human rights violations."[112]

The TRC's internal critique is muted but important. Instead of using restorative justice to depoliticize investigations of the past, these passages argue that the TRC falls short of the goals associated with restorative justice precisely because of the way that it depoliticizes its analysis. The *TRC Report* acknowledges that the focus on individual suffering and guilt undermines the original goal of challenging denial regarding the abuses of apartheid. It also acknowledges that the focus on therapeutic healing is at cross-purposes with political responses to the legacy of apartheid's injustices. In these passages, the *TRC Report* suggests that restorative justice requires an ongoing process of political change and a political judgment of systemic injustices. It insists on acknowledging ongoing divisions rather than obfuscating them with a focus on shared wounds and common suffering. This approach to restorative justice builds on earlier ideas articulated by the ANC lawyers and healers who influenced the development of the TRC, but has been omitted from theoretical debates on the legacy of the South African approach to transitional justice.

[111] *TRC Report* vol. 1, 133.
[112] *TRC Report* vol. 4, 43. The final addition to the *TRC Report*, released in March 2003, recommends that all beneficiaries contribute to a reparation fund for victims (*Truth and Reconciliation Commission of South Africa Report* [Cape Town: Juta, 2003], Vol. 6, 8).

CONCLUSION

Just as the Nuremberg Trials came to exemplify the promise of legalism, South Africa's TRC has become an extraordinarily influential model for those who champion restorative justice. These institutions are widely viewed as the inspiration for today's international criminal tribunals and truth commissions. What is lost in most contemporary debates on the legacies of the Nuremberg Tribunal and the South African TRC is that both institutions were initially developed as vehicles for political, as well as moral judgment. Scholars that were instrumental in defending the legitimacy of these institutions against legalist critics did so by insisting that just responses to state-sponsored atrocity would have to be informed by political judgment.

Like Shklar and Nino, South African lawyers affiliated with the ANC associated political judgment with a common set of goals: the goal of judging the political institutions and practices that facilitated past injustices, the goal of persuading a divided people to accept that judgment, and the goal of influencing a process of transformative political change. Shklar argued that the Nuremberg Trials were successful because they combined a legalistic approach to justice with an effective political judgment of the Nazi regime. Lawyers associated with the ANC, such as Asmal, defended the importance of political judgment in guiding the pursuit of alternative approaches to justice for past wrongs. The TRC's restorative approach to justice was not simply window dressing for the compromises that shaped South Africa's response to apartheid's injustices. It was not simply the creation of religious leaders or therapists involved with the commission. Nor was it a "translation" of global human rights practices into a local vernacular.[113] Its development was informed by a theoretical critique of legalism that emphasized the limits of criminal prosecution and individualized accountability as moral responses to legacies of legalized brutality, institutionalized racism, and political exclusion.

It is not surprising that this critique has been all but forgotten in theoretical debates on the legacy of the TRC. Over time, the TRC would replicate the very problems its originators had hoped to avoid. By its own acknowledgment, the Commission abandoned the goal of analyzing political responsibility for apartheid in favor of a focus on individual responsibility. Although authorized to examine the context of "gross human rights violations," the Commission stated that an analysis of racism in South Africa was beyond the scope of its mandate. Given that human rights law would have required the TRC to place

---

[113] See Sally Engle Merry, *Human Rights and Gender Violence: Translating International Law into Local Justice* (Chicago and London: University of Chicago Press, 2006).

the system of apartheid at the very center of its investigations, the Commission relied on humanitarian law to draw a bright line between justice and politics. Rather than investigate the historical and political context of apartheid-era violence, it put forth a largely psychological theory of political violence and its aftermath.

These developments were not simply the result of methodological choices, or evidence that the TRC's critique of legalism was insincere. Rather, they reflect the way in which restorative justice became associated with the goal of depoliticizing the TRC's investigations. The effort to depoliticize the work of the TRC was seen as a basis for establishing its independence and legitimacy as a critical response to competing parties. Instead, it legitimated the compromises that shaped the work of the Commission. In the process, the scope of historical investigation and official remembrance was narrowed, through the framework of humanitarian law, to the "unnecessary suffering" associated with combat and to the trauma experienced by victims and perpetrators of extralegal violence in the struggle over apartheid. In this context, the meaning of restorative justice became closely identified with therapeutic adaptation and closure, rather than ongoing remembrance and political change. Just as Nuremberg became associated with an approach to legalism that would center on "individualizing guilt," the TRC became associated with the view that truth commissions can promote restorative justice by fostering therapeutic encounters between individual victims and perpetrators. Like human rights legalism, then, restorative justice would function to obfuscate the "gray zone" of systematic violence and reframe institutionalized injustices as discrete deviations from common norms.

In the context of post-apartheid South Africa, as in other countries struggling with legacies of state-sponsored violence and systematic atrocity, the political process is associated with violent division and mutual hostility. Politics may appear entirely futile, yet also suffocating and omnipresent. People may be fatigued by politics, weary of the way in which even the most intimate experiences of grief and mourning are politicized. People yearn for spaces that are beyond the reach of political conflict, in which to heal, to speak, and to reflect. And the process of establishing such spaces, the process of withdrawing from politics, may play a profound and constructive role in recovery and conflict resolution.

That kind of space, a space that is divorced from politics, will not be found in transitional justice institutions, to the extent that such institutions are tasked with judging state-sponsored violence and politically authorized atrocity. Transitional justice institutions cannot establish their critical authority by denigrating or avoiding politics, but only by defending the integrity of the political judgments that inform or qualify their moral responses to past wrongs. The trouble is that it is not clear what considerations ought to guide political judgment in contexts characterized by the failure or collapse of political institutions, in which the task at hand is to judge the very systems or practices that might have informed political judgments in times past. In the absence of such guidance, depoliticization appears as the only legitimate strategy for establishing critical moral authority. In the following chapter, I consider how Hannah Arendt addressed this problem and argue that her analysis provides useful guidance for contemporary debates on transitional justice.

4

Political Judgment and Transitional Justice: Actors and Spectators

Hannah Arendt was bitterly attacked for her controversial coverage of the Eichmann trial and even accused of betraying "a conscious desire to support Eichmann's defense,"[1] yet she is now treated as a significant authority in theoretical debates on transitional justice. Like many contemporary human rights advocates, Arendt supported the development of international criminal justice institutions and argued that success or failure in dealing with crimes against humanity "can only lie in the extent to which this dealing may serve as a valid precedent on the road to international law."[2] At the same time, Arendt's critique of the Eichmann trial and her writings on forgiveness have influenced scholarship addressing the limitations of legalism as a response to systematic atrocities.[3] South African leaders and activists associated with the TRC developed Arendt's argument that in contrast with revenge, forgiveness "does not merely re-act, but acts anew."[4] A number of legal and political theorists have argued that Arendt's reflections on forgiveness provide important insights for contemporary responses to political violence.[5]

[1] Elisabeth Young-Bruehl, *Hannah Arendt: For the Love of the World* (New Haven, CT and London: Yale University Press, 1982), 358.
[2] Hannah Arendt, *Eichmann in Jerusalem: A Report on the Banality of Evil* (New York: Penguin, 1965), 273.
[3] Carlos Nino, *Radical Evil on Trial* (New Haven, CT: Yale University Press, 1998), 15, 135, 141–2, 191; Mark Osiel, *Mass Atrocity, Ordinary Evil, and Hannah Arendt: Criminal Consciousness in Argentina's Dirty War* (New Haven, CT and London: Yale University Press, 2001); Minow, *Between Vengeance and Forgiveness*, 4, 47–8.
[4] Boraine, *A Country Unmasked*, 241; Pumla Godobo-Madikizela, "Radical Forgiveness: Transforming Traumatic Memory Beyond Hannah Arendt," in *Justice and Reconciliation in Post-Apartheid South Africa*, ed. Francois du Bois and Anje du Bois-Pedain (New York: Cambridge University Press, 2008).
[5] Donald Shriver, *An Ethic for Enemies: Forgiveness in Politics* (Oxford: Oxford University Press, 1995); Peter Digeser, *Political Forgiveness* (Ithaca, NY: Cornell University Press, 2001), 16–21, 34–5, 99–100. Trudy Govier, *Forgiveness and Revenge* (New York: Routledge Press, 2002); Jean Bethke Elshtain, "Politics and Forgiveness," in *Burying the Past: Making Peace*

Missing from these debates has been serious attention to one of Arendt's central theoretical concerns, which was to reconsider the role of *political judgment* in the aftermath of twentieth-century atrocities. Transitional justice institutions aspire to judge systematic political violence and advance political change, but their investigations are typically framed as apolitical responses to the deeds and experiences of individual victims and perpetrators. Influential thinkers such as Judith Shklar, José Zalaquett, Carlos Nino, and South African leaders associated with the TRC defended the role of political judgment as part of a moral response to past atrocities. However, such scholars have not directly addressed the problem of how to establish a basis for political judgment in contexts characterized by the absence or collapse of political communities and pervasive despair in the political process. In such contexts, depoliticization has been seen as the only legitimate avenue for establishing the critical moral authority of transitional justice institutions, and their contributions to political reconciliation. Yet efforts to depoliticize transitional justice institutions have undermined their critical role by obfuscating the compromises that frame their mandates and by narrowing the scope of their inquiries in such a way that avoids systemic patterns of violence and injustice.

This chapter argues that Arendt's writings on the theme of political judgment offer a constructive response to this problem. The first section of the chapter examines Arendt's assessment of human rights, international criminal justice, and forgiveness as responses to massive atrocities. Like contemporary proponents of transitional justice, Arendt championed the development of international criminal justice, insisted on the importance of confronting "factual truth," and explored the potential of forgiveness. However, Arendt's support for such strategies was informed and qualified by her critique of depoliticization. Arendt recognized the desire to escape politics and to avoid political judgment as a logical response to despair in the collapse of political community, yet she saw this as a self-defeating response – one that would only reinforce passivity, alienation, and denial.

The second section of the chapter looks at how Arendt's writings on political judgment address this predicament. Arendt's defense of political judgment as guided by "enlarged mentality" offers an approach that is not grounded in inherited traditions or an appeal to apolitical criteria, but in a process that strives to account for diverse perspectives on a common problem. In some

and Doing Justice after Civil Conflict, ed. Nigel Biggar (Washington DC: Georgetown University Press, 2003); Andrew Schaap, *Political Reconciliation* (New York: Routledge, 2005); Mark Amstutz, *The Healing of Nations: The Promise and Limits of Political Forgiveness* (New York: Rowman and Littlefield, 2006); Thomas Brudholm, *Resentment's Virtue: Jean Améry and the Refusal to Forgive* (Philadelphia: Temple University Press, 2008), 148–9.

writings, Arendt suggests that good political judgment requires persuasion, dialogue, and active involvement in politics. In other writings, however, Arendt associates political judgment with the detached and imaginative reflections of the historian. This apparent discrepancy has been a source of perplexity and a great deal of debate among political theorists.[6] I suggest that Arendt's two ways of thinking about political judgment are instructive as a basis for developing and examining implicit claims about the political role of transitional justice. In doing so, I argue that transitional justice requires *both* approaches to establishing the validity of political judgment – that of the actor, and that of the spectator – but that the two are in tension with one another.

Instead of seeking ways to resolve or elide this problem, I suggest, transitional justice institutions and practices might alternatively locate strategies for *mediating* the tension between their role as political actors and critical spectators. The third section of this chapter develops and illustrates this argument by reconsidering Aeschylus's trilogy, *The Oresteia*, as a drama of transitional justice.

DEPOLITICIZATION AND DESPAIR

Arendt was a Jewish refugee who had fled, first from Germany and then from France, after the Nazis seized power. She was also a member of Amnesty International, and her writings address many themes that have been central to the work of human rights scholars and advocates.[7] Yet she dismissed the human rights advocates of her time as "a few international jurists without political experience" and "professional philanthropists supported by the uncertain sentiments of professional idealists."[8] In *Origins of Totalitarianism*, Arendt observed that the human rights framework aspires to transcend the authority of the nation state and to challenge government-sponsored terror, yet relies on the nation state for enforcement.[9] Paradoxically, the plight of refugees and

---

6   Ronald Beiner, "Hannah Arendt on Judging," in *Hannah Arendt's Lectures on Kant's Political Philosophy*, ed. Ronald Beiner (Chicago: University of Chicago Press, 1982); Seyla Benhabib, "Judgment and the Moral Foundation of Politics in Arendt's Thought," *Political Theory* 16 (1988): 29–51; Lisa Disch, *Hannah Arendt and the Limits of Philosophy* (Ithaca, NY: Cornell University Press, 1994); Dana Villa, *Politics, Philosophy, Terror: Essays on the Thought of Hannah Arendt* (Princeton, NJ: Princeton University Press, 1999).

7   Jeffery Isaac, "A New Guarantee on Earth: Hannah Arendt on Human Dignity and the Politics of Human Rights," *American Political Science Association Review* 90 (1996): 61–73.

8   Hannah Arendt, *The Origins of Totalitarianism* (New York: Harcourt Brace, 1966), 292.

9   Douglas Klusmeyer, "Hannah Arendt's Critical Realism: Power, Justice, and Responsibility," in *Hannah Arendt and International Relations: Reading Across the Lines*, ed. Anthony F. Lang, Jr. and John Williams (New York: Palgrave McMillan, 2005); Isaac, "A New Guarantee on Earth."

those subjected to government-sponsored terror inspired the elaboration of human rights as a set of principles that must apply to all, but also revealed the extent to which the exercise of human rights is premised on political membership. Without citizenship, she argued, those who are to be empowered by rights are placed in a position of radical inequality and dependence, unable to mobilize on their own behalf.[10]

Arendt defended the view that genocide ought to be condemned as a "crime against humanity." However, she rejected the assertion of "humanity" as a category independent of history and politics.[11] Arendt developed this position in a speech that she gave in Germany upon receiving the Lessing Prize in 1959. She argued that in the context of the Nazi period, "it would scarcely have been a sign of humanness for friends to have said: Are we not both human beings?"[12] To do so, "would not have been resisting the world as it was," she added, but would rather function as a "dangerous evasion of reality." A commitment to "humanity" in the abstract or based on a belief in enduring human sameness cannot serve as a substitute for acts of solidarity and resistance based on friendship across lines of division and difference.[13]

Arendt also rejected the basic premise that rights ought to be defended as "self-evident truths."[14] The assertion of self-evidence is a way to demand recognition or allegiance to principles by denying the validity of opposing views. The trouble with this approach, Arendt argued, is that it abandons the task of persuasion that is necessary to achieve genuine political support for common values. As she put it, truths that are asserted in this way "stand above" people, but not "*between*" them.[15]

Although Arendt supported the expansion of international law, she rejected the idea that a global community could be established through some kind of "universal agreement on one religion, one philosophy, or one form of government."[16] She favored a kind of "world wide federated structure" as a

[10] Arendt, *Origins of Totalitarianism*, 294.
[11] See Hannah Arendt, "On Humanity in Dark Times: Thoughts about Lessing," in *Men in Dark Times* (New York: Harcourt, 1968), 23.
[12] Arendt, "On Humanity in Dark Times," 23.
[13] As Hanna Pitkin puts it, Arendt's concept of solidarity entails "making common cause with the sufferers as one's peers without losing track of one's own separateness from them or confusing their suffering with one's own" (1998, 266).
[14] In a recent, widely reviewed history of human rights, Lynn Hunt argues that the assertion of "self-evidence" has been central to the appeal of human rights and intrinsic to their success. See Lynn Hunt, *Inventing Human Rights: A History* (New York: W.W. Norton, 2007).
[15] Hannah Arendt, *Between Past and Future: Eight Exercises in Political Thought* (New York: Viking, 1969), 247.
[16] Arendt, *Men in Dark Times*, 90. For an expanded discussion of Arendt's modest cosmopolitanism and how it differs from that of contemporary cosmopolitan thinkers, see Patricia

possible alternative, but warned that the advance of communications tech-
nologies along with atomic weapons seemed to be generating a shallow,
"negative solidarity, based on fear of global destruction.[17] Arendt suggested
that "solidarity of mankind" might be meaningful in a positive sense, "if it
is coupled with political responsibility." In contrast with the legalistic framework for accountability, this type of solidarity would be based on "our political
concepts, according to which we have to assume responsibility for all public
affairs within our reach regardless of personal 'guilt.'"[18]

In her writings on the Eichmann trial, Arendt supported international criminal justice as a response to crimes against humanity, but she also observed
that the criminal trial was limited as a framework for judging politically authorized atrocities. Like Shklar, Arendt noted that legalism may be compatible
with, or mobilized to legitimate, systematic atrocities. Those who were complicit in Nazi atrocities were, as she put it, "very well acquainted with the letter
and the spirit of the law."[19] Yet in contrast with Shklar, Arendt warned that the
use of individual criminal trials to teach history could undermine the integrity of the trial as well as the quality of the history.[20] Arendt also articulated
a more fundamental set of concerns regarding the use of criminal trials to
judge politically authorized abuses. She thought that the court's reliance on
established legal categories obfuscated the novelty of the genocide and evaded
the problem of how to establish a basis for judgment.[21] And she argued that
the court's reliance on the basic concept of "criminal intent," premised on an
understanding of crime as deviance, was in tension with the goal of judging
the way in which the Nazi regime operated as a system.[22]

Arendt's contributions to debates on truth commissions and restorative
justice may be better understood in the context of this critique of depoliticization. Proponents of restorative justice have been inspired by her endorsement of forgiveness as an alternative to vengeance. Yet for Arendt, the act
of forgiveness is only meaningful in the context of a political community.

Owens, *Between War and Politics: International Relations and the Thought of Hannah Arendt*
(Oxford: Oxford University Press, 2007), 128–48.

[17] Arendt, *Men in Dark Times*, 83.

[18] Arendt, *Men in Dark Times*, 83.

[19] Hannah Arendt, "Personal Responsibility under Dictatorship." in *Responsibility and Judgment*, ed. Jerome Kohn (New York: Shocken, 2003), 40.

[20] Arendt, *Eichmann in Jerusalem*, 5–10.

[21] See Leora Bilsky, "When Actor and Spectator Meet in the Courtroom: Reflections on Hannah
Arendt's Concept of Judgment," in *Judgment, Imagination, and Politics*, ed. Ronald Beiner and
Jennifer Nedelsky (New York: Rowman and Littlefield, 2001): 257–86.

[22] Arendt, *Eichmann in Jerusalem*, 276. See also Osiel, *Mass Atrocity, Ordinary Evil, and Hannah
Arendt*.

She situates her analysis of forgiveness in the context of a relationship that is "eminently personal (though not necessarily an individual or private) affair, in which *what* was done is forgiven for the sake of *who* did it."[23] Arendt argues that the act of forgiveness *can* be politically useful as a way to free people from "relentless cycles of action and reaction" even where intimacy and love are lacking, but only if there is already a basic foundation of respect.[24]

Like contemporary proponents of truth commissions, Arendt argued that "factual truths" regarding past events ought to be preserved and defended against inevitable distortion and denial.[25] For Arendt, "reconciliation with reality," or an acceptance of basic facts was a necessary basis for common ground in a political community. Similarly, contemporary truth commissions aim to foster reconciliation by establishing "the facts" regarding past atrocities, in the form of statistics or decisive findings on matters such as contested massacres, disappearances, or claims regarding chain of command. Payam Akhavan also invoked Arendt's defense of "factual truth" to argue that international criminal tribunals could contribute to reconciliation by establishing certain basic facts, despite ongoing conflict over how to interpret their meaning.[26] Yet Arendt's defense of "factual truth" was qualified in important ways. She argued that factual truths could never be fully removed from the narratives in which they appear, and she observed that factual truth is characterized by a disturbing "fragility" in the face of organized lying, propaganda, and self-deception.[27] Simply stating the facts, in her view, would have little impact in contexts where propaganda has undermined the capacity for critical thought and judgment.

Arendt's analysis of human rights and international law contains certain affinities with the tradition of international relations realism. Like many realists, Arendt rejected narratives and theories of historical progress in favor of a tragic view of history. Instead of seeking to "master" the past, she argued, we must reconcile ourselves to it. "The best that can be achieved," she wrote, is to see precisely what it was, and to endure this knowledge."[28] Yet Arendt's tragic perspective does not rest on the premise of an essential flaw in human nature or the structure of international anarchy. Rather, she offers a tragic

---

[23] Arendt, *The Human Condition*, 241.

[24] Arendt, *The Human Condition*, 243.

[25] Arendt, *Between Past and Future*, 231, 237.

[26] Akhavan, "Justice in the Hague, Peace in the Former Yugoslavia."

[27] Arendt, *Between Past and Future*, 231. In such a context, writes Lisa Disch, "both truth and falsehood 'stick' equally well." Disch, *Hannah Arendt and the Limits of Philosophy*, 114.

[28] Arendt, *Men in Dark Times*, 20.

view of history as the basis for reclaiming agency and innovation. Arendt identified the role of tragedy with Aristotlean catharsis – a "purging of all emotions that could prevent men from acting."[29] In her view, the belief in theories of progress is detrimental to human agency and innovation.[30]

Importantly, Arendt's critique of depoliticization is rooted in a defense of politics as an ongoing process of contestation among plural perspectives and opinions.[31] In some writings, she distinguishes between matters that are appropriately political and those that are appropriately private in a manner that is oddly purist and would seem to foreclose attention to the politics of economic injustices, racism, and gender.[32] Nevertheless, Arendt's basic defense of politics provides an instructive response to the logic of depoliticization in contemporary approaches to transitional justice. Arendt acknowledged that political life is often "no more than a battlefield of partial, conflicting interests."[33] "[I]t may be in the nature of the political realm," she added, "to deny or pervert truth of every kind."[34] Yet she also saw efforts to escape or avoid politics as deeply nihilistic and argued that the human potential for developing innovative interpretations of, and responses to, the tragic events of the past would depend upon an ongoing engagement in political life.[35] It is only *through* politics, Arendt maintained, through the interaction and clash of diverging opinions in debate and action, that people are able to develop a genuinely shared commitment to values such as freedom, equality, and justice.

Like Shklar, Zalaquett, and Nino, then, Arendt argued that addressing these problems would require political judgment.[36] Unlike these thinkers, however, Arendt examined the problem of how political judgments could be critical and persuasive without appealing to prevailing prejudices or relying upon standards derived from inherited traditions. "How can you judge," she

[29] Arendt, *Between Past and Future*, 262.
[30] Arendt, *Lectures on Kant's Political Philosophy*, 77. See Leslie Paul Thiele, "Judging Hannah Arendt: A Reply to Zerilli," *Political Theory* 33 (2005), 709.
[31] Arendt, *The Human Condition*, 57–8, 175.
[32] Arendt, *The Human Condition*, 28–37. On the implications of Arendt's discussion of the distinction between the public and private realms, see Hannah Fenichel Pitkin, "Justice: On Relating Private and Public," *Political Theory* 9 (1981); Mary Dietz, *Turning Operations: Feminism, Arendt, and Politics* (New York: Routledge, 2002); John Medearis, "Lost or Obscured? How V.I. Lenin, Joséph Schumpeter, and Hannah Arendt Misunderstood the Council Movement," *Polity* 36, no. 3 (2004).
[33] Arendt, *Between Past and Future*, 263.
[34] Arendt, *Between Past and Future*, 236.
[35] See Patchen Markell's discussion of "natality" ("The Rule of the People, Arendt, Arche, and Democracy," *American Political Science Review* 100 [2006], 6–7).
[36] Arendt, *Lectures on Kant's Political Philosophy*, 76.

asked, "without holding onto preconceived standards, norms, and general rules under which the particular cases and instances can be subsumed"?[37]

THE ACTOR AND THE SPECTATOR

Arendt looked to Immanuel Kant's *Critique of Judgment* for guidance in addressing this question.[38] She saw the challenges associated with political judgment as analogous, in important respects, to the difficulties that Kant associated with aesthetic judgment. First, Kant treated aesthetic judgments as reflective rather than determinative. Whereas determinative judgments apply general standards to particular cases, reflective judgments derive general principles from the particular. Second, just as taste is intensely subjective, Arendt argued, so too are moral conscience and the experience of suffering or pain. Good judgment in politics should not seek to *overcome* the plurality of subjective opinions and perspectives by organizing them in accordance with a singular truth.[39] At the same time, good judgment in politics cannot simply *reflect* those perspectives, but must also provide a basis for critically evaluating them.[40]

Arendt looked to Kant's concept of *sensus communis*, or "common sense," guided by "enlarged mentality" as a kind of model for the considerations that ought to guide political judgment. Kant characterizes "enlarged mentality" as a way of thinking that consists of "being able to think in place of everyone else."[41] "Enlarged mentality" is a kind of impartiality that is not achieved through appeals to scientific objectivity or universality, but through the work of examining a problem from the perspectives of others who may see things very differently. The power of judgments guided by enlarged mentality, she writes, rests "on potential agreement with others." Arendt suggests that the process of testing one's views against those expressed by others – imagining a problem from the perspective of someone else – provides a way to liberate judgment from its purely subjective character and partisan prejudices. However, such judgments cannot fully transcend their partial character and are never universally valid.[42]

---

[37] Hannah Arendt, "Personal Responsibility under Dictatorship," in *Responsibility and Judgment*, ed. Jerome Kohn (New York: Schocken Books, 2003), 26.

[38] Arendt, *Between Past and Future*, 221–2; Arendt, *Lectures on Kant's Political Philosophy*; Immanuel Kant, *Critique of Judgment* (1790), trans. Werner S. Pluhar (Indianapolis, IN: Hackett, 1987).

[39] Arendt saw this tendency in Western political thought, beginning with Plato, as inherently violent (*The Human Condition*, 230–6).

[40] Arendt, *Lectures on Kant's Political Philosophy*, 40–3.

[41] Arendt, *Between Past and Future*, 220.

[42] Arendt, *Between Past and Future*, 221. Lisa Disch refers to this as "political impartiality."

Arendt's analysis not only defends political judgment as a response to twen-tieth-century atrocities but also offers a basis for distinguishing political judg-ment as a critical and transformative response to the past, from uncritical assertions of opinion or manipulative power plays. At the time of her death, however, she had only just begun to develop what was intended to be an entire book devoted to the theme.[43] Scholars have been perplexed by two ways of thinking about political judgment that appear in her work. In some of her ear-lier essays, Arendt seems to associate political judgment with Aristotelian *phro-nesis*, or practical wisdom, which guides us in deliberating and acting well.[44] However, in other writings, Arendt characterizes political judgment as the task of the spectator, "onlooker" or historian.[45] Ronald Beiner has argued that Arendt presents two distinct theories of political judgment – one grounded in active engagement, and the other premised on isolation and detachment.[46]

These two ways of characterizing political judgment – as a guide for action and as a guide for critical reflection – bear a striking resemblance to two ways in which political judgment has been characterized in debates on transitional justice. That is, as responses to political violence, transitional justice institu-tions are political actors that seek to inform a process of reform, yet they are also critical spectators that strive to challenge conventional political wisdom and evaluate past events. A closer look at Arendt's analysis of political judg-ment reveals tensions between these two roles that are masked by the logic of depoliticization. At the same time, her analysis suggests alternative strategies for addressing these tensions.

In some essays, Arendt presents "enlarged mentality" as a guide for action and the unique virtue of "the statesman." She stresses that judgment depends on publicity and argues that political judgment "cannot function in strict iso-lation or solitude; it needs the presence of others."[47] She compares Kant's claim that "enlarged mentality" requires an effort to "woo" others to one's own per-spective to the way in which persuasion operates in a political context. The validity of political judgment, she suggests, depends on this quality of per-suasion. In developing this claim, Arendt distinguishes political persuasion from violent forms of coercion, as well as assertions of truth by means of some kind of compelling proof. In contrast with warfare and philosophical or moral

---

[43] This was to be the third volume in a work entitled, *The Life of the Mind* (Beiner, "Hannah Arendt on Judging," 89).

[44] Aristotle, *Nichomachean Ethics*, 1142a.

[45] See for example, Arendt, *Lectures on Kant's Political Philosophy*, 5, 59, 61. Beiner argues that Arendt offers two distinctive theories of judgment ("Hannah Arendt on Judging," 91).

[46] Beiner, "Hannah Arendt on Judging," 91.

[47] Arendt, *Between Past and Future*, 220.

judgment, she argues, good *political* judgment entails "the judicious exchange of opinion about the sphere of public life, and the decision of what manner of action is to be taken in it."[48]

Arendt's case for basing political judgment on a process of persuasion and deliberation resonates with Shklar's claim that legal strategies are only effective when relevant audiences can be persuaded to accept their findings and judgments. It resonates with Nino's concern that a formal, international "duty to prosecute" would be damaging or counterproductive absent a process of argumentation designed to establish common ground. It also resonates with arguments advanced by South African leaders, such as Sachs, Villa-Vicencio, and Asmal, all of whom argued that the TRC would advance a common basis for justice and reconciliation by cultivating a process of political dialogue and by persuading diverse parties to accept its findings. Such thinkers have characterized persuasion and dialogue as a basis for praxis, for connecting moral judgments to political action and change.

However, Arendt's posthumously published lectures seem to move away from her earlier Aristotelian approach, by identifying political judgment as the task of the historian – a faculty for "dealing with the past" rather than a guide for action.[49] She argues that "enlarged mentality" is guided by *imagined* rather than *actual* dialogue, and that the validity of political judgment can be evaluated in relation to the extent to which it is based on "anticipated communication."[50] It is the force of the imagination, she contends, that makes it possible to consider alternative points of view and establish a degree of freedom from one's own partial perspective, without passively accepting the prejudices and opinions of others.[51] Arendt stresses that the political actor never "sees the meaning of the whole," which requires disinterest and *dis*engagement.[52] The power and danger of prejudice, she argues, "lies in the very fact that it is always anchored in the past." To dispel prejudice, then, requires an examination of the "past judgments contained within them."[53]

Arendt's discussion of the role of the critical spectator resonates with a second way in which political judgment has appeared in debates on transitional justice. Transitional justice institutions are not only active political interventions, but also strive for the critical posture of the historian or spectator. Thus,

---

[48] Arendt, *Between Past and Future*, 223.
[49] Arendt, *Lectures on Kant's Political Philosophy*, 5, 58, 77.
[50] Arendt, *Between Past and Future*, 220.
[51] Arendt, *Lectures on Kant's Political Philosophy*, 43.
[52] Arendt, *Lectures on Kant's Political Philosophy*, 43.
[53] Arendt, "Introduction *into* Politics." In *The Promise of Politics*, edited by Jerome Kohn, 93–200 (New York: Random House, 2005), 101.

Shklar saw the historical records generated by the Nuremberg Trials as their greatest contribution.[54] Truth commissions are designed to challenge denial regarding historical events and to reflect on the broader causes and consequences of historical patterns of violence.[55] ANC lawyers involved in developing South Africa's TRC, such as Kader Asmal, championed this approach to political judgment in calling for a truth commission that would critically evaluate mythologies associated with past injustices, while simultaneously exposing the limitations of transitional compromises.

These are not exactly two entirely different theories of political judgment. Arendt is consistent in arguing that "enlarged mentality" is the basis of good judgment for political actors as well as spectators.[56] However, her analysis does illuminate two distinctive *stances* or forms of political judgment that are implicit in theoretical debates on transitional justice – that of the actor and that of the spectator. These two forms of political judgment are mutually constitutive. The historical investigations of transitional justice institutions are framed and limited by mandates established through the process of political deliberation. At the same time, the historical reflections of transitional justice institutions also frame the terms of political deliberation, and narrow or expand the parameters of political action.

Nevertheless, Arendt's effort to establish criteria for evaluating the validity of political judgment reveals profound tensions between the two stances. As a guide for action, political judgment must appeal to prevailing perspectives in an effort to persuade people to reach a common understanding. An Aristotelian approach to political judgment, argues Beiner, would ground the validity of political judgments within the context of the "substantive ends and purposes of political deliberation, rhetoric, and community."[57] The trouble with the Aristotelian approach is that systematic political violence or injustice implies the absence or failure of common values and traditions. Appealing to prevailing opinions and airing multiple perspectives on past injustices may simply legitimate the myths and ideologies that rationalize atrocity or reward the loudest and most powerful voices in the political arena.

Dana Villa argues that Arendt came to associate political judgment with the critical spectator in response to her overriding concern with the question of how to judge in the *absence* of shared criteria, where community-based

---

54 Shklar, *Legalism*, 169. See also, Bass, *Stay the Hand of Vengeance*, 302–304.
55 Hayner, *Unspeakable Truths*, 16.
56 Arendt, *Lectures on Kant's Political Philosophy*, 63.
57 Beiner, "Interpretive Essay," 138.

judgments are no longer viable or meaningful.[58] As form of critical reflection, political judgment requires an effort to stand apart from prevailing perspectives and community traditions in order to see and evaluate patterns that may not be apparent to those immersed in political struggle or to those suffering from profound emotions of loss, guilt, shame, and fear. Transitional justice institutions do not typically have the luxury of reflecting on events in the distant past, nor do they enjoy the insulation from political scrutiny associated with the work of academic historians.[59] They must seek other ways to establish critical distance, yet without presuming agreement on general standards and their application.

Arendt's primary exemplar in this regard is Socrates, who achieves critical distance by withdrawing from public life and engaging in a process of relentless questioning in pursuit of truth.[60] Socrates withdrew from public office and had a bleak perspective on the political community that he inhabited.[61] However, he did not retreat into isolation to engage in his pursuit of truth and justice. Instead, he established critical distance by soliciting various opinions and perspectives, while simultaneously subjecting them to rigorous, relentless, critical scrutiny. The Socratic approach does not say what to do in the future or how to act, but exposes the limitations and contradictions inherent in prevailing approaches. It implies that the task of establishing critical distance requires an *ongoing* process of questioning. From this vantage point, no single perspective is sacred – not the threats issued by those who wield power and not the shushing of those who claim that too much critique will undermine a fragile democratic transition or negotiated peace. The critical judgments of contemporary transitional justice projects may be as profoundly unsettling as Socrates' relentless questioning was for democratic Athens.[62] This Socratic stance is a response to despair in the failures or inadequacies of

---

58 Villa, *Politics, Philosophy, Terror*, 99. For a discussion of this theme as applied to scholarly traditions, see John G. Gunnell, *Between Philosophy and Politics: The Alienation of Political Theory* (Amherst: University of Massachusetts Press, 1986), 103.

59 Charles Villa-Vicencio, who directed the writing of South Africa's *TRC Report*, writes that "a fair amount of inevitable internal political squabbling and external political pressure" influenced the work of the commission. That, along with limited amount of time they were allotted to complete the report, made the work of the commission very different from "academic history," he argues ("On the Limitations of Academic History: The Quest for Truth Demands Both More and Less," in *After the TRC: Reflections on Truth and Reconciliation in South Africa*, ed. Wilmot James and Linda Van de Vijver (Athens, OH: Ohio University Press, 2001), 26).

60 Arendt, *Lectures on Kant's Political Philosophy*, 37–8, 41.

61 Plato, "The Apology," trans. Hugo Treddenick, in *The Last Days of Socrates*, ed. Hugo Treddenick (London: Penguin, 1954), 31–71.

62 For a discussion of transitional justice in Athens following the defeat of oligarchs in 411 and 403 BCE, see Elster, *Closing the Books*, 3–23.

political community, but it cannot provide a basis for reestablishing community. It remains critical and negative, rather than constructive.

In debates on Arendt's scholarship, this tension has sometimes been treated as a problem to be resolved, whether in favor of a single stance or by identifying a unifying logic. In contemporary debates on transitional justice, legalism and restorative justice frameworks have become strategies for eliding this tension by depoliticizing investigations of past abuse and avoiding overtly political claims and judgments. The trouble with these responses is that the stance of the actor and that of the spectator are *both* vital to good political judgment, and both are required for any transitional justice project that aspires to play a critical and transformative role in response to systematic atrocities.

Critical judgment requires us to check our perceptions and opinions against those of others because we are each limited as to what we can perceive and comprehend. Yet critical judgment also requires the Socratic capacity to step outside of the "common sense" of the day, to distance oneself from conventional wisdom. Efforts to judge systematic political violence vary tremendously in scope and context, but all are marked by this tension between the goal of establishing their validity as persuasive political interventions and establishing their authority as critical spectators who strive to remove themselves from present-day imperatives in order to discern and address broader patterns or logics in historical events. Where transitional justice practices merely legitimate the aspirations and decisions of political actors, they abandon their critical role. Where they operate only as critical spectators, they may undermine the goal of establishing a basis for common ground, advancing change, and attaining remedies.

Instead of identifying transitional justice with the goal of *resolving* this set of tensions, we might alternatively consider how transitional justice might be understood as an effort to *mediate* between the goals associated with the role of the actor and the role of the spectator. How might transitional justice investigations inform political reform and reconciliation without abandoning a critical response to the systemic dimension of past wrongs? How might investigations of systemic atrocities challenge conventional wisdom and expose the failures of inherited communities without jeopardizing efforts to identify new possibilities for reform, recovery, and solidarity?

IMAGINATION AND REFLECTION

Arendt's writings on political judgment suggest two strategies for addressing this set of problems. The first might be drawn from her claim that "enlarged mentality" depends on the capacity of the *imagination* to mediate between the tasks of taking the perspectives of others into account and the task of establishing a critical distance from those perspectives. This dimension of Arendt's argument is troubling to many who are otherwise sympathetic to her case for political judgment as "enlarged mentality." After all, it is quite easy to *imagine* that we have accounted for competing views when we have done nothing of the kind. What we imagine to be the experiences and perspectives of others is shaped by dynamics of power and inequality in ways that are often imperceptible to us and may have very little to do with reality.

In identifying imagination as an important dimension of "enlarged mentality," however, Arendt does not suggest that imagination ought to *substitute for* or displace actual dialogue. As Benhabib observes, Arendt's "enlarged mentality" requires that we "know 'how to listen' to what the other is saying, or when the voices of others are absent, to imagine oneself in conversation with the other."[63] The imagination is also active in our efforts to understand the views of those who are present. Speech is limited as a means of conveying experiences, and when we encounter perspectives that are unfamiliar to us, we assimilate them into our own understanding only with the aid of imagination. By emphasizing the role of imagination in enlarged mentality, Arendt suggests that political judgments must strive to account for diverse perspectives, yet also acknowledge the limits of doing so. By acknowledging these limitations, Arendt's conception of political judgment avoids masking imbalances of power or ongoing conflicts.[64] It also underscores the limitations of dialogue as a basis for political change. Where political judgment is simply viewed as a matter of attaining *consent*, it may amount to little more than a ratification of the most basic or obvious of shared viewpoints.[65]

With this in mind, one strategy for mediating the tensions between persuasion and critical reflection is to acknowledge the limited and partial character of both dimensions of transitional justice. As political interventions, transitional justice practices strive to establish a common basis for judgment that accounts for relevant perspectives, to generate a compelling basis for consent. Yet to some extent, their decisions and judgments also depend on an effort to imagine possibilities for a consensus that does not yet exist. As critical spectators, transitional justice institutions strive to establish a kind of distance from

---

[63] Seyla Benhabib, "Judgment and the Moral Foundation of Politics in Arendt's Thought," *Political Theory* 16 (1988), 44. Romand Coles argues that democratic theory itself must move beyond an emphasis on dialogue to encompass practices of listening ("Moving Democracy," *Political Theory* 32, no. 5 [2004]: 678–705).

[64] Disch, *Hannah Arendt and the Limits of Philosophy*, 163, 4.

[65] See Linda Zerilli, "'We Feel Our Freedom': Imagination and Judgment in the Thought of Hannah Arendt," *Political Theory* 33 (2005): 181.

political imperatives and prevailing forms of conventional wisdom, but to some extent, this distance is also imagined and therefore limited. To recognize the role of imagination in transitional justice, then, is not naively utopian. Perhaps paradoxically, it is actually a form of realism.

A second strategy for addressing the tensions between the role of actors and spectators in transitional justice may be drawn from Arendt's discussion of "exemplary validity." Arendt argues that as a form of reflective judgment, political judgment must rely on the imaginative use of examples to reveal generalities that could not otherwise be defined.[66] Exemplars illuminate the significance of general principles and make them meaningful to a wide audience, yet also retain their uniqueness and particularity. Arendt's discussion of "exemplary validity" offers an alternative approach to addressing the tensions associated with political judgment – between the potentially destabilizing impact of the Socratic critic and the limitations of Aristotelian persuasion.

In *Eichmann in Jerusalem*, Arendt uses "exemplary validity" to dissent from the conventional view that the genocide is best understood as the most extreme example in a long history of anti-Semitic violence.[67] Instead of searching for ways to apply existing legal, moral, or historical categories to the problem, she insists that we must confront the task of establishing new concepts to understand and condemn genocide. She does so by recasting the Holocaust as an example not only of crimes against the Jewish people, but also a "crime against humanity." It was, she writes, "an attack against human diversity as such, that is, upon a characteristic of the 'human status,' without which the very words 'mankind' or 'humanity' would be devoid of meaning."[68] Alessandro Ferrara has referred to this as "negative exemplarity."[69] The concept of "crimes against humanity" and the case for global solidarity in prohibiting such crimes are thus given meaning with reference to the example, rather than through an appeal to pre-existing principles in international laws or traditions.

Arendt also makes use of exemplary validity as a way to draw guidance from the past. This strategy might be better understood in the context of her reflections on the work of Walter Benjamin. "Benjamin knew that the break in tradition and loss of authority which had occurred in his lifetime were irreparable," Arendt wrote, and "he concluded that he had to discover new ways

---

[66] Arendt, *Lectures on Kant's Political Philosophy*, 77.
[67] Arendt, *Eichmann in Jerusalem*, 268, 269, 276. See also Bilsky, "When Actor and Spectator Meet," 268.
[68] Arendt, *Eichmann in Jerusalem*, 269.
[69] Alessandro Ferarra, *The Force of the Example: Explorations in the Paradigm of Judgment* (New York: Columbia University Press, 2008), 80.

of dealing with the past."[70] He did so by developing an eccentric approach to working with quotations, taking them out of their context and rearranging them. In contrast with the role of the storyteller, which is to fit experiences into a narrative that is handed down in collective memory, Benjamin saw his work as a destructive act of preserving fragments of the past by destroying the context in which they are handed down to us. Arendt likened his work to "pearl diving" and argued that "there is no more effective way to break the spell of tradition ... than to cut out the 'rich and strange' corals and pearls, from what had been handed down in one solid piece."[71] In contrast with traditional narratives and histories, which systematically put the past in order, the work of the "collector" or "pearl diver" is interested in the intrinsic worth or meaning of fragments.

Arendt employs a similar method to draw fragments from the work of exemplary thinkers out of the ideological, theoretical, and historical contexts in which they appear.[72] She preserves "pearls" of wisdom from canonical works, while simultaneously exposing the collapse or inadequacy of the broader systems of thought in which they appear. She appropriates historical examples creatively – some would say too creatively – as a way to identify possibilities for political action and community in a context marked by despair and disengagement.[73] However, her use of examples is also destructive in the sense that it reveals the collapse of traditional guidance and exposes the inadequacy of standards that have been taken for granted.

In *Eichmann in Jerusalem*, Arendt uses the example of Anton Schmidt to reveal the limitations of the criminal justice framework. Anton Schmidt had aided Jewish partisans by supplying them with forged papers and military trucks for several months in 1941 and 1942 before he was arrested and executed. Recounting testimony concerning Schmidt's resistance, Arendt suggests that everything in the world would be "utterly different" if more such stories could have been told.[74] Schmidt's story functions as a way to strengthen Arendt's indictment of those who were complicit in the machinery of Nazi brutality. The story of Schmidt also functions to demonstrate Arendt's claims regarding the inadequacy of a morality premised on

[70] Hannah Arendt, "Introduction: Walter Benjamin: 1892–1940," in *Illuminations*, ed. Hannah Arendt (New York: Schocken, 1968), 38.
[71] Arendt, "Introduction: Walter Benjamin," 51.
[72] Kirstie McClure, "The Odor of Judgment: Exemplarity, Propriety and Politics in the Company of Arendt," in *Hannah Ardent and the Meaning of Politics*, ed. Craig Calhoun and John McGowan (Minneapolis, MN and London: University of Minnesota Press, 1997), 60.
[73] See Dietz, *Turning Operations*, 183–200.
[74] Arendt, *Eichmann in Jerusalem*, 231.

obedience and deference to a set of principles, laws, or standards. At the same time, the story illuminates possibilities of solidarity and agency in the face of widespread complicity, which are peripheral to legal narratives.

Arendt's 1961 volume of essays, *Between Past and Future*, begins with a quote from René Char: "Notre héritage n'est précédé d'aucun testament" ("Our inheritance was not willed to us"). Arendt explains that Char articulated this "strangest" of his "abruptly strange" aphorisms as he reflected on his role in the French resistance from the vantage point of the immediate postwar period and on his odd realization that the postwar years had brought despair, disappointment, and even some degree of nostalgia for the struggle of war. The work of the resistance movement was a terrible burden, but it involved people in a collective struggle for freedom. Although the resistance was underground, hidden, and members often did not know one another, they had created, "without knowing it or even noticing it," what Arendt refers to as a kind of "public space."[75] After the liberation, they returned to the "empty strife of conflicting ideologies," which "divided former comrades-in-arms into innumerable cliques."[76]

To locate a basis for political community without relying on a tradition, which "selects and names, hands down and preserves," Arendt argues, is like trying to locate an inheritance that was left without a testament.[77] She does not conclude from this that political community is rendered impossible for the future and that we must learn to live without it. Instead, she develops Char's aphorism as a way of urging readers to locate the "inheritance" that was *not* willed to us, by identifying possibilities for political engagement and community that have appeared – even in the darkest moments of history – before fading into obscurity. She invokes the French resistance not only to exemplify such possibilities, but also to destroy the delusion that all of France supported the resistance.

Paradoxically, the critical role of transitional justice requires action *and* disengagement, persuasion and critique. It requires acceptance of the horrors of the past but *also* a basis for hope in the future. It requires an approach to historical reflection and remembrance that exposes the limitations of transitional justice remedies, yet also identifies possibilities for community and innovation beyond the limitations of political compromise. Contemporary approaches to transitional justice have avoided these tensions by depoliticizing responses to the past.

[75] Arendt, *Between Past and Future*, 4.
[76] Arendt, *Between Past and Future*, 4.
[77] Arendt, *Between Past and Future*, 5.

Critical responses to political violence require constructive strategies for mediating the tensions between these goals. Arendt's analysis of political judgment offers two such strategies. One strategy would be to acknowledge the partial and provisional character of efforts to establish a common basis for judging past wrongs – the extent to which such efforts imagine a basis for consensus that does not actually exist. Another strategy is to identify examples that illuminate general principles without appealing to pre-existing standards. Like contemporary human rights activists Arendt thought that exemplary cases could be constructive as a way to persuade people to accept novel standards of judgment. Yet for Arendt, exemplary validity was powerful not as a strategy for defending abstract principles but as a tool for reflective judgments that would allow for innovation in response to the particularities of each case. In contrast with contemporary proponents of transitional justice, Arendt also argued that investigations centered on the experiences of victims and perpetrators would be limited as a basis for judgment and reconciliation in the aftermath of systematic atrocities. She suggested that examples of resistance might offer a uniquely promising basis for addressing the limitations of legal judgment, as well as a forgotten form of guidance for the project of identifying new forms of solidarity, action, and community.

THE ORESTEIA AS A DRAMA OF TRANSITIONAL JUSTICE

The *Oresteian Trilogy* by Aeschylus has been widely discussed as a drama of criminal justice. It has been read as a story of the triumph of impartial institutions over senseless cycles of revenge, as a story of the institutionalization of patriarchal power, and as a story of the power of pardon and amnesty. Here, I reexamine *The Oresteia* as a drama of transitional justice. Drawing on an essay by Peter Euben, I suggest that *The Oresteia* exemplifies how the strategies that Arendt associates with "enlarged mentality" might usefully inform the pursuit of justice and reconciliation in the aftermath of political violence.

The *Oresteian Trilogy* dramatizes the transformation of a society scarred by brutality and revenge killings to an ordered polis in which previously warring parties voice their commitment to unity and harmony. In the first two plays, *Agammemnon* and *The Libation Bearers*, the land of Argos appears fated to replay endless cycles of violence and revenge. King Agammemnon sacrifices his own daughter to save his kingdom, and his wife, Clytaemnestra, takes her revenge by killing him and seizing power. Clytaemnestra characterizes the killing as just retribution for his actions: "Act for act, wound for wound ... here you are repaid!"[78] In the second part of the trilogy, the chorus urges her children to murder Clytamenestra in revenge for their father's death: "Justice turns the wheel, word for word, curse for curse … Justice thunders, hungry for retribution."[79] Euben observes that for Orestes, the past is both an inheritance and a curse. Orestes kills his mother in order to claim a home and citizenship, yet he is aware that in so doing, he will also inherit the cycles of revenge and death that cloud the history of his family and kingdom.[80] Orestes proclaims that he is not to be blamed for killing his mother, "who was herself/Marked with my father's blood, unclean."[81] Yet he is soon approached by the Furies, "the great fulfillers of memory and grief," who scream at him in rage and demand that he be punished in return for what he has done. Clytaemnestra's ghost also returns to call for revenge. "Will you not wake?" she cries out to the chorus, "Does grief not touch you?"[82]

The Goddess Athena confronts this horrific landscape in the third play of the trilogy, *The Eumenides*. Athena is called on to resolve the conflict and presides over a hearing that would, in contemporary parlance, be considered a successful case of transitional justice. Athena listens carefully to the claims made on behalf of the parties to the conflict. She acknowledges that she is concerned not only with the legal question of Orestes's guilt, but also with the political implications of an acquittal. "Your accusers' claims are not to be dismissed," she tells Orestes. "And should they fail to win their case," she adds, "their anger falls/Like death and terror, blight and poison, on my land."[83] It seems as though Athena is faced with an impossible decision. She must decide in favor of the Furies and punish Orestes, or she must banish the Furies altogether to avoid further bloodshed, yet "either course," she observes, "is peril and perplexity."[84] Faced with a seemingly impossible decision, Athena conceives of a way to transform the situation and chart a new course. She decides to establish a perpetual court and urges both sides to "[b]ring your evidence," and to "call witnesses, whose oaths shall strengthen Justice's hand."[85] The Furies warn that if such a court were to pardon Orestes, his acquittal would erode traditional moral standards: "His act shall now to every man/Commend the easy path of crime." The Furies also threaten further bloodshed and revenge: "If we should

[78] Aeschylus, *The Oresteia*, trans. Robert Fagles (New York: Penguin, 1966).
[79] Aeschylus, *The Oresteia*, 315–8.
[80] Peter Euben, *The Tragedy of Political Theory: The Road Not Taken* (Princeton, NJ: Princeton University Press, 1990), 76.
[81] Aeschylus, *The Oresteia*, 141.
[82] Aeschylus, *The Oresteia*, 151.
[83] Aeschylus, *The Oresteia*, 164.
[84] Aeschylus, *The Oresteia*, 164.
[85] Aeschylus, *The Oresteia*, 164.

fail to win this case ... we will infest the land with plagues unspeakable."[86] Yet Athena nevertheless casts the deciding vote in favor of pardoning Orestes and she persuades the Furies to accept her decision, to accept an offer of membership in the newly established order, and to trade their fury and sorrow for a commitment to bestow their blessings on the city.[87]

One way to interpret *The Oresteia* is to see it as a drama about the triumph of legalism (and patriarchy) over the chaos of revenge.[88] Char lamented the loss of commitment and passion in the aftermath of transition, as principled struggle gave way to petty squabbling and a retreat into private life. The Furies represent the opposite concern – that the passions and anger associated with past struggles will "poison the land." The two problems are related in that it is fear associated with the image of the Furies – the fear of endless destabilizing conflict over the meaning of the past – that is often invoked to justify forgetting the demand for justice.[89] Athena's pardon did not abandon justice, as the Furies warned, nor did it lead to further revenge or violence. The incorporation of the Furies into this new order of justice represents the taming, cooptation, and harnessing of the revenge impulse by an official judicial order. By granting the Furies a place of honor in the new regime, the fear of revenge, the fear of what would ensue in the absence of an established legal order, is kept alive as a way to legitimate the judicial system, while the desire for revenge is maintained and channeled into institutionalized forms of punishment.

George Bizos, who served as a lawyer to Nelson Mandela and was actively involved in the drafting of South Africa's TRC legislation, has interpreted *The Oresteia* in a very different way – as a drama about the transformative power of pardons.[90] For proponents of restorative justice, cycles of violence and revenge cannot be overcome through impartial legal accountability alone, but only by broadening our view of justice beyond the confines of retribution. Athena's success in transforming the situation in Argos is not only due to the development of an impartial court, but also to the responsive and inclusive process that she used in reaching the decision to pardon Orestes, which aimed not only at reaching a just verdict, but also at establishing a basis for social peace. For those restorative justice theorists that have emphasized therapeutic healing, the main problem in Argos, as represented by the Furies, is not the absence of

[86] Aeschylus, *The Oresteia*, 171.
[87] Aeschylus, *The Oresteia*, 179.
[88] See David Luban, *Legal Modernism: Law, Meaning, and Violence* (Ann Arbor, MI: University of Michigan Press, 1997), 299–321.
[89] Robert Meister, "Human Rights and the Politics of Victimhood," *Ethics and International Affairs* 16 (2002): 91–108.
[90] Interview, Cape Town, March 30, 1999.

an impartial legal system, but the unhealed wounds and traumatic memories associated with past violence. Athena's genius is to transform the Furies and secure their blessing in the new order by acknowledging their suffering.

The legalistic and restorative interpretations of *The Oresteia* are both persuasive. The development of impartial legal institutions and rule of law is a vital response to political violence, but also limited as a basis for remembrance and reform. Pardon and the acknowledgment of the victim's suffering may broaden our understanding of remedy for past abuse. These may be useful strategies for integrating marginalized or stigmatized populations, or for striving to transform factions still motivated by a desire for revenge and recrimination. Yet both interpretations are also missing something important, namely the role of political judgment in guiding both dimensions of Athena's decision.

For Peter Euben, Athena's pardon of Orestes represents the way in which political judgment, when guided by "enlarged mentality," might contribute to a broader approach to justice that encompasses a provisional kind of reconciliation. He argues that justice requires judgment in the Arendtian sense that entails "the capacity to see things from another's point of view and so accept the human condition of plurality."[91] Euben does not elaborate on this idea because this is not the primary purpose of his essay. However, his analysis provides a useful starting point for thinking about how Arendt's idea of "enlarged mentality" can be brought to bear on contemporary transitional justice debates.

One way to develop the argument is to take a closer look at how Athena's decision exemplifies "enlarged mentality." In many respects, her judgment resembles the Aristotelian approach to political judgment articulated by Beiner—one that is grounded in an active process of deliberation within a political community. Athena listens to the Furies and treats them with respect. "Your greater age claims my forbearance," she tells them. However, in making her decision, she does not simply ratify the lowest common denominator of public opinion, but rather imagines a new basis for transforming the conflict and persuading the Furies to accept the new order. "Force is needless," she tells them, "let persuasion check/ The fruit of foolish threats before it falls to spread Plague and disaster."[92] Athena develops institutions that are to foster transparency in decision making and inclusive membership in a plural society. Evidence and arguments are to be presented in an open hearing, and the Furies are granted a home in the new polis. These dimensions of

---

91 Euben, *The Tragedy of Political Theory*, 81.
92 Aeschylus, *The Oresteia*, 175.

her judgment enhance its contributions to the broader vision of justice that prevails at the conclusion of the drama.

Euben does not discuss tensions between the Aristotelian and Socratic dimensions of Arendt's theory of political judgment, but his comments regarding the judgment of the intended audience, or spectators, of *The Oresteia* are evocative in this regard. Euben observes that the spectators Aeschylus had in mind as the intended audience of *The Oresteia* were unlikely to have been persuaded by the reconciliation that occurs in the concluding scenes of the trilogy. The Furies abandon their demands for revenge and exemplify the possibility of reconciliation, yet the ending of *The Oresteia* is haunted by what has come before, reminding us that the harmony that prevails at the conclusion of the play is likely to be temporary.[93]

Athena has not established a moral consensus regarding her judgment of past events. The moral perspectives of the Furies and Orestes are still irreconcilable, but they assent to compromise in the name of membership in an imagined community. The persuasion and compromise involved in Athena's decision establish the possibility of political community and agency, yet the drama of the previous acts awakens the audience to the horrors of past violence in a manner that exposes the fragility and the limitations of the play's final resolution. *Without* this tension, between the political judgment of Athena's intervention and the critical historical perspective revealed to spectators, the drama would merely function as an exercise in political legitimation.

Athena does not attempt to mask this tension by disavowing the limitations or the partial character of her judgment. Euben's analysis stresses the positive outcomes of the decision and the inclusiveness of the process, yet Aeschylus's Athena is strikingly frank in noting the ways in which her decision reflects some degree of bias and inequality. "There is no mother anywhere who gave me birth," she proclaims as she casts her ballot, "So, in a case where the wife has killed her husband, lord of the house, her death shall not mean most to me. And if the other votes are even, then Orestes wins." Although she acknowledges that Orestes's accusers have a valid moral perspective, she also makes it clear that the Furies represent a less valued segment of the new order, the losses that they mourn are deemed less significant, their lives less valuable than those of longstanding members of the polis. Athena's persuasive efforts rely heavily on flattery and the promise of future happiness and healing. She offers the Furies "glistening thrones covered with praise," a "royal share of

---

[93] Euben, *The Tragedy of Political Theory*, 89. Luban similarly argues that Aeschylus presents the cooptation of the Furies as necessary, while simultaneously and subversively revealing the injustice of the transition.

our land," a place "[w]here all the pain and anguish end," if they accept her verdict.[94] Yet Athena also reminds them of her own position of power and warns that she is the only one with the key to Zeus's thunderbolts.[95]

To evaluate the role of political judgment in Athena's decision is not to downplay the significance of the legal institutions that she establishes or the transformative potential of her pardon. Rather, it is to examine the process of judgment that informs the role of these strategies as responses to injustices that are systemic in nature. Athena's judgment exemplifies the role of the engaged actor, who seeks to "woo" the consent of a divided people. At the same time, the play also dramatizes the role of the critical spectator in exposing the limited and tentative nature of that consent. The legacies of the two most prominent exemplars for contemporary approaches to transitional justice – the Nuremberg Trials and the South African TRC – may be better understood with attention to the relationship between their role as political actors and critical spectators.

The Nuremberg Trials departed from the premises of academic legalism by allowing the victors in a war to sit in judgment over atrocities committed by the vanquished. The court effectively used legalistic strategies as a basis for establishing a limited form of impartiality by granting defendants a fair hearing and analyzing evidence in a persuasive manner. Yet to a large extent, Nuremberg also displayed the political judgments that animated its mandate. The court's judgment of individual cases was premised on, and designed to illuminate, a decisive condemnation of the political regime with respect to its institutions and its ideology. The Nuremberg Trials were also a major historical drama that used the example of Nazism to persuade an international audience of the need to accept new limitations on Westphalian sovereignty by prosecuting political authorities for crimes against their own citizens.[96]

Arendt's analysis of political judgment suggests an alternative way to draw on this legacy in evaluating the role of criminal prosecution as a response to systematic political violence. Instead of evaluating these institutions as manifestations of uncompromising legalism or dismissing them as merely reflections of political power dynamics, we might critically evaluate the role of political judgment in their development and execution. As responses to politically authorized violence, these institutions must persuade local and international audiences to accept their authority and mandates. At the same time, they must establish their critical authority as a response to systemic violence by distancing themselves from prevailing local and international interests.

94 Aeschylus, *The Oresteia*, 819–20, 898, 903.
95 Aeschylus, *The Oresteia*, 837–38.
96 See Esquith, "Re-enacting Mass Violence."

The analytic framework of the criminal trial may be useful in pursuing both of these goals, but it can also mask and exacerbate the tension between them. The history of war crimes trials and human rights prosecutions in the decades following the Nuremberg Trials suggests that the adversarial character of the trial may be uniquely persuasive as a basis for presenting evidence, but it may also be extremely polarizing and divisive. The Nuremberg Trials advanced a broad condemnation of the Nazi regime, but did so in a context where the Nazi regime had been decisively defeated. More commonly, where war crimes trials are used to examine and condemn the broader regime or system, they have also been challenged as destabilizing or illegitimate. Proponents of human rights legalism have responded to this problem by calling for more narrowly framed, exemplary trials. However, their focus on individualizing guilt is in tension with their aspiration to offer a critical response to politically authorized violence, by exposing the extent of atrocities that may have been committed and challenging denial regarding who bears responsibility for such acts.

Arendt's discussion of "enlarged mentality" also sheds light on the legacy of South Africa's TRC as model for the ways in which truth commissions might address these limitations. South Africa's truth commission aimed to acknowledge varied perspectives on the conflict while issuing a decisive judgment. In contrast with the blanket amnesties issued by outgoing military governments in countries such as Argentina and Chile, the amnesty provisions in South Africa were established through a broad process of negotiation that would institutionalize an inclusive basis for membership and power sharing. Just as Athena established a space for the Furies in the new order with the goal of neutralizing their destructive anger, so too did the TRC aim to establish a space for remembering and acknowledging the abuses and killings of the past in the hopes that the process would alleviate the trauma associated with such experiences. Yet while the process acknowledged diverse viewpoints, the amnesty in South Africa could not be characterized as the result of a moral consensus, but only an agreement among major players to compromise their own moral goals in the name of an imagined, future community, the precise character of which would remain unpredictable.

Although South Africa's amnesty process was based on a successful compromise, it was also a process with winners and losers that reflected past inequalities to the extent that those previously in power had the most to gain from amnesty. Like Athena's pardon, South Africa's amnesty was presented and accepted in a context of promises regarding the benefits of the compromise, including the promise of reparations and the claim that participation in the process would facilitate healing at the individual, local, and national levels.

Such promises were made with little evidence to suggest that they could be ful-filled and would exacerbate anger and frustration among those for whom the reparations process proved disappointing, and when initial feelings of catharsis and emotional release gave way, in some cases, to a sense of betrayal.[97] South Africa's amnesty provision was also accepted against the backdrop of a threat – that failure to compromise would mean endless bloodshed.[98]

Athena established a space for the Furies with their memories of grief and loss in the hopes that this official acknowledgment would facilitate a cathartic healing process and transform violent desires for revenge into a commitment to bless the new order. The role of public remembrance in truth commis-sions might also be understood and assessed in relation to Arendt's analysis of the relationship between the judgment of actor and spectator. The frame-work for historical judgment and official memory that guides the work of truth commissions is established through the political dialogue, negotiations, and compromises that shape truth commission mandates and the broader terms of transitions. Although the TRC was committed to establishing a space for remembrance, the compromises that informed the amnesty would dramati-cally limit the TRC's role in acknowledging and commemorating the losses suffered as a result of apartheid. The TRC addressed this conflict by depoliti-cizing its work. The TRC would only investigate the stories of "victims" and "perpetrators" defined in relation to forms of violence that were illegal even under the apartheid regime, excluding the stories of those who resisted, and benefited from, the apartheid system.

Arendt's analysis of political judgment suggests an alternative way to think about the contribution of truth commissions to transitional justice. The criti-cal role of truth commissions depends on how these institutions mediate the tension between their efforts to persuade a wide and diverse audience on the one hand and efforts to expose the limitations of conventional wisdom on the other hand. Truth commissions can achieve critical distance from transitional

97 Based on interviews with individuals who participated in the TRC process as victims, a recent study concluded that "the lack of adequate support and follow-up by the commission left most survivors with a sense of having been abandoned and not having their needs understood or their stories acknowledged." Phakathi and Van der Merwe, "The Impact of the TRC's Amnesty Process," 137. See also, David Backer, "Exit, Voice and Loyalty in Transitional Justice Pro-cesses: Evidence on Victims' Responses to South Africa's Truth and Reconciliation Commis-sion." Paper presented at the annual meeting of the American Political Science Association, Hilton Chicago and the Palmer House Hilton, Chicago, IL, September 02, 2004.
98 Erik Doxtader, "Easy to Forget or Never (Again) Hard to Remember? History, Memory and the 'Publicity' of Amnesty," in *The Provocations of Amnesty: Memory, Justice and Impunity*, ed. Charles Villa-Vicencio and Erik Doxtader (Cape Town: Institution for Justice and Reconcili-ation, 2003).

compromises by establishing a space for remembering what cannot be remedied or forgiven.

This analysis of political judgment also underscores what is problematic about an implicit assumption that has been associated with truth commissions and human rights advocacy more generally – that in remembering political violence we have a dichotomous choice between avoiding the stories of those who cannot be characterized as passive victims in need of healing, or opening the door to vengeful Furies bent on poisoning the land with their grief and rage. To structure investigations of political violence in accordance with this perceived dichotomy is to condone the forgetting of those who took action in the name of solidarity and change. The stories of those who organize various forms of resistance are complicated for contemporary transitional justice institutions. They are stories of people who acted politically, and how they are remembered is a source of potentially explosive controversy. Yet to forget them, as Char reminds, is also to abandon a potentially valuable, if "unwilled," inheritance.

CONCLUSION

Arendt's analysis of political judgment addresses an important problem at the center of two theoretical frameworks that have dominated transitional justice debates. Legalistic and restorative approaches to transitional justice both aim to judge political violence and advance political change, but are premised on a view of crime as a discrete deviation from shared norms. Both frameworks have functioned to depoliticize transitional justice investigations by using the experiences of individual victims and perpetrators to obfuscate the problem of widespread complicity and the absence or breakdown of common standards as a basis for judgment. In contrast with contemporary human rights advocates, Arendt rejected the use of human rights claims as a basis for depoliticizing responses to political violence. In her view, such efforts would not aid but only undermine the task of building common ground, solidarity, and political responsibility. Yet Arendt also rejected a stance of tragic acceptance or resignation to the view that we inevitably inherit divisions and conflicts. Instead, she saw political judgment as a basis for recovering what Char had referred to as the "inheritance that was not willed" by learning from the past without relying on the guidance of inherited community and tradition.

Political judgment is intrinsic to the critical role of transitional justice, but it may also be mired in prejudice and may simply serve to justify what is really just an assertion of power or narrowly defined interest. Where massive atrocities and political violence have occurred, or continue to occur, where people despair in the possibility of political community, political judgment appears inherently divisive or immoral. Thus, contemporary transitional justice institutions have aimed to establish their moral authority and their contributions to reconciliation by depoliticizing their investigations of past wrongs. Arendt offers an alternative approach to establishing a common basis for judging politically authorized atrocities. Instead of avoiding or disavowing political judgment, she developed a set of criteria for distinguishing the critical and transformative exercise of political judgment from narrow and uncritical assertions of opinion.

Arendt's concept of "enlarged mentality" provides a way to move beyond dichotomous thinking that pits justice against politics, international law against local values, or trials against forgiveness. It does so by establishing guidelines for seeking commonalities without claiming to transcend political conflict altogether through an appeal to prepolitical or apolitical criteria. "Enlarged mentality" entails two distinctive stances that are in tension with one another – the stance of the active, engaged political actor that appeals to prevailing "common sense," and the stance of the detached historian who imaginatively reflects on past events to identify examples that might illuminate possibilities for the future. It entails thinking with and without community by striving to transcend the confines of past beliefs, yet also acknowledging the limitations of such efforts. Arendt uses exemplary validity as a way to appeal to the possibility of common ground, while also exposing the absence of inherited communities.

Examining the role of political judgment in the development of international criminal justice and truth commissions means thinking about how such institutions navigate this tension: How they simultaneously appeal to prevailing opinions, yet also stand apart to challenge and expose the inadequacy of inherited views; how they strive to generate dialogue and consent, but are nonetheless shaped by compromise, negotiation, and imagination; how they seek to learn from the past not only through compiling evidence and documenting abuse, but also through the selection and interpretation of events and experiences that exemplify new possibilities for justice and community.

Arendt's analysis of political judgment does not provide a blueprint for resolving the dilemmas associated with transitional justice. However, it does suggest strategies for addressing or mediating tensions that have been overlooked in contemporary debates on transitional justice. One strategy is to acknowledge the limited and partial character of the judgments that animate transitional justice institutions and practices, the extent to which they rely on imagination as a basis for establishing general claims. Acknowledging the limitations of the judgments and partial remedies of transitional justice institutions is one way to ensure that those decisions do not foreclose ongoing efforts to expand the scope of accountability or develop further remedial responses for past abuses. In the following chapter, I consider how this strategy might inform efforts to reconsider the role of restorative justice as a response to systematic political violence and state-sponsored atrocities.

A second strategy is to identify examples that illuminate possibilities for political community and consensus in the future, while exposing the collapse or failure of political community in the past. To some extent, "exemplary validity" captures what has become a standard strategy of transitional justice – the use of individual cases to exemplify demands for justice and possibilities for reconciliation beyond the limitations of what is possible to realize in a divided and fearful political setting. Yet Arendt uses "exemplary validity" as a way to move beyond the limitations of legalism. She does so by suggesting that reflecting on the stories of those who resist systematic atrocities might be instructive for efforts to evaluate the problem of complicity in the past and efforts to establish new forms of solidarity, agency, and community in the future. In Chapter 6, I consider what it would mean to build on this argument by integrating the theme of resistance into the theory and practice of transitional justice.

5

Rethinking Restorative Justice

South Africa's TRC articulated an ambitious and influential challenge to human rights legalism. In so doing, the TRC also challenged conventional wisdom regarding the path of innovation and change in human rights norms and practices. However, scholarly debate on the legacy of the TRC has been limited in important ways. Most notably, critics and supporters alike have tended to identify restorative justice very closely with therapeutic justice. This close identification of restorative and therapeutic justice departs from the theoretical premises that animated the early development of the TRC and elides the theoretical innovations of those who contributed to the TRC's restorative justice framework.

In this chapter, I develop a conceptual distinction between restorative and therapeutic justice and suggest an alternative way to understand how truth commissions might contribute to restorative justice. The first section of the chapter takes a closer look at restorative justice theory as articulated by scholars that have defined the field. It argues that what makes restorative justice appealing, but also problematic, as a response to systematic injustices and political violence is the fact that the framework allows political judgment to influence the adjudication process. More specifically, restorative justice is based on the view that addressing individual harms requires a response to underlying conflicts and inequalities. However, it relies on a communitarian approach to political judgment that is in tension with this commitment. The analogy to therapy is a way of eliding fears regarding the role of political judgment in the restorative justice process, but it also abandons much of what is promising in the theory.

How, other than by analogy to therapy, might truth commissions contribute to restorative justice? The second section of the chapter examines three distinctive responses to this question offered by thinkers who influenced the debate on restorative justice in South Africa: Desmond Tutu, Charles

Villa-Vicencio, and Mahmood Mamdani. These thinkers shared the view that the TRC had been limited and disappointing as a basis for restorative justice. They also shared the view that restorative justice could not simply be applied, but would have to be *adapted* to the context of systematic atrocity and political violence. However, they offer very different ideas about what this should entail and what it implies for the role of truth commissions. Tutu and Villa-Vicencio both associate the framework with an approach to political judgment that is grounded in active persuasion, compromise, and transformative dialogue. In contrast, Mamdani suggests that restorative justice requires a critical and historical approach to political judgment—one that exposes denial and examines the legacy of the past in the present. Building on the argument developed in Chapter 4, I suggest that restorative justice requires both forms of political judgment and consider how truth commissions might better mediate the tensions between them.

RESTORE WHAT?

Restorative justice theory emerged out of the experiences of people who became involved in experimental Victim-Offender Reconciliation Programs in Canada, Australia, and North America in the 1970s. Over time, a wide range of groups engaged in developing alternatives to prosecution united under the banner of restorative justice, encompassing religious leaders, indigenous rights activists, and feminist critics of the justice system. This somewhat eclectic collection of activists shared a common concern with shifting the focus of criminal justice away from punishment toward redress and rehabilitation. In the 1980s and 1990s, restorative justice was popularized by a number of scholars and activists as an alternative to retribution and a basis for criminal justice reform.[1]

Restorative justice theory has many variants, but scholars and practitioners tend to converge on four basic principles: participation, personalism, reparation, and reintegration.[2] According to Tony Marshall's widely accepted definition, restorative justice is a "process whereby all the parties with a stake in

[1] Tony F. Marshall, *Alternatives to Criminal Courts: The Potential for Non-Judicial Dispute Settlement* (Brookfield, VT: Gower Publishing Co., 1985); Zehr, *Changing Lenses*; Mark Umbreit, "Restorative Justice through Victim-Offender Mediation: A Multi-Site Assessment," *Western Criminology Review* 1, no. 1 (1998); Burt Galaway and Joe Hudson, *Restorative Justice: International Perspectives* (Monsey, NY: Criminal Justice Press, 1996); Gordon Bazemore and Lode Walgrave, *Restorative Juvenile Justice* (Monsey, NY: Criminal Justice Press, 1999); Braithwaite, *Restorative Justice and Responsive Regulation*; Heather Strang, *Repair or Revenge: Victims and Restorative Justice* (Oxford: Clarendon Press, 2002).
[2] Declan Roche, *Accountability in Restorative Justice* (Oxford: Oxford University Press, 2003).

a particular offence come together to resolve collectively how to deal with the aftermath of the offence and its implications for the future."[3] Restorative justice programs use a range of strategies to facilitate participation from victims, offenders, and communities. For Braithwaite, what is crucial about such efforts is that they aim for an "undominated dialogue" about the consequences of injustice and "what is to be done to put them right."[4] Beyond participation in the adjudication process, restorative justice also entails a pluralist approach to defining the very terms of justice, which builds on dialogue among distinct cultural traditions. Restorative justice holds that victims and perpetrators, as well as communities, should play an active part in the process of addressing crime.

"Personalism," a second principle of restorative justice, requires attention to the "concrete harms" and consequences of crime as experienced by victims.[5] It also requires attention to the way that individual harms are related to underlying social practices and conflicts. In practice, this means that victim participation in restorative justice is not limited to their assistance in establishing "who did what to whom," but includes testimony that sheds light on the impact of their injuries or losses.

Third, restorative justice entails a commitment to reintegrating offenders back into a broader community. Restorative justice programs typically involve offenders in the process of "making amends" through various forms of mediation, dialogue, and ritual. Braithwaite maintains that such processes must also be complemented with efforts to promote values that support restorative justice, such as empathy, reconciliation, and forgiveness. However, restorative justice does not require forgiveness from victims, but rather establishes spaces where forgiveness might be possible.[6] The restorative justice commitment to reintegration is not an abdication of accountability, nor does it abandon punishment.[7] Instead, restorative justice stipulates that punishments are to be administered with the long-term goal of reintegration, rather than stigmatization or exclusion. Central to restorative justice theory is the premise that offenders are capable of transformation, and that prosecution and punishment often prevent such transformation from occurring, while exacerbating the underlying conflicts and social problems that fuel crime. If perpetrators of

3 Tony Marshall, "The Evolution of Restorative Justice in Britain," *European Journal on Criminal Policy and Research* 4, no. 4 (1996): 21–43, 37.
4 Braithwaite, *Restorative Justice and Responsive Regulation*, 11.
5 Zehr, *Changing Lenses*, 185.
6 Braithwaite, *Restorative Justice and Responsive Regulation*, 11.
7 See Daniel Philpott, "Religion, Reconciliation, and Transitional Justice: The State of the Field," *Social Science Research Council Working Papers* (2007).

crime work toward reintegration by offering apologies for their actions, confessions, or contributions to the process of repair, then restorative justice may
generate a more meaningful degree of accountability than is possible in contexts where perpetrators have an incentive to evade responsibility in order to
avoid permanent exclusion.

Finally, the most important principle of restorative justice is that justice
requires repair, or restoration. When a wrong occurs, writes Howard Zehr, we
should not ask, "What does the offender deserve?" but rather, "What can be
done to make things right?"[8] Addressing this question is not a simple matter,
and when I asked people in South Africa what they thought about restorative
justice, the most common response I received was a question: "Restore *what?*"
Restorative justice theory offers three kinds of responses to this question. One
response is that restorative justice aims to locate some mechanism, however
imperfect, for addressing the needs of victims in the aftermath of crime or
abuse. Restorative justice programs, such as Victim-Offender Reconciliation,
will often establish some form of compensation or restitution to victims as a
direct payment from the offender. Another response is that restorative justice
implies attention to the underlying systemic injustices and conflicts that contribute to individual harms. Braithwaite develops a sweeping approach to conceptualizing repair that encompasses material compensation, a restored sense
of security and dignity, as well as the restoration of deliberative democracy.[9]
Llewellyn and Howse argue that restorative justice requires a commitment to
establish social equality, regardless of the social dynamics that prevailed in
the past. This implies that *restoration* of political community requires broad
social and political *transformation*. A third response has been that the theory
of restorative justice leaves open the question of what is to be "restored" and
posits that the terms of restoration must be established through the participatory process.[10]

It is now easier to see why restorative justice is appealing, but also problematic, as a model for addressing systematic political violence. Restorative justice
requires an adjudicative process that aims to foster qualities that Arendt associated with "enlarged mentality" as a guide for political judgment. That is,
restorative justice calls for a process of persuasion designed to identify agreement on a common standard of judgment by urging participants to consider
multiple perspectives on a common problem. Restorative justice provides a
direct response to the dehumanization associated with systematic atrocity by

---

[8]   Zehr, *Changing Lenses*, 186.
[9]   Strang, *Repair or Revenge?*
[10] See Llewellyn and Howse, "Institutions for Restorative Justice."

providing space for the voices of victims and perpetrators to be heard in a process designed to compel perpetrators to confront their own responsibility for the consequences of abuses that they may have committed. The restorative justice commitment to persuasion and participation is also appealing in the aftermath of systematic political violence because it provides a basis for establishing the legitimacy of the transitional justice process in local contexts. By contrast, international criminal justice has often been perceived as physically distant and philosophically removed from the communities affected by the crimes under investigation.[11]

Restorative justice theory, like Arendt's "enlarged mentality," calls for reflective judgment that is responsive to the particularities of the context in which harms are committed, rather than determinative judgment that would apply formal law or doctrine to a given case. Restorative justice is particularly appealing as a response to political violence because it requires attention to the connections between individual harms and systemic conflicts or injustices. This means restorative justice allows for flexibility in addressing recurring forms of violence in novel ways that are responsive to changing circumstances, constraints, and dynamics associated with local context. It calls for investigations that examine how specific harms are related to underlying conflicts, as well as remedies that address such conflict. The flexibility inherent in restorative justice also allows for a broader approach to remedy and repair, which may be tailored to address the particular damages or needs experienced by those harmed. By stipulating a process of adjudication guided by reflective judgment, the restorative justice framework also allows for flexibility in addressing culpability and is, at least in theory, particularly well positioned address what Levi referred to as the "gray zone" of responsibility.

Thus, much of what makes restorative justice so *appealing* as a response to political violence requires a process of adjudication that is designed to accommodate a direct role for political judgment. What makes restorative justice *problematic*, particularly as a response to political violence, has been the way in which restorative justice theorists and programs have generally relied on communitarian theory of political judgment.

This communitarian approach to political judgment is evident in the writings of the two scholars that have been perhaps most influential in shaping the development of restorative justice theory: Nils Christie and John Braithwaite.

---

[11] See Laurel Fletcher and Harvey M. Weinstein, "A World unto Itself? The Application of International Justice in the Former Yugoslavia," in *My Neighbor, My Enemy*; Eric Stover, "Witnesses and the Promise of Justice in the Hague," in *My Neighbor, My Enemy*; Peter Uvin and Charles Mironko, "Western and Local Approaches to Justice in Rwanda," *Global Governance* 9 (2003).

Nils Christie's 1974 article, "Conflicts as Property," is considered one of the most important early texts in restorative justice theory.[12] Conventional wisdom holds that justice can only be distinguished from revenge by establishing institutions that formalize the process and remove it from the influence of those most affected by crime. Christie rejected this vision and argued that the process of resolving conflicts associated with crime should be understood as an important opportunity to clarify fundamental community values. A second seminal text of restorative justice theory is John Braithwaite's *Crime, Shame, and Reintegration*.[13] Braithwaite's main claim is that the shame and condemnation that accompany punishment are counterproductive without an effort to reintegrate the offender into society. Without community involvement in the process of moralizing about the causes and consequences of crime, argued Braithwaite, the rule of law will amount to little more than a "meaningless set of formal sanctioning proceedings."[14] The key to crime control, in his view, is a cultural commitment to forms of public shaming that are "reintegrative." He argued that shaming may control crime when it is bounded by ceremonies or rituals to reintegrate the offender back into the community.[15] Braithwaite's discussion of shaming has affinities with the Confucian argument that social norms are strongest when internalized through community rituals and traditions on the model of the family.

Following Braithwaite and Christie, restorative justice theorists generally presume a basic consensus on who should be understood as "victims," who should be addressed as "offenders," and what constitutes a "crime." Implicit in restorative justice theory, as influenced by the work of Christie and Braithwaite, is the premise that such judgments may be effectively guided by the shared norms, traditions, and practices of communities. In his work on reintegrative shaming, Braithwaite suggests that where criminal law does not reflect the majoritarian morality, the theory will fail.[16]

This reliance on political judgment guided by the practices and traditions of local communities is in tension with major goals associated with transitional justice. Transitional justice institutions aim to hold community leaders accountable for their role in sponsoring systematic abuses, to critically examine patterns of political violence that may have been justified in the name of political community, and to identify ways that community-based practices

---

[12] Nils Christie, "Conflicts as Property," *The British Journal of Criminology* 17 (January 1977): 1–15.

[13] Braithwaite, *Crime, Shame and Reintegration.*

[14] Braithwaite, *Crime, Shame and Reintegration*, 8.

[15] Braithwaite, *Crime, Shame and Reintegration*, 4.

[16] Braithwaite, *Crime, Shame, and Reintegration*, 13.

and institutions may be implicated in atrocities under investigation. The communitarian approach to political judgment that animates restorative justice is also in tension with the theory's own commitment to critically examine the relationship between individual harms and underlying political or social conflicts. To the extent that restorative justice relies on prevailing community norms to define standards of judgment and guide the process of adjudication, it may function to reify or exacerbate existing inequalities and hierarchies.[17] Because restorative justice allows for so much flexibility in the adjudication process, it may be particularly vulnerable to manipulation in a context of gross inequality or repression.

The identification of restorative justice with a therapeutic response to individuals has become a prominent way to adapt the framework as a response to political violence while avoiding the problematic implications of communitarian political judgment. The analogy implies that a "body politic" may be likened to an individual, and that addressing the legacy of political violence is comparable to confronting the traumatic experiences that have harmed an individual. Therapeutic justice, as well as restorative justice, recast crime as injury and identify justice with the goal of healing. Yet therapeutic justice also abandons much of what is promising about restorative justice. Whereas restorative justice theory calls for approaches that are responsive to the particularities of the local context, therapeutic justice tends to locate the causes of conflict in the idea of a dysfunctional culture or a psychological disorder within affected societies.[18] Restorative justice requires attention to the way in which individual injuries are connected to social injustices. In restorative justice theory, addressing psychological trauma is only one dimension of a much broader conception of harm and repair. In contrast, therapeutic justice identifies injury with psychological harms and associates remedy and repair with adaptation, adjustment, and closure. Where restorative justice insists upon efforts to remedy past wrongs through reparation and reform, the close identification of justice with therapy has obfuscated the political causes and consequence of systematic violence, and may be used to rationalize the decision to abandon material and political redress of past wrongs.

The close identification of restorative justice with therapeutic healing has been a distraction for critics as well as proponents of the theory. It has allowed defenders of restorative justice to avoid grappling with the internal

---

[17] Sally Engle Merry, "The Social Organization of Mediation in Nonindustrial Societies: Implications for Informal Community Justice in America," in *The Politics of Informal Justice*, ed. Richard Abel (New York: Academy Press, 1982); James A. Ptacek, ed. *Restorative Justice and Violence against Women* (Oxford: Oxford University Press, 2010).

[18] Pupavac, "International Therapeutic Peace and Justice."

tensions of the theory and led them to downplay the dimensions of the theory that are most promising as a response to political violence. The identification of restorative justice with therapeutic healing has also allowed critics to write it off all too easily without grappling with the significance of the challenges that restorative justice scholars pose for human rights legalism or considering the potential of the theory to inform responses to the limitations of legalism. Finally, the identification of restorative justice with therapeutic healing has also obfuscated the originality of theoretical debates in South Africa.

BEYOND THERAPY

Although South Africa's TRC has become influential as an exemplar of restorative justice, very little attention has been given to the way in which thinkers that influenced South Africa's restorative approach to justice reconsidered the theory as they reflected on the disappointments associated with the TRC process. As discussed in Chapter 3, the TRC did not directly analyze the apartheid system or the theme of racism in South Africa. It was not empowered to grant reparations, but only to make recommendations regarding reparations. The final reparations package was far smaller than the TRC had hoped it would be. The TRC had associated restorative justice with accountability through the amnesty process. However, the majority of those who refused to participate in the process has not been prosecuted and probably never will be.[19] South Africa's TRC was far better funded than the average truth commission, but provided victims with very little information other than what they already knew.[20] Many people who participated in the process reported that the experience had been unsettling or otherwise unhelpful, rather than healing or cathartic.[21]

Many of these disappointments were already evident in the late 1990s, as Tutu, Villa-Vicencio, and Mamdani became influential in shaping theoretical debates on the role of restorative justice in South Africa. These thinkers did not simply apply restorative justice theory to the South African context. They also reconsidered restorative justice theory in light of the disappointments associated with the TRC. Tutu and Villa-Vicencio both worked for the TRC and defended it against prominent critics, such as Mamdani. However,

[19]   Hugo Van der Merwe and Audrey R. Chapman "Conclusion: Did the TRC Deliver?" in *Truth and Reconciliation in South Africa: Did the TRC Deliver?*
[20]   Phakathi and Van der Merwe, "The Impact of the TRC's Amnesty Process on Survivors of Human Rights Violations."
[21]   Quoted in Hayner, *Unspeakable Truths*, 142.

they share Mamdani's view that that restorative justice theory is limited to the extent that it is premised on the availability of common norms and consensus on how to define the categories of "victim" and "perpetrator." Although Mamdani became influential as a critic of the TRC, he did not reject the TRC's appeal to restorative justice. Instead, he took issue with the therapeutic interpretation of restorative justice that prevailed in the TRC's report. All three thinkers share the view that restorative justice requires strategies for persuading people to accept a common political judgment of past injustices. They also shared the view that as a response to political violence, restorative justice could not be premised on traditional community values or on apolitical criteria for defining harm and remedy.

These thinkers agreed, then, that restorative justice could not be applied, but would have to be adapted to the context of systematic political violence. However, they offer very different ways of thinking about how truth commissions might contribute to restorative justice without relying on the premise of shared community values. These differences can be usefully categorized in relation to Arendt's distinction between the judgment of political actors and that of spectators. That is, Tutu and Villa-Vicencio both suggest that the TRC's contribution to restorative justice depended on its role in fostering an active process of persuasion that would enable conflicting parties to identify new possibilities for political community and a common basis for judgment. In contrast, Mamdani suggests that the contribution of truth commissions to restorative justice depends on their capacity to reflect on past wrongs as detached critical spectators who examine the ways in which inherited understandings of community have been shaped by the legacies of past injustices. Instead of seeing these as competing ways of conceptualizing the role of truth commissions, I suggest that they are better understood as complementary. Although they are in tension with one another, each is limited on its own.

Ubuntu, Ritual, and Gesture

Desmond Tutu was the first to publicize the case for viewing South Africa's TRC as a restorative approach to justice. In doing so, Tutu used the concept of *ubuntu* to adapt restorative justice to the South African context. *Ubuntu*, or "humaneness," had been integrated into South Africa's interim constitution, which articulated "a need for understanding, but not for vengeance, a need for reparation, but not retaliation, a need for *ubuntu*, but not victimization."[22] As discussed in Chapter 3, this constitutional reference to *ubuntu* was cited in the

[22] *Constitution of the Republic of South Africa Act no. 2* (1993)

opinions of major Constitutional Court cases, including the case that upheld the legitimacy of the TRC in response to a complaint against its amnesty provisions. For Tutu, *ubuntu* was not only significant as a basis for legitimizing the TRC. It was also a way to address the limitations of restorative justice theory as a response to South African apartheid. For many, Tutu's use of *ubuntu* appeared naïve or depoliticizing. A closer look at his reflections on the disappointments of the TRC process suggests a somewhat different interpretation.

Tutu's theory of *ubuntu* blends African philosophy and Anglican theology. He characterizes *ubuntu* as a personal quality, a value system, and a worldview. A person with the quality of *ubuntu*, writes Tutu, is "open and available to others, affirming of others."[23] Such a person does not feel threatened by the accomplishments or successes of others because "he or she has a proper self-assurance that comes from knowing that he or she belongs to a greater whole and is diminished when others are humiliated or diminished." *Ubuntu* entails a spirit of generosity, hospitality, friendship, caring, and compassion rather than competition and resentment. *Ubuntu* also refers to the value system that elevates this kind of personal quality – one in which social harmony is the greatest good.[24] Finally, *ubuntu* refers to a way of understanding the world that views all human beings as interdependent.

Tutu argued that the constitutional emphasis on *ubuntu* should be read as a preference for restorative justice over legalism and he used the concept to identify restorative justice with traditional African justice practices. Tutu associates *ubuntu* with the restorative justice values that promote the "healing of breaches, the redressing of imbalances, and the restoration of broken relationships," and with a worldview that sees crime in personal terms, as a rupture of relationships.[25] "It is not, 'I think therefore I am,'" he writes of *ubuntu*, "It says rather: 'I am human because I belong. I participate.'"[26]

Ubuntu is not only a worldview and an ethic for Tutu, but also a quality that can be cultivated in people or neglected and undermined. As a quality, *ubuntu* entails the ability to see human interdependence, to experience empathy. He argues that cultivating the quality of *ubuntu* would mean humanizing the oppressors in the eyes of the majority black population.[27] In his view, the TRC aided in cultivating the quality of *ubuntu* by helping people "understand the

[23] Tutu, *No Future without Forgiveness*, 31.
[24] Tutu, *No Future without Forgiveness*, 31. See also, Lynn Graybill, *Truth and Reconciliation in South Africa: Miracle or Model?* (Boulder, CO: Lynne Rienner, 2002), 33.
[25] Tutu, *No Future without Forgiveness*, 54
[26] Tutu, *No Future without Forgiveness*, 31.
[27] See Michael Battle, *Reconciliation: The Ubuntu Theology of Desmond Tutu* (Cleveland, OH: The Pilgrim Press, 1997), 47

perpetrators and so have empathy, to try and stand in their shoes and appreciate the sort of pressures and influences that might have conditioned them."[28]
This dimension of Tutu's interpretation of *ubuntu* is strongly influenced by
Christian theology. "[T]heology reminded me," he writes, "that, however diabolical the act, it did not turn the perpetrator into a demon."[29] Tutu also identifies *ubuntu* as a basis for humanizing the oppressed by demonstrating that
those who suffer injustice are not morally destroyed by their experiences or
destined to inflict vengeance on others.

Just as Braithwaite's discussion of shaming has parallels in Confucianism,
so too does Tutu's discussion of *ubuntu* resemble the Confucian concept of
ren, which is also translated as "humane."[30] In *The Analects*, it is argued that
an emphasis on addressing crime through regulation will only undermine
the effort to cultivate *ren*. Whereas regulations undermine *ren* by external-
izing norms, according to *The Analects*, ritual internalizes social norms and
breeds harmony.[31] Similarly, Tutu suggests that an emphasis on resolving past
conflicts and addressing abuses through the courts is in tension with the goal
of establishing a sense of shared community in South Africa because it will
undermine the quality of *ubuntu*. In contrast, he suggests, truth commissions
might foster the quality of *ubuntu* by establishing spaces for rituals of atonement, apology, and forgiveness. Truth commissions in Sierra Leone, East
Timor, and elsewhere have followed a similar logic to the extent that they
have identified restorative justice with efforts to incorporate traditional rituals
associated with conflict resolution and community reintegration.

With this in mind, Tutu's use of *ubuntu* might seem to suffer from the same
problem that is inherent in restorative justice theory – an uncritical reliance
on community traditions to guide the process of judgment. Thus, Tutu has
been criticized for invoking a romanticized, ahistorical image of *ubuntu* and
traditional justice practices in order to legitimate a compromised vision of
justice.[32] Tutu's theory of *ubuntu* also seems to justify the TRC's effort to base
reconciliation on the identification of shared forms of suffering and victimhood, as divorced from political context. At times, Tutu has invoked *ubuntu* in

---

[28] Tutu, *No Future without Forgiveness*, 271.
[29] Tutu, *No Future without Forgiveness*, 83.
[30] Arthur Waley, "Introduction," *The Analects of Confucius*, trans. Arthur Waley (New York: Vintage Books, 1989), 27–9.
[31] "Govern the people by regulations, keep order among them by chastisements, and they will
flee from you, and lose all self-respect. Govern them by moral force, keep order among them
by ritual, and they will keep their self-respect and come to you of their own accord" (*The Analects of Confucius*, 88).
[32] Wilson, *The Politics of Truth and Reconciliation in South Africa*, 11.

ways that suggested that the black population was uniquely willing to forgive. This was interpreted by some as a message that the black population should also be willing to assume the burdens of the transition by sacrificing their demands for redress.[33]

Although these are certainly valid criticisms of *ubuntu* discourse, they do not capture the complexity of the logic animating Tutu's reflections on restorative justice. Tutu presented the TRC as a basis for reconciliation and restorative justice, but also insisted upon the importance of acknowledging that the TRC's mandate was not the product of "idealistic upstarts," but rather "hard-nosed politicians."[34] As a result of that compromise, the TRC mandate called for investigations that would center on the abuses that were illegal under apartheid, rather than the abuses of the apartheid system. As Kader Asmal and Mahmood Mamdani observed, the TRC could have interpreted its mandate more broadly, particularly given that the mandate offered a very broad definition of "ill-treatment" and called for attention to the political context of individual abuses. Tutu defended a more narrowly framed investigative process. However, Tutu also stressed that this framing ought to be understood as the product of a painful political compromise rather than consensus. This would suggest that the TRC's contribution to restorative justice could not be evaluated in relation to the limited terms of its own mandate, but would depend on the extent to which the TRC could inform a broader process of investigation and redress in response to the legalized injustices of the apartheid system.

Tutu's discussion of *ubuntu* might be better understood as a strategy for *adapting* restorative justice to a context characterized by the absence of community values and lack of consensus on the basis of judgment. Tutu does not defend the TRC's narrow mandate in order to endorse an anemic or apolitical conception of justice. Rather, he suggests that by examining common injuries, the "shared wounds" suffered by all South Africans, the TRC would awaken the quality of *ubuntu* among those who remained in a state of denial over the inhumanity of apartheid. He suggests that over time, this expansion of *ubuntu* would also provide the basis for an expanded sense of political responsibility for the legacy of systematic injustices and racism in South Africa. Tutu is commonly misinterpreted as arguing that unconditional forgiveness or amnesty will generate political reintegration and reconciliation. Instead, he characterizes forgiveness as a kind of *gesture* of generosity, a manifestation of

[33] Tinyko Sam Maluleke, "The South African Truth and Reconciliation Discourse: A Black Theological Evaluation," *Journal of Black Theology* 12 (1998): 35–58.

[34] Tutu, *No Future without Forgiveness*, 57.

ubuntu, which must be *reciprocated* with acknowledgment and repentance if it is to become a meaningful basis for political reconciliation.

In this regard, Tutu's theory of *ubuntu* may be usefully compared with Arendt's discussion of "enlarged mentality." Arendt characterizes "enlarged mentality" as a basis for political judgment that might persuade or "woo" common agreement on contested problems by anticipating how such problems might be understood from the standpoint of distinct and conflicting perspectives. Instead of relying on traditional values or formal standards of judgment, Arendt suggests that political judgments must rely on the imaginative use of examples that offer possibilities for common ground, but also reveal the limitations of inherited communities, the absence of consensus. Arendt makes it very clear that "enlarged *mentality*" does not mean enlarged *empathy* and suggests that confusing the two would detract from the critical role of judgment or result in a presumptuous, perhaps misleading identification with the suffering of others. In contrast, Tutu's *ubuntu* suggests an approach to establishing common ground based on an effort to empathetically imagine the standpoint of those that represent an enemy camp or oppressor. However, Tutu's use of *ubuntu* resembles Arendt's use of "exemplary validity" as a way to exemplify the possibility of community in the future, while simultaneously exposing its absence in the present.

Tutu is often seen as a naïve figure that trumpeted forgiveness a transcendent cure-all for the brutalities of apartheid. This depiction of Tutu is out of step with his actual reflections on the immediate aftermath of the TRC process, which are marked with disappointment, sadness, and even anger that the gesture of amnesty had not been met with a reciprocal commitment to acknowledge and repair the legacy of apartheid. "Many white people in South Africa," he writes, "have come to see themselves as entitled to reconciliation and forgiveness without their having to lift so much as a little finger to aid this crucial and demanding process."[35] He puts this even more bluntly in his introduction to the *TRC Report*, writing that the reluctance on the part of most white South Africans to participate in the TRC process was akin to "spitting in the face of the victims."[36] In his writings on restorative justice and forgiveness, Tutu wrestles with the question of how to respond to this disappointment. He notes that the failure to acknowledge responsibility for apartheid is not surprising: "They were descendents of their forbears and behaving, true to form in being in denial mode."[37] He acknowledges that

---

[35] Tutu, *No Future without Forgiveness*, 164.
[36] Desmond Tutu, "Chairperson's Foreward," in *Truth and Reconciliation Commission of South Africa Final Report*, Volume 1 (Cape Town: Juta, 1998), 17.
[37] Tutu, *No Future without Forgiveness*, 83.

many white people grew up knowing no other system, and that black townships were usually out of sight in white South Africa.[38] At the same time, Tutu warns that the failure of the TRC to challenge denial regarding the systemic injustices of apartheid will undermine the process of reconciliation over the long term.

Tutu's discussion of *ubuntu* in the context of the TRC resembles James Baldwin's reflections on love and race in the United States. In *The Fire Next Time*, Baldwin wrote that, "[i]t demands great spiritual resilience not to hate the hater whose foot is on your neck, and an even greater miracle of perception and charity not to teach your child to hate."[39] Although Baldwin praised this quality of resilience and insisted on the transformative potential of love, he also warned that "the intransigence and ignorance of the white world might make … vengeance inevitable."[40] Tutu calls for truth commissions to cultivate *ubuntu* and empathy, but his reflections suggest that in the absence of community, *ubuntu* appears in the form of gestures – potentially transformative, but not solutions in and of themselves. And he issues his own sort of warning: "[U]nless houses replace the hovels and shacks in which most blacks live," writes Tutu, "we can just as well kiss reconciliation goodbye."[41]

Tutu's comments on *ubuntu* and the TRC have important implications for more recently developed truth commissions that similarly emphasized traditional values and rituals. Some scholars have suggested that traditional community-based rituals may be more important than the investigations associated with truth commissions as a basis for establishing a sense of justice and reconciliation.[42] Tutu's emphasis on *ubuntu* and on rituals of repentance and forgiveness may seem to validate this perspective. However, his reflections on the TRC serve as a warning regarding the limitations of these practices as a basis for restorative justice. As a response to political violence, truth commissions cannot advance restorative justice by promoting forgiveness or incorporating traditional rituals and principles of community restoration. In contexts characterized by radical inequality and exclusion, such practices are better understood as gestures. Such gestures are potentially very powerful, but only to the extent that they are followed by meaningful reciprocation.

---

38 Tutu, *No Future without Forgiveness*, 274.
39 James Baldwin, *The Fire Next Time* (New York: Vintage Books, 1993), 100.
40 Baldwin, *The Fire Next Time*, 105.
41 Tutu, *No Future without Forgiveness*, 274.
42 Tim Kelsall, "Truth, Lies, Ritual: Preliminary Reflections on the Truth and Reconciliation Commission in Sierra Leone," *Human Rights Quarterly* 27 (2005): 361–91.

Democratic Dialogue

As director of South Africa's *Truth and Reconciliation Commission Report*, Charles Villa-Vicencio published a series of essays reflecting on role of the truth commission in advancing restorative justice. Whereas Tutu is responsible for publicizing South Africa's restorative approach, Villa-Vicencio has probably done the most to develop the broader theoretical case for truth commissions as a form of restorative justice. The two thinkers worked together at the TRC and have many ideas in common. Like Tutu, Villa-Vicencio observed that restorative justice is premised on a consensus, missing in the aftermath of systematic political violence, regarding what constitutes a crime, a victim, and a perpetrator.

Villa-Vicencio offers a distinctive way of adapting restorative justice to this context, which he refers to as "political restorative justice."[43] As a response to systematic political violence he argues, restorative justice cannot be premised on any kind of "pure unencumbered theory." Instead, it is influenced by "messy negotiations" and "experimental initiatives."[44] This political restorative justice requires strategies for locating common ground, while also acknowledging the reality of compromise. Like Tutu, Villa-Vicencio defends the narrow investigative framework of the TRC as a continuation of the political compromises that informed its mandate. He concedes that the TRC softened its approach to truth seeking and justice "in the interests of non-confrontation."[45]

At the same time, Villa-Vicencio also insists that the TRC's contribution to restorative justice depends on the extent to which it contributes to a broader process of investigation and repair. To contribute to a "long-term restorative process," writes Villa-Vicencio, the debate must move past a focus on victims of gross violations of human rights "to a more systematic view of victim-age and its redress that addresses the gap between rich and poor in South Africa."[46] This position is consistent with the approach to reconciliation and justice outlined in the *Kairos* document, as discussed in Chapter 3. It also builds on Villa-Vicencio's earlier theological writings that argue that social

---

43 Charles Villa-Vicencio, "Restorative Justice: Ambiguities and Limitations of a Theory," in *Provocations of Amnesty: Memory, Justice, and Impunity*, ed. Charles Villa-Vicencio and Erik Doxtader (Cape Town: David Philip Press: New Africa Press, 2003), 31.
44 Villa-Vicencio, "Restorative Justice: Ambiguities and Limitations," 31.
45 Villa-Vicencio, "Restorative Justice: Ambiguities and Limitations," 45.
46 Villa-Vicencio, "Restorative Justice: Ambiguities and Limitations," 42.

reconstruction in South Africa must be premised on economic justice and insist on the indivisibility of economic and political rights.[47]

Villa-Vicencio argues that "political restorative justice" requires an effort to connect analyses of individual victims and perpetrators to broader strategies for political reform. He develops this point by drawing on the writings of Karl Jaspers to argue that restorative justice requires political responsibility. In the immediate aftermath of the Second World War, Jaspers argued that it would be important to address the problem of collective responsibility without making attributions of group criminality. To do so, Jaspers offered a nuanced analysis of the meaning of "German guilt" as a way to open what he referred to as a "radical dialogue" about the Nazi period.[48] Jaspers argued that criminal guilt could only be attributed to individuals, but that all members of society bear some degree of political responsibility for addressing past abuses. "A people answers for its polity," wrote Jaspers, and "[e]very German is made to share the blame for the crimes committed in the name of the Reich."[49] Similarly, Villa-Vicencio argues that restorative justice must address the responsibility not only of those who were directly involved in committing past abuses, but also those who "simply allowed them to happen, or who chose to look the other way."[50]

Villa-Vicencio also follows Jaspers in arguing that "radical dialogue" ought to be the primary strategy for moving beyond defensive denial to genuine acknowledgment and for widening the scope of political responsibility for past wrongs. Villa-Vicencio's "political restorative justice" is consistent with the process-based definition of restorative justice offered by Tony Marshall. Villa-Vicencio argues that the role of restorative justice is not to establish unity, but rather to cultivate the "stable reciprocity of expectations" that Lon Fuller identified as the premise for rule of law.[51] Villa-Vicencio also integrates the commitment to protect rights associated with democratic deliberation, such as the right to free speech and the right to organize, into his definition of restorative justice.[52]

This distinctive way of adapting restorative justice to the South African context informs Villa-Vicencio's discussion of how truth commissions might

[47] Charles Villa-Vicencio, A *Theology of Reconstruction: Nation-Building and Human Rights* (Cambridge: Cambridge University Press, 1992), 197–253.
[48] Karl Jaspers, *Lebensfragen der Deutschen Politik* (Munich: Deutschen Tagenbuch Verlag, 1963), 118–19.
[49] Jaspers, *The Question of German Guilt*, 61.
[50] Villa-Vicencio, "Restorative Justice: Dealing with the Past Differently," 71.
[51] Villa-Vicencio, "Restorative Justice: Dealing with the Past Differently," 70.
[52] Villa-Vicencio, "Restorative Justice: Dealing with the Past Differently," 76.

contribute to restorative justice. Specifically, he suggests that truth commissions ought to promote restorative justice by cultivating democratic dialogue regarding the process of judging past wrongs. "We need to learn to speak with one another after generations of rebuke and confrontation," he argues, adding that this requires a "quality of conversation that goes beyond castigating one another … it involves empathy, engaged dialogue, and listening at a new level of intensity."[53] The kind of dialogue that Villa-Vicencio identifies with restorative justice requires qualities that Tutu associates with *ubuntu*, such as empathy and a "genuine desire to understand what someone else is saying." However, Tutu's conception of *ubuntu* elevates social harmony as the greatest good and he identifies *ubuntu* with ritual gestures and reciprocity. In contrast, Villa-Vicencio explicitly calls for an *agonistic* democratic dialogue – one that exposes conflicts without demanding their resolution. "The very notion of democracy," he argues, "is undermined to the extent that differing ideas are not heard and talked through, in pursuit of a way forward."[54] Whereas Tutu views the quality of *ubuntu* as a basis for expanding political responsibility, Villa-Vicencio argues that the only way to cultivate political responsibility for ongoing reform and broader redress is through a process of persuasion.[55] Thus, he argues that truth commissions contribute to restorative justice by establishing a space for dialogue among citizens with vastly diverging perspectives, including "those who cling to the past" as well as those who reject the entire transition.[56]

Like Tutu's discussion of *ubuntu*, Villa-Vicencio's argument for democratic dialogue as the basis for restorative justice also bears a resemblance to Arendt's use of "enlarged mentality." That is, Villa-Vicencio argues that restorative justice requires a process of persuasion and deliberation that anticipates agreement from multiple perspectives. And just as Arendt's "enlarged mentality" remains partial and limited, Villa-Vicencio qualifies his approach to restorative justice by reframing it as "political restorative justice." By cultivating dialogue, truth commissions strive to move beyond the compromises and limitations of their mandates, but such efforts remain partial and political.

One limitation of Villa-Vicencio's emphasis on dialogue has to do with the difficulty of speaking about traumatic experiences. Godobo-Madikizela observes that those who testified as victims before the TRC often characterized their experiences as "unspeakable" or "indescribable."[57] They struggled

53 Villa-Vicencio, "Restorative Justice: Ambiguities and Limitations," 43.
54 Villa-Vicencio, "Restorative Justice: Ambiguities and Limitations," 43.
55 Villa-Vicencio, "Restorative Justice: Ambiguities and Limitations," 41.
56 Villa-Vicencio, "Restorative Justice: Ambiguities and Limitations," 41.
57 Godobo-Madikizela, *A Human Being Died That Night*, 85

to present their testimonies in a language that they found inadequate to the task. Primo Levi similarly observes that members of the Special Squad who were forced to work in Nazi crematoria had generally refused to speak about the past.[58] Another limitation has to do with the victim-perpetrator framework itself. Most significantly, participation in the official TRC process was largely, though not entirely, restricted to those who identified as "victims" and "perpetrators" under the narrow scope of the TRC's legislation.[59] These categories would frame and limit the scope of dialogue sponsored by the TRC regarding past wrongs.

Villa-Vicencio's "political restorative justice" resembles Arendt's more Aristotelian writings on good political judgment as a guide for action, but it is at odds with Arendt's discussion of what ought to guide the political judgments of the historian or critic. Arendt argues that political judgment requires not only persuasion and an appeal to diverse perspectives, but also an effort to stand apart from prevailing views and examine them critically. Although this was a major goal of the TRC, Villa-Vicencio contends that the role of the critical historian was at odds with the TRC's effort to cultivate democratic dialogue. To those who charged that the TRC had failed to produce a compelling history of the apartheid era, Villa-Vicencio replied that historical judgment should not be the main role of a truth commission. Rather, in keeping with his stress on democratic dialogue, Villa-Vicencio argues that the TRC instead provided a space for multiple, conflicting stories to be told.[60]

Nevertheless, Villa-Vicencio acknowledges that something important was lost along the way. Just as Tutu recognizes the limitations of *ubuntu* and forgiveness as strategies for overcoming the narrow framework of the TRC, so too does Villa-Vicencio recognize that the TRC's efforts to foster democratic dialogue did not generate the kind of political responsibility that he had anticipated. Villa-Vicencio observes that perpetrators investigated by the TRC were widely perceived as psychopaths or aberrations, which resulted in "ordinary" white South Africans avoiding a sense of political responsibility for having

---

[58] Primo Levi, "The Gray Zone," in *The Drowned and the Saved*. Trans. Raymond Rosenthal. New York: Vintage Books, 1989.

[59] The TRC involved NGOs in the process of developing strategies and policies for implementing its mandate. It also sponsored several public debates, at which a range of criticisms were aired, including challenges to the victim-perpetrator framework and the way it was defined.

[60] Charles Villa-Vicencio, "On the Limitations of Academic History: The Quest for Truth Demands Both More and Less," in *After the TRC: Reflections on Truth and Reconciliation in South Africa*, ed. Wilmot James and Linda van de Vijver (Athens, OH: Ohio University Press, 2001), 24.

benefited from the apartheid system.[61] He also notes that the narrow parameters of the TRC's investigations and the idealism surrounding the process have obfuscated the "resentment, alienation, disappointment, and compromise that some brought to the settlement."[62] Villa-Vicencio's case for a dialogical approach to restorative justice and Tutu's case for forgiveness and *ubuntu* must both be read, then, alongside their warnings regarding the limitations of these strategies absent an ongoing process of political and social change.

Critical Acknowledgment and Historical Reflection

Mahmood Mamdani was working in South Africa in the 1990s, during which time he articulated an influential critique of the TRC, which was eventually paraphrased in the text of the *TRC Report* and integrated into its theoretical legacy.[63] Mamdani's critique is often cited as evidence of what is wrong with restorative justice. However, he did not frame his own comments as an attack on restorative justice, but rather as an evaluation of the limits of the TRC as a basis for restorative justice. In contrast with Villa-Vicencio and Tutu, Mamdani argued the TRC's primary contribution to restorative justice did not depend on its efforts to promote dialogue or forgiveness, but rather its aspiration to reflect critically on South Africa's historical patterns of violence and systemic injustices. He did not go as far as he might have in elaborating on this claim. The significance of his proposal can be better appreciated once restorative justice is clearly distinguished from therapeutic justice.

Mamdani's main critique of the TRC, which was briefly addressed in Chapter 3, centers on the narrow scope of its investigations. More specifically, Mamdani rejected the TRC's decision to restrict its investigations to the categories of "victim" and "perpetrator" as outlined in the terms of its legislative mandate. As Tutu and Villa-Vicencio acknowledge, the TRC defined these categories in relation to the excesses of apartheid and the struggle against it, rather than the institutionalized violence and injustice of apartheid itself. Both Tutu and Villa-Vicencio acknowledge that the TRC's ultimate contribution to restorative justice would depend on ongoing efforts to broaden the scope of political responsibility and redress to encompass the systemic harms of apartheid. However, they also defended the narrow scope of the TRC's investigative framework, arguing that such compromises would enable the

---

[61] Villa-Vicencio, "Restorative Justice: Dealing with the Past Differently," 74.
[62] Villa-Vicencio, "Restorative Justice: Ambiguities and Limitations of a Theory," 32.
[63] Christodoulidis, Emilios, and Scott Veitch, "Reconciliation as Surrender: Configurations of Responsibility and Memory," in *Justice and Reconciliation in Post-Apartheid South Africa*, 15.

TRC to establish a modest basis for common ground that might give rise, over time, to a broader and more critical response to past wrongs. Mamdani rejected this logic, particularly the last point. Instead of opening a space for meaningful dialogue and a broader sense of political responsibility, he argued, the narrow focus of the TRC merely served to legitimate the denial of responsibility and "suffocated a much-needed social debate on how to go beyond the compromises of 1994."[64]

Mamdani evaluates the TRC's contribution to restorative justice in relation to a minimalist version of the way in which the concept was formulated in South Africa. Stripping the concept from the therapeutic discourse associated with the TRC, Mamdani characterizes restorative justice in South Africa as an agreement to provide "acknowledgment followed by reparation for the victim, along with amnesty for the perpetrator."[65] Given that the TRC was not empowered to grant reparations, this suggests that the commitment to *acknowledgment* would be central to the TRC's role in advancing restorative justice. However, for Mamdani, this means acknowledging the systemic violence of apartheid. To do this, he suggests, the TRC should not only have expanded the way in which it defined the category of "victimhood," but also taken steps to move beyond the limitations of the victim-perpetrator framework.

In accordance with this basic formulation, Mamdani argues that the TRC ought to have investigated and acknowledged victims of forced removals and the brutal enforcement of pass laws. The idea of investigating apartheid-era abuses without attention to forced removals, he argues, is as preposterous as the idea of investigating Soviet-era abuses without attention to the gulag.[66] The TRC did observe that forced removals created a climate of fear that silenced opposition to apartheid and forced millions into deeper poverty, yet did not systematically investigate this form of violence or include its victims in the formal process of acknowledgment.

The pass law system in South Africa was a way of monitoring the black population by requiring those defined by the state as "native" to carry passbooks. Pass laws also served as a way to target political opposition. The TRC found that as much as 25 percent of the South African prison population consisted of pass law offenders in the 1960s and 1970s.[67] In order to cope with the demands on the prison system, the state either induced or compelled prisoners to labor on farms. The Commission observed that pass law arrests also evolved

---

[64] Mamdani, "Amnesty or Impunity? A Preliminary Critique."

[65] Mamdani, "Amnesty or Impunity? A Preliminary Critique," 33.

[66] Mahmood Mamdani, "A Diminished Truth," in *After the TRC: Reflections on Truth and Reconciliation in South Africa*, ed. Wilmot James (Athens, OH: Ohio University Press, 2001), 59.

[67] TRC, *TRC Report*, vol. 4, 200.

as a way to guarantee cheap labor for the farms and noted that prison laborers were subjected to violence and abuse. Forced removals not only involved violent dispossession, but also racial and ethnic cleansing. Pass laws not only generated mass incarceration, but also became a form of enslavement. However, the TRC did not acknowledge those imprisoned, killed, and forced into labor under the system as "victims."

What Mamdani is proposing, then, is that restorative justice requires a form of acknowledgment that does not simply register diverse perspectives and experiences of past violence, but also critically examines how prevailing perspectives have been informed by legacies of systemic violence and abuse. The decision not to investigate consequences of forced removals and pass laws not only meant that the TRC would neglect to acknowledge victims of some of the worst brutalities of the apartheid system, suggests Mamdani, but also that it would abandon its own goal of investigating and acknowledging the legacy of apartheid in contemporary political and social relationships.

Mamdani's most well-known intervention in debates on transitional justice grew out of his argument that the TRC should have examined not only "perpetrators" of "gross violations of human rights," but also *beneficiaries* of the apartheid system.[68] Acknowledging how one segment of the population has benefitted from an unjust system is a necessary step to beginning a dialogue about political responsibility without making attributions of intentional criminality. Attention to beneficiaries means acknowledging the economic legacy of civil and political rights violations, as well as economic injustices that are not necessarily rooted in civil and political rights abuses. In contrast with the investigations that focus narrowly on victims and perpetrators, acknowledging that some people have benefitted from past injustices is an important basis for examining the connections between past abuses and ongoing conflicts and inequalities. To acknowledge the responsibility of beneficiaries is also to acknowledge *continuities* that may not in evidence when transitional justice institutions frame their work as a response to discrete wrongs committed in the past.

One objection to Mamdani's argument has been that truth commissions have limited resources and must find some way to place reasonable parameters on their investigations.[69] It is true that truth commissions operate with limited budgets. They are temporary institutions, designed to produce reports within a couple of years, generally in the immediate aftermath of a regime change or negotiated political settlement. It is unrealistic, in this view, to compare the

---

[68] Mamdani, "Reconciliation without Justice," 22–5.
[69] See Tutu, *No Future without Forgiveness*, 104–5.

work of truth commissions to that of historians, who are insulated from immediate political pressures and generally reflect on past events from a greater distance in time.

However, this objection is misleading to the extent that it suggests that the primary constraints on truth commissions concern the simple need for a manageable chunk of the past to investigate. The parameters of truth commission mandates are shaped by political jockeying over the basis for judgment and the extent of acknowledgment. The work of truth commissions may simply reflect these compromises, or it may call them into question. Although Guatemala's Historical Clarification Commission had a very narrow mandate and was not permitted to name individuals, it developed a report that critically situates its discussion of the abuses covered under the terms of the mandate in the context of a broader historical analysis of colonialism, racism, and Cold War interventionism.[70]

Mamdani's case for widening the scope of the TRC's investigations in such a way as to critically examine and challenge transitional compromises is at odds with the therapeutic approach to restorative justice that dominates much of the TRC's report. Rather than focusing on common experiences of loss and suffering, Mamdani posits that the truth commission ought to have engaged in a kind of critical historical reflection that might be unsettling and even generate backlash. When restorative justice and therapeutic justice are disentangled, however, it is easier to see that Mamdani's proposal is consistent with a core commitment of restorative justice theory as articulated by scholars such as Braithwaite. That is, restorative justice requires attention to the ways in which individual harms are associated with systemic conflicts and injustices. Mamdani's proposal for the TRC does this by dismantling the very legalistic binaries that restorative justice purports to reject in order to examine the linkages between individual guilt and political responsibility, individual injury and systemic conflict, censure of past wrongs and remedies for their present consequences.

At the same time, Mamdani's proposal addresses a major problem at the center of restorative justice theory. Restorative justice is appealing because it outlines strategies for developing flexible, novel responses to past wrongs that connect remedial action with conflict resolution. Restorative justice does this by allowing political judgment to influence the definition of crime and the

---

[70] Guatemalan Commission for Historical Clarification, *Guatemala Memory of Silence: Report of the Commission for Historical Clarification* (1996). See also, Amy Ross, "The Creation and Conduct of the Guatemalan Commission for Historical Clarification," *Geoforum* 37, no. 1 (2006): 69–81.

process of adjudication. However, the communitarian approach to political judgment that has influenced restorative justice theory seems to accede to an uncritical or romantic reliance on local traditions and practices.

Mamdani's proposal incorporates an alternative approach to political judgment that resembles, in certain respects, the way that Arendt characterizes the judgment of the critic or spectator. Of course, Mamdani's take on the role of the TRC differs from Arendt's discussion of the "spectator" in important ways. Arendt stresses the role of historical imagination and "exemplary validity" as a basis for innovation and action that might delineate a break from the past. In contrast, Mamdani calls for a form of historical reflection that reveals the continuities that are obfuscated by the very terminology of transitional justice with its focus on the "aftermath" of violence. However, Mamdani suggests a role of truth commissions that is similar to that of Arendt's critic in that it would seek to establish a stance of detachment from prevailing views and political imperatives in order to evaluate patterns that may not be evident or convenient for those engaged in the day-to-day business of political action. Like Arendt, Mamdani suggests that the project of establishing a basis for common ground in the future requires this kind of critical historical reflection, which confronts the absence or failure of inherited traditions. Arendt suggested that in the aftermath of the Nazi era, examples of resistance might provide guidance for efforts to establish new forms of solidarity and community. Similarly, Mamdani suggests that the TRC could have looked to the history of South African resistance for guidance in the project of reconciliation. "If power sought to impose a racial/ethnic grid on society," he asks, "to what extent was resistance able to break out of it? Where else but in the history of resistance can we locate the roots of reconciliation?"[71]

Mamdani's proposal also resembles Arendt's discussion of the role of the historical "critic" in the sense that it appears to be in tension with the goals of political actors. Thus, Villa-Vicencio has objected to Mamdani's critique by arguing that a decisive and critical interpretation of South Africa's past would have been in tension with the TRC's effort to foster democratic dialogue. In making this claim, Villa-Vicencio seems to suggest that truth commissions cannot generate a common basis for judging systemic injustice by defending decisive verdicts on events that remain controversial, but only by making space for competing interpretations and by identifying points of minimal, provisional consensus. However, the work of truth commissions and all forms of transitional justice entails a process of condemning as "abuses" or "atrocities," practices that were once widely accepted or even mandated. The question is

---

[71] Mamdani, "Reconciliation without Justice."

not whether or not this implicates truth commissions in historical judgments (it does), but whether such judgments will merely ratify prevailing perspectives and accommodations or whether they will critically engage conventional wisdom and reveal the limits of political compromise. Although Tutu and Villa-Vicencio defend the TRC's narrow investigative framework, they also acknowledge the limits of dialogue and ritual in the absence of a critical response to ongoing denial. As an approach that strives to address individual harms by analyzing underlying conflicts and inequalities, restorative justice cannot rely on traditional practices or democratic dialogue, but also requires the kind of critical historical reflection that Mamdani is proposing.

CONCLUSION

As truth commissions have been associated with the goal of restorative justice, they have also moved away from their defining mission, which was to examine historical patterns of violence. Instead, truth commissions have been promoted as strategies for healing individuals, communities, and nations. Critics of this "healing" approach to justice have tended to dismiss restorative justice as an inherently depoliticizing theory or to reject truth commissions as a manifestation of therapeutic justice. I have argued that therapeutic justice is only a variant of restorative justice, one that abandons much of what is promising in the theory while obscuring much of what is problematic about it as a response to political violence.

The close identification of the TRC's legacy with a therapeutic approach to transitional justice has also obfuscated the originality of theoretical debates on restorative justice in South Africa. In their reflections on the disappointments associated with the TRC process, Desmond Tutu, Charles Villa-Vicencio, and Mahmood Mamdani all acknowledged the limitations of the communitarian premises of restorative justice theory and offered distinctive ways to adapt restorative justice to a process designed to address politically authorized abuses in a context characterized by the absence of shared norms.

Despite their significant differences, the three thinkers offer a common set of guidelines for thinking about what restorative justice requires in such contexts – one that reframes restorative justice as an approach characterized by internal tensions. First, restorative justice calls for institutions that are responsive to local political contexts, values, and practices. Although the theory outlines a basic set of governing principles, it calls for a great deal of flexibility in how these principles are institutionalized. Yet restorative justice cannot rely uncritically on local values and practices, but rather requires attention to the ways that political communities are implicated in, and constructed by, patterns of political violence. Second, restorative justice requires active participation in the process of framing responses to past abuse. However, restorative justice also requires acknowledgment of past abuses in the form of a critical response to ongoing denial, justification, and rationalization. Third, in contrast with legalism, restorative justice calls for attention to the personal experience of suffering and efforts to repair the consequences of past abuses. It also calls for mechanisms to reintegrate individuals who are responsible for causing past suffering. However, restorative justice also requires critical attention to the link between individual harms and systemic injustices. Thus, restorative justice challenges the emphasis on civil and political rights or "personal integrity rights," which is dominant in transitional justice institutions and requires mechanisms to address economic and social injustices.

Tutu, Villa-Vicencio, and Mamdani offer three distinctive ways to conceptualize restorative justice practice or policy in response to these tensions. Tutu connects restorative justice in South Africa to his own interpretation of the African principle of *ubuntu* and to rituals of forgiveness and atonement. He offers these as strategies for revealing possibilities for common ground, yet also suggests that in contexts characterized by gross inequality and compromise, they are better understood as gestures that will amount to little in the absence of a critical challenge to denial regarding systemic injustices of the past. Villa-Vicencio suggests that establishing a space for democratic dialogue regarding past wrongs ought to be a primary strategy for advancing what he terms "political restorative justice." However, he also acknowledges that the parameters of dialogue as established by transitional justice institutions are shaped and limited by political compromise, as well as the victim-perpetrator framework itself.

Mamdani suggests that truth commissions might further restorative justice by adhering to their defining goal, which is to critically examine historical patterns of violence. As critical spectators truth commissions may call into question the tentative agreements established by political negotiations and may question the terms of emerging dialogue in ways that seem disruptive or entirely negative. Whereas the work of critical history implies an ongoing process of evaluation, and an effort to attain some kind of distance or detachment from the events that are under scrutiny, truth commissions are political creatures, bound to produce their findings under intense scrutiny. Yet the unique contribution of truth commissions to restorative justice depends on their role as institutions that are designed to reflect critically on *patterns* of political violence.

It is not self-evident that the proposals offered by Tutu, Villa-Vicencio, and Mamdani are mutually exclusive, though they are in tension with one another.

It is possible for a truth commission to defend a single judgment of historical wrongs while simultaneously following South Africa's TRC in acknowledging ongoing controversies, alternative perspectives, and the limitations inherent in their mandates. It is possible for a truth commission to provide a space for rituals that might encourage individual gestures of empathy, forgiveness, and atonement while simultaneously establishing a critical historical assessment of prominent rationalizations for past abuses.

The main obstacle to bridging these goals is not logistical or technical in nature, but fear that the kind of critical historical reflection that Mamdani is proposing would jeopardize the fragile compromises that are seen as the starting point for deepening a process of political reconciliation. This concern is not only raised in response to truth commissions or even to transitional justice institutions. It is cited as a general objection to all efforts to broaden and publicize critical responses to historical wrongs, whether in the form of truth commissions, criminal trials, textbook reforms, reparations, commemorations, or apologies. Mamdani, like Arendt, hints that examining the role of resistance to past wrongs might provide an important and neglected response to this concern. In the following chapter, I examine this proposition by considering what it would mean to integrate the theme of resistance into the theory and practice of transitional justice.

6

Remembering Resistance

Anton Schmidt was a German officer under the Nazi regime who had aided Jewish partisans with forged papers and military supplies for several months before he was caught, arrested, and executed. Schmidt's story was told by Abba Kovner as part of his testimony before the Jerusalem court during the trial of Adolf Eichmann. In her report on the Eichmann trial, Arendt described Kovner's testimony as a cathartic and transporting experience, "like a sudden burst of light in the midst of impenetrable, unfathomable darkness."[1] The impact of the story was so powerful, adds Arendt, that among those who witnessed it, "a single thought stood out clearly, irrefutably, beyond question – how utterly different everything would be today in this courtroom, in Israel, in Germany, in all of Europe, and perhaps in all countries of the world, if only more such stories could have been told."[2]

Whereas Arendt lamented the dearth of stories about resistance to Nazism, Kader Asmal insisted that the South African Truth and Reconciliation Commission ought to have documented stories of resistance to apartheid, alongside testimony from victims and the confessions that were presented to the Amnesty Committee. In his 1995 volume on the TRC, Asmal, along with coauthors, Louise Asmal and Ronald Suresh Roberts, illustrate this point by recalling a book that Joe Slovo put together to honor the memory of his wife, Ruth First. Slovo and First were both leaders in the anti-apartheid movement, when First was assassinated by a bomb planted by state security forces. Slovo's tribute to his wife included an image of First making a toast in an "undying gesture of celebration" of the resistance.[3] Remembering the lives and deaths of people like Ruth First, they argue, ought to have been part of the TRC's mission.

---

[1] Arendt, *Eichmann in Jerusalem*, 231.
[2] Arendt, *Eichmann in Jerusalem*, 231.
[3] Asmal et al., *Reconciliation through Truth?* 12.

Stories of those who engage in acts of resistance against systematic atrocities and oppression are often powerful and inspiring. Yet, the theme of resistance is almost entirely absent from the theory and practice of transitional justice. Contemporary responses to political violence have been framed as inquiries into the roles of victims and perpetrators. This framework is in keeping with the basic premises of legalism and the tendency to elevate war crimes trials as the most important moral response to politically authorized brutality. However, it is at odds with the claim that transitional justice institutions offer a way to critically investigate and remedy *systematic*, politically authorized forms of abuse. Truth commissions have been championed as a way to address this problem by analyzing systematic patterns of violence and advancing a restorative approach to justice that would encompass responses to underlying conflicts and systemic harms. However, these institutions have generally framed their investigations in relation to the same victim-perpetrator framework that animates the criminal trial.

This emphasis on analyzing the roles of victims and perpetrators is associated with the view that transitional justice institutions must depoliticize their investigations in order to establish moral clarity and legitimacy, particularly in contexts where political rationales have been mobilized to justify abuse. Depoliticization has also been a major strategy for promoting political reconciliation in the aftermath of conflict. This helps explain why transitional justice institutions have generally avoided the theme of resistance. What is more puzzling is that the theme of resistance receives so little attention in more general theoretical debates on judgment, remembrance, and reconciliation in the aftermath of political violence.

If political judgment is recognized as an indispensable dimension of the process of evaluating systematic atrocities, then it will be important to consider strategies for addressing the limitations of the victim-perpetrator framework. This chapter does so by considering what it would mean to incorporate the theme of resistance into truth commission investigations. It takes the writings of Arendt and Asmal as a starting point for examining three different forms that such inquiries might take. First, following Arendt's reflections on the Eichmann trial, truth commissions could investigate the *failure to resist* or to withdraw support from political systems that are engaged in atrocities. Second, truth commissions and other quasi-adjudicatory institutions or commissions of inquiry could follow Asmal's call to investigate and acknowledging the role of *political resistance* to atrocities committed under a prior regime. A third approach, found in the arguments presented by both Arendt and Asmal, would investigate examples of what I refer to as *privileged* resistance, acts of resistance by individuals who broke ranks with their own communities to protest atrocities that were committed in their name.

One goal of the analysis is to take a closer look at the unique objections that might be raised in response to different approaches to analyzing resistance, and to consider how such objections might be addressed without avoiding the theme of resistance altogether. A common concern that animates such objections has to do with the way that resistance, in all of its forms, entails a struggle against power – most commonly the power of the state. Transitional justice and political reconciliation have been associated with the goal of shedding the oppositional posture that characterizes resistance and counterinsurgency in order to cultivate a common commitment to the project of reconstruction. Returning to Primo Levi's essay, "The Gray Zone," I suggest that truth commissions might address such concerns by acknowledging shades of gray, not only in various forms of complicity, but also in acts of protest, resistance, and refusal.

The argument developed here also addresses more general debates on the problem of what it means to pursue justice and reconciliation in response to systematic, politically authorized violence. It takes issue with the view that investigating the theme of resistance is inherently destabilizing and therefore threatening to the project of political reconciliation. Against this view, I suggest that investigating the theme of resistance illuminates possibilities for agency, solidarity, and innovation that are obscured by the victim-perpetrator framework, and offers a more promising basis for political reconciliation that what are often dubious efforts to emphasize common experiences of suffering across lines of conflict and difference.

THE FAILURE TO RESIST

One way that truth commissions could investigate the theme of resistance would be to examine its absence or failure. Why didn't people refuse to comply with orders to commit atrocities? Why did people not do more to resist an oppressive system? Why did they participate or just keep quiet instead of taking some other course of action? Arendt poses such questions in her report on the Eichmann trial. Her analysis is useful in that it demonstrates how this kind of investigation could address an important problem in prominent approaches to international justice. However, Arendt's analysis also illustrates the pitfalls associated with such inquiries and how they can go awry.

Although Arendt was highly critical of many of the ideas that are now associated with human rights legalism, she was also convinced that international criminal prosecution offered a vital response to systematic atrocities.

She found criminal prosecution appealing, despite her awareness of its limitations, because the logic of the criminal trial, as she saw it, insists on the human capacity for resistance. Arendt makes this point by characterizing the criminal trial as a particularly useful response to what she refers to as the "cog" defense – the claim that there was no other choice but to support the Nazi regime, or to participate in the genocide, because one was merely a "cog" in a larger machine whose ultimate purposes were not known or subject to challenge. The great advantage of the criminal trial, wrote Arendt, "is that this whole cog business makes no sense in its setting ... if the defendant claims he was simply a cog, that everyone would have done it in his place, this will be ruled out as immaterial."[4] Confronted with the "cog theory," writes Arendt, the court should ask, "why, if you please, did you become a cog, or continue to be a cog under such circumstances?"[5] In so doing, criminal prosecution would confront systematic atrocity by demanding that people be prepared to question the logic of their own political system and to disobey the orders of their superiors.

This argument identifies the promise of international criminal justice with a principle that is often seen as troublesome. The Nuremberg Principles, codified in 1950, not only established a basis for holding leaders criminally accountable for crimes against their own people, but also invalidated the defense of superior orders. Specifically, the Nuremberg Principles hold that, "[t]he fact that a person acted pursuant to order of his Government or of a superior does not relieve him from responsibility under international law, provided a moral choice was in fact possible to him."[6] International criminal law demands not only obedience to established standards, but also resistance to local authorities who transgress them. It requires lower-ranking members of the military to be prepared to question the authority of their commanding officers. As discussed in Chapter 2, the first case before the International Criminal Tribunal for the former Yugoslavia affirmed this principle in response to Drazen Erdemovic's claim that he would have been shot had he refused orders to participate in the Srebrenica massacre.

Although international criminal justice implicitly demands resistance, it treats politically authorized atrocities as a form of criminal deviance and identifies moral action with efforts to promote compliance and obedience. That is, proponents of international criminal justice have identified the moral force

---

4   Arendt, "Personal Responsibility under Dictatorship," 30.
5   Arendt, "Personal Responsibility under Dictatorship," 32.
6   Principles of International Law Recognized in the Charter of the Nuremberg Tribunal and in the Judgment of the Tribunal, 1950.

of war crimes tribunals with their role in condemning the worst offenders –
those who authorized and ordered brutalities and can be clearly distinguished
from ordinary participants. Scholars and activists have also argued that international criminal trials deter would-be war criminals by compelling them to
comply with international norms. Some have identified the success of international justice with the achievement of a kind of habitual obedience, such
that the basic norms associated with international justice no longer appear as
a set of rules imposed from outside, but have become "internalized" and have
a "taken for granted quality."[7]

Arendt thought that the Eichmann trial illustrated just what was wrong with
this emphasis on obedience and compliance. The trouble with Eichmann,
she wrote, was precisely that so many were like him … that they were, and
still are, terrible and terrifyingly normal."[8] She characterized him as the kind
of criminal that "commits his crimes under circumstances that make it nearly
impossible to know or feel he is doing wrong."[9] This conclusion was one of
the reasons that her reporting on the Eichmann trial shocked and horrified
many of those who read the report in the *The New Yorker* magazine, and one
of the reasons that Eichmann's prosecutor, Gideon Hausner, journeyed from
Jerusalem to New York in order to answer what he reportedly referred to as
"Arendt's bizarre defense of Eichmann."[10]

Far from letting Eichmann off the hook by reclassifying him as "ordinary,"
Arendt's analysis of Eichmann's character instead aims to widen the scope
of accountability to encompass the role of ordinary, "banal," normal people
who passively worked as "cogs" in the Nazi system instead of refusing or resisting. Nevertheless, it is impossible to read her discussion of Eichmann without
becoming concerned that she may have misunderstood him. Even in Arendt's
own reporting, Eichmann often sounds more like a zealot than a reluctant
follower. Her efforts to recast his zealotry as a radical kind of deference are
somewhat awkward.[11]

---

7 Martha Finnemore and Kathryn Sikkink, "International Norm Dynamics and Political
   Change," *International Organization* 55, no. 4 (1998): 887–917; Thomas Risse and Kathryn
   Sikkink, "The Socialization of International Human Rights Norms," in *The Power of Human
   Rights: International Norms and Domestic Change*, ed. Thomas Risse, Stephen C. Ropp, and
   Kathryn Sikkink (New York: Cambridge University Press, 1999), 17.
8 Arendt, *Eichmann in Jerusalem*, 267.
9 Arendt, *Eichmann in Jerusalem*, 276.
10 Young-Bruehl, *Hannah Arendt*, 349.
11 Arendt makes this argument by detailing how Eichmann had surprised the court by declaring
   that he had lived his whole life according to Kant's moral precepts. Yet he had distorted the cat-
   egorical imperative (act only according to that maxim whereby you can at the same time will
   that it should become a universal law) and had interpreted it to mean: "Act as if the principle

Whether or not she painted an accurate portrait of Eichmann's character, Arendt's analysis is important because of the way that it addresses a problem that she saw *represented by* Eichmann – that is, the various ways in which systematic atrocities are supported and condoned by ordinary citizens. Scholarship examining the causes and motives of those who participate in crimes against humanity has confirmed her view that the vast majority of participants are not deviants, but rather individuals who often do not differ significantly from the vast majority of people in their societies.[12] Although it is far-fetched, in many cases, to suggest that such participants do not "know or feel" that they are doing wrong, her larger concern is with the problem of how to hold people responsible for their participation in actions that do not deviate from the norm, but are rather legalized, institutionalized, authorized, and rationalized in such a way as to reinforce the view that those who commit even the worst brutalities are little more than cogs.

In light of this concern, Arendt was deeply skeptical of the way in which the criminal justice framework identifies moral action with obedience and enforcement. She warned that people who are dependent on formal moral codes and standards for guidance are unreliable as allies in a struggle against state-sponsored repression. Those who depend on habits of obedience, she suggests, will be unprepared to respond to situations where the rules or standards that once guided them no longer make sense against the backdrop of radically altered conditions. They will lack the resources to challenge leaders who subtly alter or manipulate the rules to rationalize abuse. All they are left with in such circumstances, writes Arendt, "is the mere habit of holding fast to something."[13] International criminal justice addresses this problem by demanding resistance to superior orders. Yet, this sits uneasily alongside the way in which criminal trials frame atrocity as a problem of deviance and the emphasis among advocates of international criminal justice on enforcement, compliance, and obedience.

of your actions were the same as that of the legislator or of the law of the land." She offers this anecdote, in part, to explain how he could have appeared so zealous, yet still bear the essential character traits of an obedient follower. Arendt, *Eichmann in Jerusalem*, 136.

[12] See, for example, Scott Straus, *The Order of Genocide: Race, Power, and War in Rwanda* (Ithaca, NY: Cornell University Press, 2006); James Waller, *Becoming Evil: How Ordinary People Commit Genocide and Mass Killing* (Oxford: Oxford University Press, 2005); Stathis Kalyvas, "The Ontology of 'Political Violence': Action and Identity in Civil Wars," *Perspectives on Politics* 1, no. 3 (2003): 475–94; Drumbl, *Atrocity, Punishment, and International Law*; Lee Ann Fujii, *Killing Neighbors: Webs of Violence in Rwanda* (Ithaca, NY: Cornell University Press, 2009); Mark Osiel, *Mass Atrocity, Ordinary Evil, and Hannah Arendt: Criminal Consciousness in Argentina's Dirty War* (New Haven, CT and London: Yale University Press, 2001).

[13] Arendt, "Personal Responsibility under Dictatorship," 44–5.

Thus, while Arendt recognizes that criminal trials must be narrowly framed to investigate individual guilt, she also argues that defending the goals associated with international criminal justice requires inquiries that examine the failure of resistance. She imagines an alternative verdict in the Eichmann case that would reframe his guilt as a failure to resist or refuse. Even if "80 million Germans behaved exactly as you did," she declares, this would not be an excuse because "there is an abyss between the actuality of what you did and the potentiality of what others might have done."[14] Instead of condemning Eichmann for deviating from universal principles of justice, then, Arendt accuses him of failing to withdraw support from a criminal regime. In doing so, she also articulates a basis for expanding the scope of accountability beyond a focus on those who may be categorized as "abnormal monsters" to those who represent the kind of passive, complacent followers that Arendt took Eichmann to represent.

The idea that people may be held responsible for their failure to resist systematic atrocities should not be confused with the support for collective criminal guilt. For Arendt, collective guilt was just as effective a "whitewash" as the characterization of Eichmann as an abnormal monster.[15] Instead, Arendt suggests that responsibility for the failure to resist ought to be calibrated in relation to the availability of alternatives to support or obedience. The analysis presumes that people ideally ought to be capable of making judgments regarding the legitimacy of an established political order and to act on those judgments. The Jerusalem court recognized that responsibility for the genocide decreased with proximity to the actual killings. Those who bore the greatest responsibility were the ones that gave orders from the distance of their offices.[16] Such individuals were, in Arendt's view, also more likely to be in a position to pursue alternatives. Arendt builds on this insight in her imaginary verdict. Despite his protests to the contrary, she insists that Eichmann was not bound to carry out the orders he was given and instead could have refused them without confronting great personal loss or sacrifice. Even those who may be essentially powerless, she argues, retain the capacity to withdraw or refuse support for a criminal system.[17] However, when Gideon Hausner asks Jewish witnesses why they did not protest, Arendt dismisses this as a "cruel and

---

[14] Arendt, *Eichmann in Jerusalem*, 278. For an insightful, extended analysis of Arendt's imaginary verdict in the Eichmann trial, see Jennifer Culbert, "The Banality of Death in Eichmann," *Theory and Event* 6, no. 1 (2002).

[15] Arendt, Eichmann in Jerusalem, 21.

[16] Arendt, *Eichmann in Jerusalem*, 247.

[17] Arendt, "Personal Responsibility under Dictatorship," 45.

silly question," observing that in Amsterdam, a group of Jews who attacked a German security police detachment were tortured to death.[18]

Although Arendt demonstrates why it is so important to investigate failed resistance, her own efforts to do so reveal some of the potential pitfalls and challenges associated with this kind of inquiry. One reason that her analysis was troubling to many readers was that it seemed to displace the victim-perpetrator framework altogether. By recasting Eichmann as a person who failed to resist, Arendt seems to downplay the role of those who organize and authorize brutalities – those who may be uniquely "evil," or deviant. At the same time, the idea of widening the scope of accountability to include ordinary followers seems unmanageable and potentially destabilizing in light of the kinds of protests that accompany far more narrowly framed exercises in accountability for past wrongs.

A second potential concern is that Arendt's analysis slips into blaming victims for their own suffering by recasting it as the outcome of their failure to resist. The actions of Jewish council leaders who negotiated with Nazi authorities in exchange for lives spared, she argues, demonstrated the same kind of instrumental logic and status seeking that had rationalized participation in the Nazi regime. Arendt certainly does not imply a moral equivalence between Jewish collaborators and Eichmann himself. However, she does argue that by collaborating with the Nazi regime, Jews made it easier for the German population to engage in mass denial and self-deception. Everyone who demanded to have an exception made in his case, she argues, implicitly recognized the rule. She went so far as to suggest that in doing so, "they convinced their opponents of the lawfulness of what they were doing."[19] Her point here is to demonstrate how victim participation comes to play a powerful role in the logic of atrocity.[20] However, her emphasis on the role of individual choice led her to formulate the discussion in a manner that was sometimes strangely detached from the context of violence and coercion that she had set out to examine. In a response to her critics, Arendt insisted that, "if someone points a gun at you and says, 'Kill your friend or I will kill you,' he is tempting you, that is all."[21] In the postscript to *Eichmann in Jerusalem*, Arendt castigated the "American literati" for their "naïve belief that temptation and coercion are the same thing" by likening the situation of being ordered to kill one's friend at gunpoint to the dilemma confronting the winner of a quiz show who has discovered that the

[18] Arendt, *Eichmann in Jerusalem*, 124.
[19] Arendt, *Eichmann in Jerusalem*, 133.
[20] On this theme, see Corey Robin, *Fear: The History of a Political Idea* (Oxford: Oxford University Press, 2006), 124–5.
[21] Arendt, "Political Responsibility under Dictatorship," 18.

win was a hoax and cannot "resist" taking the money anyway.[22] The person with a gun to his or her head is no longer a victim in this odd formulation, but someone who is "tempted" into complicity.

This raises a third concern, which is that it seems presumptuous to judge people for actions that are taken under conditions of unimaginable deprivation and pressure. Primo Levi, himself a survivor of Auschwitz, observes that these are the kinds of judgments that people prefer to entrust "only to those who found themselves in similar circumstances and had the opportunity to test for themselves what it means to act in a state of coercion."[23] A related problem is that it is impossible to know exactly what alternatives were available to people who opted to support, rather than resist, systematic atrocity. Possibilities for resistance that may appear obvious to those observing from a safe distance are not necessarily evident in times of chaos.

A fourth concern raised by Arendt's analysis is that in judging people for failing to resist, we may lose sight of the dilemmas and complexities of moral action in a context of systematic atrocity, and fail to understand the conditions under which the capacity for resistance is eroded. In a letter written in response to the controversy surrounding her assessment of the Jewish Councils, Arendt observes that the council leadership became involved in negotiations with the Nazi authorities in a way that was so gradual that it was difficult to see when they came to "cross a line which never should have been crossed."[24] Pragmatic or instrumental bargaining might have appeared as a way to minimize suffering, to choose the "lesser evil"; it also functioned, in her view, to legitimate the evil of Nazism. Arendt acknowledges that this makes their actions more understandable. However, instead of seeing this as indicative of the moral complexity involved in these decisions, she interprets it as further evidence that the choice as to whether to resist or comply must be understood in black-and-white terms.

These kinds of concerns generally cause people to avoid inquiries into the failure or absence of resistance. Yet, these problems do not follow logically from Arendt's decision to investigate the failure of resistance, but from the specific way that she went about it. Although she recognizes the limitations of victim-perpetrator binary, Arendt retains the simple moral logic of the criminal justice framework and frames the problem of resistance as an individual choice between what is right and what is wrong. She finds this framework appealing because it insists on the possibility of clear moral choice and

[22] Arendt, *Eichmann in Jerusalem*, 295.
[23] Levi, *The Drowned and the Saved*, 44.
[24] Young-Bruehl, *Hannah Arendt*, 345.

agency as against helplessness and moral confusion. However, she adopts it at the expense of a genuine effort to examine the different forms that resistance might take, the complex and agonizing dilemmas that might be associated with acts of resistance, and the social and political factors that might explain the absence of resistance.

Primo Levi's essay, "The Gray Zone," suggests an alternative approach to investigating failed resistance that would move away from Arendt's emphasis on individual choice. Like Arendt, Levi suggests that responsibility for complicity ought to be calibrated in relation to the costs of refusal or resistance. Levi also rejects claims made by accused war criminals that invoked the defense of superior orders. Most such individuals, he argues, could have refused to carry out their orders through "some maneuver, some slowdown in career, moderate punishment, or in the worst of cases, the objector's transfer to the front."[25] In contrast with Arendt, however, Levi insists on humility in judging those who become complicit under conditions of extreme coercion and deprivation. He writes that his judgment is "tentative and varied" for those who occupied commanding positions, the chiefs or *Kapos* and if forced to judge, he would "lightheartedly absolve all those whose concurrence in the guilt was minimal and for whom coercion was of the highest degree."[26] Levi argues that "no one is authorized to judge" the Sonderkommandos, or Jewish prisoners who were in charge of running the gas chamber. For Levi, collaboration under such circumstances is best understood as *Befehlnotstand*, the "state of compulsion following an order."[27]

"With equal frequency, and an even harsher accusatory tone," observes Levi, "we [concentration camp survivors] are asked: 'Why didn't you rebel?'"[28] This question cannot be answered by insisting that resistance is always an option, but requires an effort to imagine the experience of coercion. Arendt's analysis of victim resistance does not suffer from insufficient empathy, as some of her critics have suggested, but from a failure of imagination. Her analysis of victim resistance is more like an exercise in legal judgment than the kind of reflective, political judgment guided by "enlarged mentality" that she called for in response to Nazi atrocities. For those who would stand in judgment over collaborators within the camps, Levi responds with a thought experiment:

Let him imagine if he can, that he has lived for months or years in a ghetto, tormented by chronic hunger, fatigue, promiscuity, and humiliation; that he

25 Levi, *The Drowned and the Saved*, 60.
26 Levi, *The Drowned and the Saved*, 44.
27 Levi, *The Drowned and the Saved*, 59.
28 Levi, *The Drowned and the Saved*, 158.

has seen die around him, one by one, his beloved; that he is cut off from the world, unable to receive or transmit news; that, finally, he is loaded onto a train, eighty or a hundred persons to a boxcar.[29]

Levi characterizes the desire for simple moral judgments as a universal response to atrocity, yet maintains that the logic of collaboration under the Nazi regime and within the concentration camps can only be understood as a "gray zone," peopled with those who could not easily be classified as innocent victims or as evil criminals. In place of the either/or logic that Arendt applies to her analysis of the failure to resist, Levi contends that strategic collaboration is not always or necessarily a slippery slope to responsibility for atrocity. He observes that some of the prisoners working in the camp facilities were able to gain access to secret information that became essential to compiling the history of the regime, or assisting fellow prisoners in more concrete ways. Some prisoners used the privileges they gained through collaboration to determine which SS officials could be "dissuaded from cruel decisions," or blackmailed. Others used their positions as collaborators to mask covert resistance activities.

Although Levi urges his readers to acknowledge the "gray zone," he also draws an analytic distinction between the exercise of examining the logic of victim complicity and the kind of thinking that would abandon the categories of victim and perpetrator altogether. He makes this point by reflecting on a comment made by film director, Liliana Cavani, who had summarized her film with the statement that, "We are all victims or murderers, and we accept these roles voluntarily."[30] The *TRC Report* contains a passage that makes a similar point, observing that "a little perpetrator" exists within all of us. For Levi, such claims are speculative as a general matter, but self-serving or manipulative as a response to mass murder. "I do not know and it does not interest me," he replies, "whether in my depths there lurks a murderer, but I do know that I was a guiltless victim and I was not a murderer. I know that murderers existed and still exist ... and that to confuse them with their victims is a moral disease."[31]

Given that truth commissions are designed to investigate systematic patterns of violence, they are in a position to conduct investigations that examine the failure of resistance. Together, Arendt and Levi shed light on how such investigations could address a problem, or gap, in advocacy on behalf of international criminal justice. International criminal justice cannot simply

---

[29] Levi, *The Drowned and the Saved*, 59.
[30] Levi, *The Drowned and the Saved*, 48.
[31] Levi, *The Drowned and the Saved*, 48.

become effective through a process whereby people shift their allegiance from one moral code to another, or internalize international norms due to concern with reputation. It also requires people to take responsibility for critical judgment and refusal in response to leaders who organize and authorize atrocities.

If truth commissions were to investigate the failure of resistance, they would likely confront the concern that such investigations might widen the scope of accountability in a manner that is destabilizing, or that they would undercut the moral clarity associated with the goal of identifying victims and perpetrators. Instead of seeing these concerns as reasons for turning away from inquiries into the failure of resistance, however, truth commissions might offset them by following Levi in examining the specific conditions, unique to each case, that undermine or diminish the capacity for resistance, and by considering how forced complicity can become a powerful strategy for consolidating the helplessness and isolation of victims. This would entail an effort to examine the shades of gray in stories of collaboration as well as stories of refusal without abandoning the categories of victim and perpetrator along the way.

POLITICAL RESISTANCE

A second way that truth commissions might examine the theme of resistance would be to investigate the role of organized political resistance. Kader Asmal made the case for this kind of investigation in his reflections on the South African TRC. Specifically, Asmal argued that the TRC ought to have acknowledged the actions, losses, and suffering of those who worked with the liberation movements in the struggle against South African apartheid. He envisioned a process of public investigation and remembrance that would look something like the book that Slovo put together in honor of Ruth First. Slovo's booklet contained the basic facts of First's murder, but also the story of her commitment to the resistance. Years later, when Slovo passed away, Asmal recalls that Slovo's memorial was carefully carved, but "jagged edged," to symbolize the "rough edges of every person's character and also Joe's unfinished work in progress – the country's work, and the world's."[32]

Asmal is widely credited with having been responsible for convincing the ANC to support a truth commission. However, his proposal for investigating the role of political resistance was not followed and has been largely ignored in scholarship on the TRC and its legacy. The image of First's gesture of celebration is very different from the images of victimization that are at the center

---

[32] Asmal et al., *Reconciliation through Truth?* 13.

of most truth commissions and those that dominated South Africa's *TRC Report*. And Slovo's jagged edged memorial is at odds with the prominent understanding of truth commissions as therapeutic institutions that seek closure and adaptation through cathartic testimony, and aim to advance a common sense of political community through the memory of shared suffering.

Of course, stories of political resistance *have* emerged in the context of the TRC as well as most other truth commissions – stories that might not otherwise have been preserved. The TRC characterized the struggle against apartheid as a "just war.[33] However, its investigations were framed as an analysis of *jus in bello* (justice in war), rather than *jus ad bellum* (justice of war). As discussed in Chapter 3, the focus on justice in war has been a pragmatic approach to minimizing wartime suffering by avoiding volatile political judgments. For South Africa's TRC, *jus in bello* provided a framework for acknowledging the suffering of victims on both sides of the struggle while condemning abuses committed in the name of the liberation movements as well as the state.

Not all truth commissions explicitly rely on *jus in bello*, yet most implicitly invoke its logic by focusing on victims and perpetrators from all sides of a conflict. This does not lead inexorably to moral equivalence and can, in fact, be a powerful basis for challenging moral equivalence. For example, Guatemala's Historical Clarification Commission (CEH) decisively rejected the "theory of two devils," which had posited that the state and the resistance were equally accountable for devastating the country. The CEH challenged this logic with the finding that state forces were responsible for 93 percent of the violations documented in the report.[34] Although the human rights legal framework emerged as a way to hold states accountable for the treatment of individual citizens, human rights organizations recognized that private entities, including resistance organizations, are often responsible for massive atrocities and repression. Peru's truth commission found that the Communist Party of Peru-Shining Path was responsible for launching the internal armed conflict, and for a greater share of abuses than the state.[35]

However, the centrality of *jus in bello* logic in truth commission investigations has also meant that those who resisted systemic abuse or repression may participate in the process of giving testimony only to the extent that they are willing or able to present themselves as "victims" or "perpetrators" as defined in the terms of the truth commission's mandate. In the case of South Africa's

[33] *TRC Report* vol. 1, 66–70.
[34] Guatemalan Commission for Historical Clarification. *Guatemala Memory of Silence: Report of the Commission for Historical Clarification* (1996), Concluding Section, no. 82.
[35] Truth and Reconciliation Commission of Peru, *Final Report* (2003), Conclusions, part IIA, no. 12–13.

TRC, this meant that members of the liberation groups were less likely to participate in the process by giving statements or presenting testimony.[36] Those that *did* appear before the TRC were directed to answer questions geared at establishing their identities as official victims or perpetrators under the terms of the TRC Act. The therapeutic framework that animated much of the TRC's analysis analyzed the motivations of the resistance movements in apolitical terms, as a response to psychological stresses.[37]

By proposing that the TRC should have documented and acknowledged the history of political resistance in South Africa, Asmal challenges, and suggests an alternative to, this therapeutic framework. He argues that investigating the role of political resistance is an important dimension of a just response to past wrongs, as well as efforts to pursue reconciliation.

First, Asmal argues that acknowledging the role of resistance is a matter of justice. If truth commissions have a moral obligation to acknowledge the helpless suffering of victims, he suggests, then they also have a moral obligation to acknowledge the suffering and losses that resulted from a decision to engage in political action against the system that caused that suffering. To acknowledge such actors only to the extent that they were "victims" is diminishing. It also amounts to a kind of concession to the stigmatization and criminalization of those who "were wrongly vilified, maimed and killed" for the work that they did to resist past wrongs.[38] Under apartheid, those who participated in acts of peaceful resistance as well as those who became involved in armed resistance were criminalized, tortured, and assassinated. The parents of children who were killed as a result of their resistance activities were often told that their children were terrorists or criminals. The TRC did take steps to decriminalize the resistance, but did so by reclassifying those targeted by the state as "victims." This proposal calls for a more expansive process of acknowledgment, which encompasses not only the wrongful suffering that resulted from political resistance, but also the deeds and sacrifices of those engaged in resistance.

Like Arendt, Asmal also argues that a failure to investigate the role of resistance reinforces a problematic tendency to identify moral action with obedience. Asmal makes this point by discussing the story, now well known, of Anja Rosmus. As a schoolgirl living in postwar Germany, Rosmus interviewed community members for a class project dealing with the way that different people had acted during the Nazi era. She discovered that many

---

[36] Minow, *Between Vengeance and Forgiveness*, 80; Chapman and Ball, "Levels of Truth," 152.
[37] Truth and Reconciliation Commission of South Africa Report, vol. 5.
[38] Asmal et al., *Reconciliation through Truth?* 13.

people she had known as former resistance fighters had actually been Nazi sympathizers. More surprising, was her discovery that those who had taken steps to help the Jews were "strangely reticent" about the good things they had done. Their acts of kindness "had broken the rules," wrote Rosmus in her reflections on what she had found. "They were disobedient. And civil disobedience is thought to be a bad thing."[39] To acknowledge the role of political resistance, and challenge the stigmatization of political resistance, is to counter this kind of logic.

Second, Asmal suggests that truth commissions might play a greater role in advancing political reform and reconciliation if they were to examine the role of political resistance and establish space for people to give testimony about their experiences as members of political resistance. This argument resembles Arendt's claim that in the memory of the French, resistance to Nazism is like an "unwilled inheritance."[40] Accustomed to locating political wisdom and guidance in the idea of inherited traditions and values, Arendt observed, people do not generally search for guidance in examples of resistance. Yet in contexts where community traditions are no longer viable, or where they are implicated in past atrocities, the memory of resistance is like an inheritance that is "unwilled" by established traditions, but which may provide guidance for future change by exemplifying possibilities for agency, commitment, courage, innovation, and solidarity. Arendt's use of such examples was not only constructive, but also critical – a basis for exposing and condemning pervasive complicity in past wrongs.

To the extent that truth commissions evaluate systematic injustice as the aggregation of individual experiences of victimhood, they are limited as a basis for critically evaluating the particular logic and dynamics of political violence in a given context. Investigations confined to this framework tend to emphasize analogous features of systematic atrocities across cases and deemphasize unique features associated with a given political and historical context. By investigating the history of organized political resistance, the TRC would have been in a better position to inform a process of reform that would address the specific logic of institutionalized political violence in South Africa. The kind of investigation that he has in mind would have examined, for example, the criminalization of dissent in South Africa through legislative acts and declared "states of emergency."[41] It would also entail an approach to historical inquiry that would critically evaluate claims used to rationalize such

[39] Asmal et al., *Reconciliation through Truth?* 63.
[40] Arendt, *Between Past and Future*, 4.
[41] Asmal et al., *Reconciliation through Truth?* 90–2.

actions, rather than one that would present them as competing perspectives in an ongoing dialogue.

Asmal also suggests that the "jagged edged" history of political resistance contains important ideas and examples of agency and commitment that might inform an ongoing process of political reform. For example, Asmal cites the unique role of the ANC in the history of the human rights movement. The ANC drafted its own bill of rights in 1943 – five years before the Universal Declaration of Human Rights was signed. The ANC's 1955 Freedom Charter became an influential document in the global struggle for human rights. The Freedom Charter "remains a global model of inclusive politics," which "both anticipated and contributed to the global human rights consensus."[42] Recalling these stories of resistance, Asmal suggests, illuminates possibilities for the kind of political agency and innovation that ought to guide South Africa's transitional process. Asmal reinforces this point by describing the perseverance demonstrated by a crowd of protesters who came together to support their leaders during the Rivonia trial. "When women protesters fell, hostile onlookers laughed ... From the window of a building, hostile occupants threw water on the protesters. Yet they were proud."[43] These reflections recall Char's recollection of the French Resistance, and his concern with the way that the political engagement and shared commitment generated in periods of crisis and historic struggle can give way to apathy, disillusionment, and disengagement in response to the day to day work of political transition.

Several concerns might be raised in response to this proposal. One concern has to do with the oppositional stance associated with political resistance. Arendt observes that the commitment and solidarity associated with the French resistance were lost in the aftermath of the war. The dedication to action and the sense of commitment that accompanied it were animated by the imperative of struggle against an overwhelming common enemy. If resistance derives its energy from this oppositional stance, then the ideas and practices associated with resistance are unlikely to resonate in the aftermath of a struggle marked by an overwhelming common threat. As Hannah Pitkin puts it, commenting on Arendt's reflections on the French Resistance, "[t]he commitment and power of the resistance had to be transferred into normal politics so that the amalgam became more than resistance and more than normal."[44] To the extent that the memory of resistance does continue to

42 Asmal et al., *Reconciliation through Truth?* 113.
43 Asmal et al., *Reconciliation through Truth?* 61.
44 Hannah Fenichel Pitkin, *The Attack of the Blob: Hannah Arendt's Concept of the Social* (Chicago and London: University of Chicago Press, 1998), 113.

animate post-conflict politics, this is often considered damaging or threatening to the project of political reconciliation. In this context, the oppositional, "jagged edged" stance of resistance appears to conflict with the stated goal of "national unity and reconciliation."[45] How is it possible to draw guidance from the legacy of political resistance in a context where the goal is to forge alliances across former divides, to establish a new basis for legitimate authority, and to sustain a commitment to political engagement in normal times?

A second, related concern is that acknowledging the role of armed resistance entails glorifying or legitimating violence committed in the name of resistance. When the ANC complained about the way the movement had been depicted in the text of the *TRC Report*, the TRC and major human rights organizations perceived this as a plea for double standards regarding the treatment of "gross violations of human rights" that were the focus of the commission's investigation.[46] In contexts where an armed resistance movement assumes the role of governing party, the fear is that transitional justice will become little other than "victor's justice." For example, the Rwandan government has refused to allow the International Criminal Tribunal for Rwanda (ICTR) to investigate atrocities that were committed by the Rwandan Patriotic Front during the invasion that stopped the genocide and brought President Kagame to power.[47]

With regard to this second concern, there is no reason to presume that acknowledging the contributions of organized resistance will inevitably sanitize or glorify the violence committed in the name of resistance. The ANC's complaint to South Africa's TRC bore little resemblance to the Rwandan government's response to the ICTR. Prior to the transition, the ANC had voluntarily submitted to the scrutiny of two independent commissions. The first commission was formed in 1991, after a group of thirty-two former detainees held by the ANC developed a committee to confront the organization's leadership regarding abuses in the ANC detention camps that were located throughout Southern Africa. The report documented what it referred to as "staggering brutality" in the camps, including regular torture, killings, and other abuses.[48] Nelson Mandela subsequently accepted

45 On this theme, see Meister, "Ways of Winning."
46 African National Congress, Submission of the African National Congress to the Truth and Reconciliation Commission in Reply to the Section 30 (2) of Act 34 of 1996 on the TRC "Findings on the African National Congress," October 1998.
47 "Rwanda: Academic Scholars Call for ICTR to Fulfill Mandate and Prosecute RPF/RPA Members," *World News Journal*, June 1, 2009.
48 Hayner, *Unspeakable Truths*, 60–1. Hayner writes that the ANC is the only armed resistance group that independently established a commission to investigate and publicly report on its own abuses (60).

responsibility for the abuses on behalf of the ANC leadership. He then named a new commission to carry out an even more thorough and independent investigation. It was following the completion of these reports, which were made public, that members of the ANC began to call for a nationwide truth commission process.[49]

Instead of avoiding or "forgetting" the role of political resistance because of its association with violence, truth commissions might critically evaluate the role of violence in the resistance. Asmal is said to have played an important role in urging the ANC to accept the proposal for a truth commission that would critically examine the violence of the liberation movements. He argued that such an evaluation should be guided by the principle that "resistance fighters should repent and acknowledge wrongdoing wherever they overstepped the bounds of international law or norms; but where they merely contravened unjust laws … no such acknowledgment is required."[50] The critical evaluation of specific violations ought to be complemented with an analysis of the historical events that preceded the armed conflict and the way in which asymmetries of power inform the dynamics of violent conflict.

Asmal also suggests that truth commissions could challenge the tendency to glorify or sentimentalize violence by providing a space for open-ended testimony regarding the experience of armed resistance. He illustrates this point by relating the story of Andrew Sibusiso Zondo, who was hanged for causing an explosion that killed five people in 1985. Zondo had joined the ANC after the police attacked a prayer service at his place of worship. He was eventually arrested and, according to his father, he became "mentally deranged" as a result of abuse experienced while he was imprisoned. Zondo told the court that he was "happy to be arrested so as to face it because the outcome of what I did … five people dead … If I ever have part of flesh to give to those who remain I can do it with pleasure." Zondo added, "[a]s an ANC member, I was supposed to prove the difference between the South African Defense Force and the MK [the armed wing of the ANC], and to ensure that civilians did not get hurt."[51] Zondo's narrative reveals the complicated and sometimes ambiguous landscape of organized resistance commonly obscured in truth commission reports that center on helpless victimization. To incorporate such oral histories into the work of truth commissions would enable these institutions to better satisfy their claim to analyze and aid in understanding the patterns and context of systemic atrocities.

---

[49] Hayner, *Unspeakable Truths*, 64.
[50] Asmal et al., *Reconciliation through Truth?* 58.
[51] Asmal et al., *Reconciliation through Truth?* 116.

This proposal does not address the concern that remembering political resistance will reinforce the kind of oppositional stance that might undermine a project of reconciliation. One way to counter this problem might be to examine multiple forms of organized political resistance and to consider variation and conflict among those engaged in organized resistance. The problem with Asmal's proposal is not that it sanitizes the violence of the ANC, but that it focuses so narrowly on the armed wing of the ANC while neglecting other forms of resistance to apartheid, such as the nonviolent strikes, community-based resistance, and the Black Consciousness movement, which emerged in the 1970s.[52] As Mahmood Mamdani observes, investigating the emergence of nonviolent protest and cross-racial solidarity within movements to resist apartheid would have shed light on how political reconciliation became a possibility in South Africa, and how it could be pursued in the future.

The armed resistance in South Africa was relatively disciplined and officially committed to the principles animating the Geneva Conventions.[53] The ANC's role in the history of the human rights movement is also unique. In other contexts, the history of armed resistance may not provide particularly useful examples or insights to inform a process of political reconstruction and reform. However, it could nonetheless be very instructive to investigate other forms of organized resistance, including nonviolent protest and strikes. Broadening the investigation of organized resistance beyond the stories of armed conflict would also allow for attention to variation and conflict in the political ideas and strategies that animated organized resistance.

Like Asmal, however, Mamdani remains focused on *successful* moments of organized resistance. Both want to remind readers that these moments of success provide a basis for pride and celebration in the past and can serve as a challenge and inspiration to move forward in the future. In South Africa, an organized resistance movement was able to win a truly decisive political victory over a repressive regime. Yet even in South Africa, there are important reasons to recall stories of resistance efforts that were crushed, suppressed, or buried. Such stories do not explain great historical changes or provide evidence that further change is on the horizon, but complicate monolithic or simplistic characterizations of resistance and complicity.

Widening the scope of investigations that examine political resistance would also enable truth commissions and other transitional justice institutions

---

52   Mamdani, "Reconciliation without Justice."

53   Oliver Tambo, "Statement on Signing Declaration, On Behalf of the ANC and Umkohnto We Sizwe, Adhering to the Geneva Conventions of 1949, and Protocol I of 1977," Headquarters of International Committee of the Red Cross, Geneva, November 29, 1980.

to address a major concern regarding the way that transitional justice investigations have been gendered. In early debates on transitional justice, gender was almost completely ignored. More recently, transitional justice institutions have worked to develop new approaches for investigating gender-based violence.[54] However, transitional justice institutions generally portray women as innocent victims of political violence rather than as agents of oppression or resistance. As Helen Kinsella has demonstrated, the distinction between civilians and combatants in international law has been animated by the premise that "women and children" may be understood as passive innocents in conflict.[55] This premise also reinforces the pervasive assumption, in war reporting and international policy, that adult males may be presumptively identified as military combatants and that the murder of adult males is therefore less egregious or tragic.[56] Investigating the role of women in resistance movements, as well as the role of groups that organize as women across political and ethnic divides, is one way to challenge this tendency. By making space for the stories of groups such as the Madres de Plaza Mayo, Black Sash, or Women in Black, truth commissions would not only gain a deeper understanding of the gendered nature of political violence, but also the importance of gender as a factor in ongoing processes of political reform.

If truth commissions were to critically examine the multiplicity of different forms of political resistance and the ambiguities and problems associated with political resistance, they would be in a better position to draw lessons from such examples in a way that would move beyond past oppositions. At the same time, Asmal's recommendation for investigating political resistance reflects the recurrent tension, in debates on transitional justice, between the goal of critical historical reflection and the goal of establishing a basis for persuasion and common action. It insists on an approach to historical reflection that is "jagged edged," one that does not necessarily challenge the validity of compromises that frame the process of dialogue about past wrongs, but does insist on exposing their limitations. The fact that this approach may be unsettling does not mean that it is inherently destructive. Asmal develops this point by discussing examples of what I term "privileged resistance."

---

[54] Emily Rosser, "Depoliticised Speech and Sexed Visibility: Women, Gender and Sexual Violence in the 1999 Guatemalan *Comisión para el Esclarecimiento Histórico* Report," *International Journal of Transitional Justice* 1, no. 3 (2007): 391–410; see also, Fionnuala Ní Aoláin and Eilish Rooney, "Underenforcement and Intersectionality: Gendered Aspects of Transition for Women," *International Journal of Transitional Justice* 1, no. 3 (2007): 338–54.

[55] See Helen Kinsella, "Gendering Grotius: Sex and Sex Difference in the Laws of War," *Political Theory* 34, no. 2 (2006): 161–91.

[56] Carpenter, *Innocent Women and Children*.

PRIVILEGED RESISTANCE

Investigating the role of "privileged resistance" is another way that truth commissions might contribute to establishing a political basis for justice and reconciliation in the aftermath of systematic atrocities. Arendt and Asmal both reflect on the significance of examples of resistance among individuals who occupy privileged positions within a regime or system, and either abandon that privilege or make use of it in an effort to protest the regime. In this context, privilege may entail an elite status within a regime or it may simply mean that the individual cannot be identified as a member of a persecuted group. Stories of privileged resistance often overlap with stories of political resistance, but may also entail isolated acts of sabotage or whistle blowing. These stories have a unique set of implications for transitional justice projects, but also raise important concerns.

Perhaps the most obvious way that stories of privileged resistance may be used is as a basis for countering the demonization of groups or the collectivization of criminal guilt that occurs in the aftermath of atrocities in which large numbers of people have participated. Proponents of human rights legalism have argued that "individualizing guilt" is the best way to address the problem of group demonization and stereotyping. South Africa's TRC attempted to counter collective blame and the demand for revenge by framing its investigation of past abuses as a collective healing process. What the two strategies have in common is that they foster reconciliation via a kind of social or political forgetting, shifting attention to the experiences of discrete victims and perpetrators and away from widespread complicity.

Stories of privileged resistance provide an alternative way to examine collective responsibility without fostering collective demonization. The story of Anton Schmidt is not just important as a story of resistance per se, but as the story of a *German* sergeant who used his position of power in order to provide supplies and forged papers to the Jewish resistance. Asmal introduces his argument for remembering resistance by summoning the story of Ruth First and Joe Slovo. Both were white and occupied positions of privilege under the apartheid regime, yet both dedicated their lives to fighting that regime. Asmal invokes their story not only as a basis for recalling the political ideas and commitment that animated resistance work in South Africa, but also as a way to challenge racial polarization with an alternative model of reconciliation built on shared political commitment. Instead of forgetting or exonerating the complicit, Arendt and Asmal use stories of privileged resistance to challenge collective attributions of blame.

One concern that might be raised regarding this approach is that stories of privileged resistance, like the individualization of guilt, can function to obfuscate the larger story of complicity. Calling attention to the resistance work of Joe Slovo and Ruth First, for example, could be just one more way to shift attention away from the fact that the majority of white South Africans did nothing of the kind and instead accepted the authority of the regime. In her essay, "Truth and Politics," Arendt notes that the mythical status of the French resistance functioned to reinforce a kind of national denial of just how small the movement actually was.[57] Asmal ruefully suggests that the "sudden elusiveness of supporters of the prior regime" is due to the way that many white South Africans now apply an "anti-apartheid gloss" to their personal histories.[58]

A related concern is that focusing on stories of privileged resistance might function to reinforce or replicate a problematic dynamic associated with the human rights movement whereby people with means and power view themselves as "saviors" of the oppressed, who are, in turn, represented as passive victims, lacking in agency.[59] In accordance with this logic, the human rights movement has developed as an advocacy movement rather than an activist movement. Arendt recognized this logic in the human rights movement that was mobilizing just prior to, and in the aftermath of, the Second World War.[60] More recently, Makau Mutua has argued that this logic undermines efforts to generate global political support for human rights because it inspires mistrust among those who are to be saved and conditions assistance on a posture of dependence.

This kind of complaint was directed at South Africa's TRC in response to Wendy Orr's prominent role in truth commission hearings on the role of the medical industry in the apartheid years. Orr was a young white doctor working at a district surgeon's office when she encountered prisoners who had been tortured. She successfully petitioned the Supreme Court for a restraining order against the police by documenting the systematic pattern of torture and abuse that had been inflicted on prisoners in her care. Orr went on to serve as a commissioner for the TRC. Yet some feared that attention to Orr's act of privileged resistance was serving to displace attention to the role of resistance among victims of apartheid. "Where are those doctors from the oppressed side," asked Dr. Baqwa, who participated in TRC's hearings on the medical community, "who have really worked and seen this ... why are they not here?"[61]

[57] Arendt, *Between Past and Future.*
[58] Asmal et al., *Reconciliation through Truth?* 165.
[59] See Mutua, "Savages, Victims, and Saviors."
[60] Arendt, *The Origins of Totalitarianism*, 292–4.
[61] Truth and Reconciliation Commission, *Mental Health Workshop*, November 21, 1997.

In response to this concern, it is important to consider that privileged resistance can also provide a powerful basis for exposing, understanding, and judging complicity in systematic atrocities. As discussed above, one of the reasons that people hesitate to judge those who "followed orders" or gave their support to systematic atrocities is that it is difficult for those who were not present to know what was actually possible: Did the people who supported this policy really *know* what was happening? Was it really possible for anyone to *do* anything about it? Such questions make people hesitant to judge or to critically assess justifications for complicity. Arendt's discussion of Anton Schmidt is intended to provide a partial response to this problem and to give meaning to the way that she frames her own verdict in the Eichmann case. Although most people may have gone along with the Nazi regime, not everyone did. Despite pervasive propaganda and fear, some people were capable of moral condemnation and protest. Similarly, Kader Asmal invokes the story of Wendy Orr's protest against apartheid-era torture as a basis for revealing the extent to which the medical community "was drafted into an ugly and partisan set of functions in defence of apartheid."[62] Orr's story is significant because it reveals just how much torture and abuse other members of the medical establishment must have seen and accepted. Asmal invokes her story not to eclipse the role of the oppressed in struggling against their own victimization, but as a way to hold the broader medical community responsible for its own acquiescence and silence. These stories also vividly convey the limits of a morality premised on conformity and obedience. Remembering small acts of privileged resistance, Asmal suggests, is a way of challenging the identification of moral behavior with in-group loyalty and obedience to authorities.

Stories of privileged resistance are also powerful because they shed light on the factors that explain widespread complicity, as well as the question of how those who once supported policies of racism and persecution may be transformed, change their minds, and even come to work alongside those they once conspired to oppress. Asmal uses the story of Bram Fischer to illustrate this point. Fischer was born into a prominent Afrikaner family, but eventually turned away from the apartheid system and went on to serve as a lawyer representing Mandela during the Rivonia trial. Fischer was excommunicated from his community, disbarred, and imprisoned for his actions. At his trial in the late 1960s, Fischer's testimony addressed his own history of racism, recalling that as a young man, he had met with a group of Africans to convert them to the apartheid policy of "separate development" and how he had recoiled when

---

[62] Asmal et al., *Reconciliation through Truth?* 154.

he realized that he was expected to shake their hands: "Could I really, as a white adult, touch the hand of a black man in friendship?"[63]

Fischer's testimony sheds light on the racist indoctrination associated with apartheid and on the way in which the legal profession was intimately bound up in supporting the system. However, it is not only Fischer's resistance that makes the story meaningful, but also the distance he traveled. Asmal strategically recounts Fischer's story to insist that "whatever the scope of complicity, it was possible to overcome it."[64] It is possible for people to recognize the illegitimacy and immorality of a system that they have been indoctrinated to support and move away from a position of acquiescence to active protest. Asmal appreciates that Fisher's story is unique and difficult to emulate, but he argues that the basic requirements for political reconciliation were contained in Fischer's commitment to "acknowledging, explicating, then fully renouncing apartheid's zoo of whiteness."[65] It is by cultivating this possibility for transformation that the pursuit of political reconciliation is distinguished from simple accommodation and compromise.

CONCLUSION

That things would be utterly different in the world "if only more such stories could have been told," was "irrefutably beyond question" for Arendt in the moments following testimony concerning Anton Schmidt.[66] Despite Arendt's emphasis on the clarity of this revelation, there is a provocative ambiguity in the way that she presents it. Read one way, she is arguing that things would be utterly different if more people had acted like Anton Schmidt, if his resistance had not been the isolated act of an individual, but part of a larger tide of organized protest. Read another way, Arendt is suggesting that things might be utterly different in the world if we made it a priority to recall stories such as these, if we recognized their value, instead of consigning them to the periphery of criminal investigations. Both arguments are of vital importance for contemporary transitional justice debates.

The first and most obvious way to interpret Arendt's claim is to see it as a call for cultivating resistance as a response to atrocity. Transitional justice has evolved as a response to the problem of how to address systematic forms of violence that are authorized by political leaders. However, it has been animated

---

[63] Asmal et al., *Reconciliation through Truth?* 166.
[64] Asmal et al., *Reconciliation through Truth?* 165.
[65] Asmal et al., *Reconciliation through Truth?* 166.
[66] Arendt, *Eichmann in Jerusalem*, 231.

by criminal justice theories that are premised on a notion of crime as deviance. The prevailing theoretical approaches to transitional justice, restorative justice and legalism differ and vary internally with respect to the extent to which crime is best addressed through coercive measures or through expressive and symbolic responses. They also differ with respect to the kinds of norms that should be authoritative in addressing political violence. Restorative justice has favored local, participatory involvement in a process of developing responsive standards of justice, whereas human rights legalism has asserted the primacy of formal international standards over local norms and practices. Similarly, debates over international criminal justice have often centered on the legitimacy of international norms and how to address conflicting ideas about what ought to be the basis of that legitimacy.

What is often taken for granted in these debates is the premise that human rights and transitional justice institutions ought to respond to atrocities by instilling obedience or deference to a superior set of norms. Yet resistance to crimes of obedience cannot be generated or motivated through the internalization of norms, but rather requires the capacity to act on moral conviction in a complex and dynamic political context. If resistance is recognized as an important response to political violence, then examining resistance must also be recognized as an important dimension of transitional justice.

This chapter has argued that more such stories, stories of resistance, *should* be told. The obligation to remember periods of systematic repression and atrocity should not be limited to efforts to establish criminal guilt or recover stories of victimization, but should also encompass stories of protest, refusal, dissent, and defiance. The commitment to learn from the past should be accompanied by an effort to understand why people failed to resist systematic atrocities. The case for political reconciliation should not be limited to the goal of establishing commonality in experiences of victimization and suffering, but should also be informed by the memory of those who sought political alternatives to a repressive order and those who took risks to stand in solidarity with targeted groups or individuals.

The institutions associated with contemporary transitional justice are not designed to accommodate such goals. Criminal trials focus narrowly on the question of "who did what to whom." Reparations are designed as responses to damages incurred by specific harms. Truth commissions, in contrast, are defined by their commitment to examining patterns of political violence and abuse. They are well suited, in theory, to investigate various forms of resistance as well as the failure to resist. That they have not done so is a reflection of the extent to which they are still framed and evaluated in relation to legalistic or therapeutic categories, as well as the way in which some truth commissions have implicitly promoted selective forgetting as the basis of reconciliation. Investigating resistance, it is feared, would be profoundly unsettling and would therefore jeopardize the moral authority of truth commissions and their contributions to reconciliation. In response to this general concern, it is worth noting that the basic goal of identifying victims and perpetrators of political violence is *also*, of course, deeply unsettling and provocative – perhaps even more so.

Instead of forgetting stories of resistance, truth commissions could address such concerns by locating ways of extracting these stories from the oppositional, Manichean framework in which they usually appear. Doing so would enable truth commissions to provide a more constructive response to the tensions associated with transitional justice, between the goal of persuading conflicting parties to locate a basis for common ground and the goal of reflecting critically on historical patterns of violence. Drawing on the writings of Arendt, Levi, and Asmal, this chapter has examined the three general ways that truth commissions or other investigatory projects might investigate the theme of resistance.

First, truth commissions could broaden debates on political responsibility by investigating the question of why people failed to resist or withdraw their support from a regime engaged in systematic atrocities or oppression. Such investigations might complement the emphasis, in criminal inquiries, on the role of those who are more easily characterized as deviant or abnormal by critically evaluating the role of complacency, passivity, and conformity in systematic injustices and atrocities. This kind of inquiry might proceed by considering what alternatives were available and what happened to those who did refuse. As Levi observes, the theme of failed resistance is better understood as a "gray zone" – one that is difficult to evaluate as an individual choice between right and wrong and difficult to understand without attention to the complicated ways in which the human impulse to resist may be subverted or crushed. At the same time, such inquires should not *displace* the categories of victim and perpetrator, by shifting attention away from those who orchestrated the worst abuses or by suggesting that there is any kind of equivalence between those who organize atrocities or oppression and those who are targeted and oppressed.

Second, truth commissions could inform the effort to imagine new possibilities for collective action, solidarity, and political engagement in the aftermath of political violence by examining the role of organized political resistance in the past. This would also be a way to deepen their contribution to understanding the unique political dynamics of violence in a given context. Such an analysis need not be seen as incompatible with the goal of using the humanitarian law as a lens through which to critically evaluate the violence of political resistance. By allowing individuals to give testimony regarding their experiences as part of organized political resistance, as distinct from their experiences as victims or perpetrators of abuse, truth commissions would broaden their contribution to the kind of democratic dialogue that Villa-Vicencio associates with restorative justice. Truth commissions would also do more to further a moral obligation to acknowledge past wrongs by acknowledging the losses experienced by those who took action to resist systematic atrocity. Truth commissions might incorporate this kind of analysis without reifying the oppositional logic of political resistance by examining multiple forms of organized resistance, including nonviolent resistance, the role of religious groups, women's resistance, and groups that organize in solidarity across political or ethnic divides.

Examples of privileged resistance may provide a powerful rejoinder to those who say that it was impossible to know that abuses were going on, to see that it was wrong, or to do anything other than to comply. In that sense, such examples offer a potentially powerful basis for condemning those who were complicit in past wrongs. However, such examples also offer an alternative to "individualizing guilt" as a strategy for challenging undifferentiated aspirations of collective blame, by serving as vivid evidence that not everyone *did* comply.

A haunting story of resistance appears at the end of Phillip Gourevitch's widely read report on the aftermath of the Rwandan genocide.[67] Gourevitch describes the testimony of a man who confessed to participating in the murder of seventeen schoolgirls and a Belgian nun that took place at a boarding school during the genocide. During the attack, the militia members ordered the schoolgirls to divide themselves and to distinguish between the Hutus and Tutsis among them. When they refused to do so, all of them were beaten and shot. For those who do not aspire to martyrdom, these stories cannot offer any kind of model or guidance in struggling against overwhelming brutality. What is perhaps most powerful and important about these stories of resistance is their potential to counter pervasive despair in the possibility of genuine solidarity and agency, which has fueled the search for ways to escape politics altogether.

---

[67] Philip Gourevitch, *We Wish to Inform You That Tomorrow We Will Be Killed with Our Families* (Picador, 1999), 353.

7

Conclusion: The Shadows of the Past

One wants to get free of the past; rightly so, since one cannot live in its shadow, and since there is no end to terror if guilt and violence are only repaid, again and again, with guilt and violence.[1]

These lines are taken from a speech given by Theodor Adorno before a German audience in 1959, yet they aptly capture the hopes and anxieties associated with the contemporary pursuit of transitional justice. Adorno's speech was entitled, "What does 'Coming to Terms with the Past' Mean?" He outlined two responses to that question. Adorno began by warning that the idea of "coming to terms with the past" had become little more than a slogan. What appeared to be a preoccupation with addressing Germany's Nazi past was an elaborate form of denial, he argued. "Coming to terms with the past" had been equated with the goal of "mastering the past" or "turning the page" by wiping the past from memory. Against this emphasis on *mastery*, Adorno called for a process of *"working through"* the past.[2] In making this distinction, he insisted that the project of addressing past injustices ought to be understood as an ongoing process – one that requires serious labor, and one that is never fully completed.

Adorno's complaint stands as a challenge to those who hold that too much attention to past wrongs is bound to open a Pandora's Box of destructive demands for redress or vengeance. Some fear that such efforts will erode

[1]   Theodor W. Adorno, "What Does Coming to Terms with the Past Mean?" trans. Timothy Bahti and Geoffrey Hartman. In *Bitburg in Moral and Political Perspective*, ed. Geoffrey Hartman (Bloomington, Indiana University Press, 1986), 114.
[2]   In the original German, this distinction is made between the concept of Vergangenheitsbewältigung, translated as "mastering the past," and "aufarbeitung de Vergangenheit." The latter is translated as "coming to terms," but uses the German noun for "working through." See Hartman, "Editor's Note," *Bitburg in Moral and Political Perspective*, 113.

possibilities for reconciliation, making it impossible for people to let go, heal, and move on. Some fear that such efforts are dangerous because they provoke backlash or resentment that threatens to undermine a fragile peace or democratic transition. Others maintain that patriotism and national unity require attention to heroic deeds rather than shameful ones.

Jurgen Habermas cited Adorno's speech to counter such sentiments as they emerged in debates over Ronald Reagan's visit to Bitburg and in the German *Historikerstreit*.[3] Adorno's 1959 speech was later included in a set of volumes edited by Neil Kritz, entitled *Transitional Justice*, which compiled some of the first writings and documents that would frame contemporary transitional justice policies and debates.[4] Transitional justice institutions have now popularized the idea that countries ought to reckon with past atrocities and injustices even as they pursue political reform. The New York-based International Center for Transitional Justice has become an influential institution, involved in consulting and training leaders around the world. A journal dedicated to the study of transitional justice, the *International Journal of Transitional Justice*, has attracted a wide audience of scholars and policy makers.

The global fascination with transitional justice practices that were developed as responses to regime change has generated new interest in using similar strategies to address abuses committed in the distant past or in long-established democracies.[5] South Africa's TRC inspired proposals to develop a truth commission that would address the history of racism and slavery in the United States. Truth commissions in Guatemala, East Timor, and elsewhere exposed new information about the role of U.S. interventions and backing for atrocities and political repression.[6] The Obama administration faced

---

3 Jurgen Habermas, *A Berlin Republic: Writings on Germany* (Lincoln: University of Nebraska Press, 1997), 17–40.
4 Neil J. Kritz ed., *Transitional Justice: How Emerging Democracies Reckon with Former Regimes*, vol. 1–3 (Washington, DC: United States Institute of Peace Press, 1995).
5 Thomas McCarthy, "Vergangenheitsbewältigung in the USA: On the Politics of the Memory of Slavery," *Political Theory* 30 (2002): 623–48; Andrew Valls, "A Truth Commission for the United States?" *Intertexts* 7, no. 2 (2003): 157–70; Fionnuala Ní Aoláin and Colm Campbell, "The Paradox of Transition in Conflicted Democracies," *Human Rights Quarterly* 27 (2005): 172–213; Stephen L. Esquith, "An Experiment in Democratic Political Education," *Polity* 36 (2003): 73–90.
6 A request from Guatemala's Historical Clarification Commission led to the declassification of thousands of U.S. documents (Hayner, *Unspeakable Truths*, 47–9). President Bill Clinton made a public apology to the people of Guatemala in response to the findings and conclusions of the Guatemalan truth commission. For a critical discussion of this set of events, see Carlos Parodi, "Apologies Under U.S. Hegemony," in *Age of Apology: Facing up to the Past*, ed. Marc Gibney, Niklaus Steiner, Jean-Marc Coicaud, and Rhoda Howard-Hassman (Philadelphia: University of Pennsylvania Press, 2007). East Timor's truth commission also succeeded in declassifying documents pertaining to the U.S. role in the 1975 invasion by

persistent pressure to prosecute human rights abuses committed under the previous administration in waging a "war on terror," as well as a proposal, tabled by Patrick Leahy, to develop a truth commission modeled on South Africa's example.[7] New efforts are underway to examine the impact of transitional justice strategies and to evaluate their effectiveness.[8] As such efforts proceed, it will be particularly important to scrutinize the basic theoretical assumptions associated with contemporary approaches to transitional justice. What does "coming to terms with the past" mean today?

THE WORK OF POLITICAL JUDGMENT

Fears regarding the danger of "too much memory" are related to the fact that systematic violence and injustice are not committed by deviants, but involve harms that were authorized by officials, legitimated by institutions, and supported in different ways by a wide range of people within a political community. To investigate such wrongs is to subject revered leaders, along with the ideologies and mythologies that underpin collective identities, to critical scrutiny. Systematic brutalities are commonly associated with starkly Manichean constructions of power and interest that fuel mutual suspicion, hostility, and a sense of helplessness or futility. To investigate them is not only destabilizing to the extent that those still invested in such constructions have the capacity to make trouble, but also disorienting and discouraging.

Human rights legalism, inspired by the legacy of the Nuremberg Trials, and restorative justice, modeled on the experience of South Africa's TRC, offer distinctive theoretical frameworks for addressing such concerns. Yet as strategies for depoliticizing transitional justice, both frameworks have been employed to alleviate fears associated with remembering political violence by analyzing it in relation to the roles and experiences of official victims and perpetrators. In other words, the most prominent theoretical frameworks that

Indonesia, and has requested reparations from the United States. See Joe Nevins, "Truth, Lies, and Accountability," *Boston Review* (2007).

7   Bobby Ghosh, "Leahy's Plan to Probe Bush-Era Wrongdoings," *Time* (February 17, 2009).

8   Snyder and Vinjamuri, "Trials and Errors"; Chapman and Van der Merwe, *Did the TRC Deliver?*; Hugo van der Merwe, Victoria Baxter, and Audrey R. Chapman, eds., *Assessing the Impact of Transitional Justice: Challenges for Empirical Research* (Washington, D.C.: USIP Press, 2009); Peskin, *International Trials in Rwanda and the Balkans*; Eric Wiebelhaus-Brahm, *Truth Commissions and Transitional Justice: The Impact of Human Rights and Democracy* (New York: Routledge, 2010). Tricia Olsen, Leigh Payne, and Andrew Reiter, *Transitional Justice in Balance: Comparing Processes, Weighing Efficacy* (Washington D.C: U.S. Institute of Peace Press, 2010). Jelena Subotic, *Hijacked Justice: Dealing with the Past in the Balkans* (Ithaca: Cornell University Press, 2009).

animate contemporary approaches to transitional justice attempt to counter the "us versus them" categories associated with violent political conflict with the "victim-perpetrator" binary of criminal justice. If the logic of depoliticization is appealing in contexts where political debate has degenerated into hostile confrontation, it is even more appealing where political leaders have been engaged in violent conflict and where genocide or violent exclusion has been justified in the name of community survival.

Despite its appeal, the logic of depoliticization that animates contemporary transitional justice is also deeply paradoxical. Institutions that are designed to investigate systematic injustice have obfuscated the systemic dimension of past wrongs. Institutions that are promoted as a basis of challenging denial have rationalized and legitimated selective forgetting and denial. Efforts to transcend volatile divisions by depoliticizing transitional justice investigations have functioned as strategies for avoiding competing claims regarding the meaning of past wrongs. In their pursuit of mastery, or "closure," that would enable people to remedy past wrongs and advance political reform, contemporary approaches to transitional justice have set aside the lessons that might be learned from those who did protest or resist the very wrongs under investigation.

This book has offered an alternative way to think about the legacies of the Nuremberg Tribunal and the South African TRC. It has argued that the dilemmas confronted by these institutions reveal the centrality, as well as the difficulty, of political judgment for any serious effort to "work through the past." Political judgments are not derived from an independent, objective standard of justice. Instead, they arise from and articulate particular political positions or approaches. Efforts to reckon with systematic political violence require judgments that evaluate not only the guilt of individuals, but also the influence of political organizations and institutions. Such efforts not only require responses to the harms suffered by individual victims, but also entail the pursuit of political change. The trouble is that it is not clear what considerations ought to inform political judgment in contexts marked by pervasive despair in politics and by the collapse or absence of political community. To affirm political judgment, many fear, is to concede to the imperatives of prevailing power dynamics or to defer to the corrosive forces of inherited prejudice.

Instead of disavowing political judgment, we might alternatively reconsider what criteria ought to inform the kinds of political judgments that animate transitional justice institutions and projects. Arendt's discussion of political judgment guided by "enlarged mentality" is useful in this regard. It outlines an approach to judging that strives for general appeal across lines of conflict and division, not by invoking universal principles, but by contemplating diverse perspectives on a common problem. It is an approach to judgment that aspires to broaden the basis of consent, but also acknowledges its own limitations in doing so. It seeks broad agreement, but remains partial, political, and provisional.

Political judgments that are guided by "enlarged mentality" require an active process of persuasion and dialogue. Persuasion may involve compromise, but it is not reducible to compromise. Instead, it must also involve an imaginative effort to consider a problem from competing perspectives. This approach to political judgment is implicit in Judith Shklar's account of what made Nuremberg a success, which centers on the role of the trials in persuading the German population to accept its legitimacy. It is also implicit in José Zalaquett's defense of truth commissions as an alternative to prosecution, and in Villa-Vicencio's insistence that truth commissions ought to promote dialogue that would reveal multiple perspectives on past events. Desmond Tutu argued that the TRC could foster *ubuntu*, or "humaneness," and mutual understanding through a process of active dialogue, alongside gestures of forgiveness and reciprocity.

These thinkers propose different avenues for advancing a common basis for judgment and change. Some are at odds with Arendt's own understanding of "enlarged mentality," yet they share her basic claim that political judgment requires efforts to examine a common problem from diverse perspectives and to generate a basis for common ground through a process of persuasion. They also share her view that such efforts are inherently limited; they do not result in objective criteria that transcend partisan views. However, they may locate previously unknown commonalities, reveal novel ways of bridging differences, or convince people to accept evidence or responsibilities they had previously denied.

Political judgment guided by "enlarged mentality" also entails historical reflection. Arendt suggests that the "spectator" or historian is uniquely positioned to consider diverse perspectives on the past because he or she is no longer personally invested in outcomes and can examine patterns and developments that are not apparent to those immersed in present-day political affairs. The work of the historian is not freed from a partisan perspective, but strives for a certain detachment from the political pressures of the day, an effort to attain critical distance from prevailing orthodoxies or conventional wisdom regarding what transpired in the past and what is possible in the future. This approach to political judgment informs Shklar's claim that the greatest accomplishment of the Nuremberg Trials was to effectively defend a historical judgment of the Nazi regime. It also informs Kader Asmal's claim that South Africa's TRC ought to have rendered a more decisive condemnation of apartheid, with attention to the role of political institutions and ideologies that supported it.

These are not two different theories of political judgment, but might alternatively be understood as two activities that are equally vital for the pursuit of transitional justice. They are mutually constitutive: Political deliberations frame the parameters of the official histories produced by transitional justice institutions, yet their historical investigations may also inform the dynamics of ongoing political debates. At the same time, the two stances are in tension with one another. As political actors, transitional justice projects aspire to further immediate goals and are responsive to the terms of debate that shape the politics of the present. They must render decisive judgments that define a break between past wrongs and present values. To the extent that they aspire to adopt the stance of the historian, they cannot allow their investigations to be subordinated to the perceived imperatives of political reform, partial remedy, or reconciliation and must instead reflect critically on the parameters of such debates. As historical critics, they inaugurate an ongoing process of reflection and remembrance, which may reveal the limitations of remedies and reforms meant to address past wrongs.

Addressing the tension between these two dimensions of political judgment presents a challenge for transitional justice projects – one that is easily misperceived as a conflict between idealism and realism or between international and local approaches to justice. Although these institutions are committed to critical historical reflection, they encounter pressure to subordinate this goal to the urgent task of locating a basis for common judgment and establishing grounds for remedial action in the immediate term. I have defended an alternative theoretical approach to transitional justice, which would aim to mediate, rather than resolve, the unsettling effects of critical historical judgment. This approach would not rely on a depoliticized version of history as the basis for reconciliation or a common sense of justice. Instead, it would pursue such goals by investigating complicity in, as well as resistance to, systematic atrocities while complicating Manichean perspectives on the past with attention to the shades of gray in such stories. In developing this argument, it is not my intention to deny the value of contemporary transitional justice institutions, such as truth commissions and war crimes tribunals. Instead, I am suggesting that we ought to reconsider the theoretical frameworks that have become the basis for evaluating, designing, and promoting these institutions, and that these institutions have helped popularize.

CONFRONTING THE LIMITS OF LEGALISM

There is a growing awareness, even among the most ardent supporters of international criminal justice institutions, that criminal prosecution is limited as a mechanism for reckoning with systematic atrocities and injustices. This book addresses ongoing debates regarding the role and limitations of international criminal justice by challenging the persistent claim that criminal prosecutions carried out in accordance with international standards invariably represent a superior form of moral action in response to political violence. Examining the role of political judgment in transitional justice provides a basis for critically evaluating the limitations of criminal justice institutions with attention to the dynamic between their political and moral aspirations. Yet confronting the limits of human rights legalism requires more than a critical look at legalistic institutions. It also requires attention to the ways in which categories associated with human rights legalism continue to influence theoretical and policy debates regarding what it means to take moral action against systemic injustice and how people ought to acknowledge and remember past wrongs.

The idea that international criminal prosecution is morally superior to other remedies for politically authorized injustices has been closely associated with the view that adherence to formal legal standards provides an effective basis for divorcing matters of justice from matters of politics. It is also associated with the view that efforts to prosecute politically authorized violence will be more effective and more just to the extent that they adhere to formal legal criteria.

Critically evaluating the role of criminal trials as a moral response to systematic injustice requires attention to the complicated relationship between the political judgments that inform them and the legal judgments that they render. Approaches to criminal justice vary significantly, even among Western countries. However, the criminal trial that is in keeping with basic standards of legality must be committed to due process, with a focus on establishing individual accountability. The judgments rendered in the context of a criminal trial are inherently depoliticizing to the extent that they condemn politically authorized violence and actions in accordance with legal criteria, and evaluate systematic patterns of violence by isolating the guilt of individual perpetrators. Where trials deviate from this in an effort to teach a history lesson or stage a political drama, they sacrifice their integrity and risk devolving into show trials. Yet even when war crimes tribunals focus narrowly on establishing individual guilt, their work is influenced by political judgment. Political judgment influences the legal standards that are applied in a given case. It informs the ways in which clashing local and international standards will be treated. It informs the selection of officials and, importantly, the selection of defendant. The development of clear international standards does not transcend the influence of local politics or the impact of global asymmetries on these decisions.[9]

The ambitious Nuremberg Trials were able to condemn the Nazi regime while revealing a great deal about its inner workings. Yet when human rights prosecutions are wide-ranging in scope and duration, they can also be polarizing, as was the case in the immediate aftermath of Argentina's transition. Proponents of human rights legalism have proposed that this kind of polarization might be offset by a limited, symbolic prosecution strategy that would target the most powerful among those allegedly responsible for past wrongs. Strategically focusing on high-profile figures *may* do much to expose and condemn broader systemic patterns, but this is not necessarily the case. Another proposal for offsetting the fears associated with human rights prosecution has been to argue that criminal prosecutions may cultivate reconciliation by clarifying that the scope of their judgment is limited to individual leaders and dramatizing common experiences of victimization and suffering. This logic influenced lobbying on behalf of the ICTY and ICTR, which became important institutional models for the post–Cold War development of international criminal justice.

The trouble with this approach is that it justifies the use of criminal prosecution as a mechanism for evading the problem of wider complicity in systematic wrongdoing. What is striking about both strategies is that they presume the inherent moral superiority of criminal prosecution and devalue alternative mechanisms, yet also accommodate political compromises that curtail the critical role of such trials as a response to systemic injustice. Instead, I have argued that we might recognize and evaluate the role of political judgment in war crimes trials without conceding to cynicism regarding their moral contributions or critical potential. Acknowledging political compromises that limit the role of human rights prosecution could be the basis for mobilizing to expand the scope of retroactive prosecution over time, as has occurred in Chile and Argentina, or for pursuing other avenues of remedy and reform.

Confronting the limitations of human rights legalism means challenging the pervasive tendency to identify moral *action* in response to atrocity with the pursuit of criminal prosecution in a court of law. To question this logic is not to deny the fact that criminal prosecution can have dramatic political

9 See Victor Peskin and Mieczylslaw P. Boduszynski, "International Justice and Domestic Politics: Post-Tudjman Croatia and the International Criminal Tribunal for the Former Yugoslavia," *Europe-Asia Studies* 55, no. 3 (2003): 1117–42.

effects, but to consider how the role of legal strategies will vary depending on the scope of their judgment and the political context. The extent to which they pose a moral challenge to systematic wrongdoing will depend on the quality of political judgment that animates them and on the kind of mobilization that develops in response to their verdicts.[10] One important implication of this is that alternatives to prosecution, including restorative approaches, ought to be taken more seriously. However, to confront the limitations of legalism is also to question the more basic idea that legal institutions can and should serve as a basis for divorcing moral action from political action. This idea has been problematic in three important ways.

First, where moral action is equated with law *enforcement*, it becomes difficult to conceive of novel responses to intractable division. The prospect of negotiations is more likely to be dismissed as immoral trafficking with perpetrators. Political change is understood to be dependent on some exertion of force, whether through punishment or military intervention. Confronting the limitations of legalism means recognizing that the interpretation, extension, and enforcement of existing legal standards cannot substitute for strategies aimed at persuading people to accept a novel standard or interpretation.

Second, the close identification of moral action with law enforcement has led to a tendency to denigrate or neglect the importance of political mobilization and resistance as responses to systematic injustice. International criminal law has evolved as a response to "crimes of obedience" and requires people to be capable of refusing orders to commit atrocity. Yet human rights legalism has been premised on the view that trained professionals ought to take the lead in enforcing human rights standards, and that in so doing, their primary goal ought to be the cultivation of obedience to, and internalization of, human rights norms. Moral action in response to systematic injustice requires more than a belief in the legitimacy of international norms, and more than the internalization of such norms. It requires the capacity to think critically about the ways in which political leaders invoke domestic and international norms to justify and sanitize abuses of power, and it requires the commitment to protest against organized atrocities.

Third, as proponents of human rights legalism have come to identify moral action with criminal prosecution, they have also tended to narrow the scope of their attention and concern to those injustices that appear to be amenable to legalistic strategies. In a world filled with miseries and brutalities, it seems to

---

[10] On the relationship between litigation and domestic mobilization, see Beth Simmons, *Mobilizing for Human Rights: International Law in Domestic Politics* (New York: Cambridge University Press, 2009).

make sense to focus on those issues that human rights lawyers and institutions are best equipped to address. And it would be absurd to dismiss the value of discrete legal victories in response to violations of "physical integrity" rights simply because they do not address underlying injustices. In following this line of thinking, though, the danger is that transitional justice institutions and the human rights movement more generally are advancing a methods-driven approach to moral action that measures achievement in relation to the elaboration of legal mechanisms and strategies, without serious attention to their role and limitations in advancing a critical response to systematic abuses of power. To the extent that they follow this logic, human rights and transitional justice institutions emphasize certain kinds of atrocities that are widely condemned, such as genocide and torture, while giving far less attention to patterns of gender and sexual violence, racism, and economic injustice, which are more difficult to address through legalistic strategies. Alternatively, we might acknowledge the political impact and potential of discrete legal victories without allowing a concern with the success and advancement of legal methodology dictate the scope of moral concern or the order of priorities in addressing past wrongs.

Finally, this book has also made the case for confronting the limitations of legalism as a basis for historical judgment. Some commentators have called attention to the discrepancies between the work of the judge and that of the historian. Others have defended the role of criminal trials in evaluating and presenting historical claims regarding systemic abuses. The format of the criminal trial may serve a useful pedagogical role, insofar as judges are bound to defend their verdicts with attention to the best arguments on both sides of a contentious debate regarding how to assign culpability.[11] Judges establish their legitimacy and critical authority by adhering to legal criteria in evaluating such claims. The drama and the high stakes attached to criminal trials may command more attention than other official commissions of inquiry. Yet all of these features of criminal trials also limit their role as a basis for evaluating systemic injustices.

Criminal trials shed light on the causes of helpless victimization and criminal guilt, but not on the more complicated roles of those who were actively complicit, passive supporters, complacent beneficiaries, or proud members of resistance efforts. Recognizing the limitations of legalism in guiding the process of historical investigation requires critical attention to the way in which the evidence, judgments, and standards established by criminal justice institutions are influenced by political judgment. It also means critically examining

---

[11] Osiel, *Mass Atrocity, Collective Memory, and the Law.*

the extent to which the categories associated with criminal prosecution have shaped and limited other approaches to commemorating and investigating systemic wrongdoing. It means confronting the limits of the victim-perpetrator framework.

EVALUATING RESTORATIVE ALTERNATIVES

South Africa's TRC became extraordinarily influential in the theory and practice of transitional justice because it developed restorative justice as an alternative to human rights legalism. Restorative justice requires a response to the underlying conflicts that animate crime and violence. It also calls for flexibility in assigning blame and establishing responsibility, allowing for measures that reintegrate offenders back into the community by taking steps to "make amends" for their crimes. In contrast with legalism, restorative-justice theory requires active participation on the part of victims and communities in the process of developing the parameters of judgment. These features of restorative justice have made it appealing as a basis for addressing systemic political violence and injustice.

Like legalism, however, restorative justice is premised on a definition of crime as deviance from the established norms of a community. To the extent that restorative justice romanticizes or uncritically appropriates traditional practices and norms, it is problematic as a framework for addressing systemic wrongdoing. The South African example has influenced a therapeutic approach to restorative justice, which emphasizes cathartic healing and closure through testimony, and locates a basis for reconciliation in common experiences of injury, suffering, and loss. As a response to systematic political violence, restorative justice has become closely identified with this therapeutic framework and with an implicit ratification of local tradition. As a result, critics have justifiably expressed concern that restorative justice may function to reify inequities based on gender, class, or ethnicity, sentimentalize judicial forms that were cultivated under colonial rule, or pacify demands for broader-based remedies and reforms.

This book offers a different interpretation of the South African TRC's theoretical contributions to debates on transitional justice. It argues that the close identification of restorative justice with therapy is not only at odds with core principles of restorative justice, but also dramatically oversimplifies theoretical debates that influenced the TRC. South Africa's restorative approach to justice was influenced by critical responses to human rights legalism that emerged within two kinds of activist communities: human rights lawyers working within the ANC and "healers," including religious leaders and medical professionals, who had engaged in the struggle against apartheid. It was not conceived of as an escape from political judgment, but as a basis for integrating moral and political responses to apartheid.

Drawing on this South African critique of legalism, along with contributions to the South African debate on the TRC's disappointments, I have proposed an alternative way of thinking about restorative approaches to transitional justice. What makes restorative justice important, but also challenging, as an alternative to human rights legalism is that it incorporates both dimensions of political judgment into the process of evaluating past wrongs – the judgment of the actor and the judgment of the spectator. Restorative justice requires a participatory process of deliberation and persuasion aimed at establishing a common basis for judgment. The specific institutional practices will vary depending on the context and the nature of the harms under investigation. At the same time, restorative justice requires a commitment to examining and addressing systemic patterns of underlying conflict associated with those harms. In this sense, restorative justice cannot simply "restore" a *particular* community, but must critically evaluate the causes of community fracture or collapse in order to restore *the possibility of* political community. This cannot be accomplished through an institutional framework that aims to establish reconciliation by depoliticizing inquiries into past wrongs. As a response to systemic injustice, restorative justice requires not only dialogue and ritual, but also a commitment to critical historical reflection and repair.

This approach to restorative justice is more ambitious and nuanced than the therapeutic variant, and it also offers a more significant response to the limitations of human rights legalism. In contrast with legalism, restorative justice requires attention to the ways in which physical harm and discrete episodes of violence are related to underlying patterns of inequality and exclusion. Thus, restorative justice challenges the legalistic tendency to privilege the pursuit of civil and political rights over efforts to address economic, social, and cultural rights. It calls for inquiries that examine not only the role of victims and perpetrators, but also the responsibilities of communities and institutions. It contains a broader vision of justice that requires efforts to remedy the legacies of institutionalized injustice. Individual reparations to officially designated victims are an important component of restorative justice, but to the extent that they are characterized as a basis for "turning the page" on the past, they may also stand in tension with this broader approach to remedy and reform.

Understood in this way, restorative justice might appear to be ridiculously broad or dangerously utopian. It sets up what seem to be impossible expectations for remedy, redemption, and transformation. Yet evaluating the role of political judgment in restorative-justice approaches also sheds light on limitations and challenges that are masked by the analogy to therapy. The fact that restorative approaches incorporate political judgment into their internal decision-making processes means that they may establish broader, more inclusive, more nuanced, and more responsive approaches to investigation and remedy. However, it also means that they may be more vulnerable to abuse and manipulation. Where restorative projects are undertaken in an atmosphere of continuing repression, they will be unlikely to facilitate genuine dialogue or critical historical reflection, and may serve as tools for marginalizing or punishing political dissent.

Evaluating the role of political judgment also sheds light on internal tensions in restorative approaches to justice between their radical commitment to exposing and addressing systemic injustices, and their more pragmatic goal of promoting dialogue and reconciliation in the immediate term. To the extent that restorative-justice projects challenge systemic wrongs, they may be unsettling and even divisive. Yet if restorative-justice projects promote reconciliation by avoiding such conflicts, they abandon one of their defining commitments. In critically evaluating the contribution of truth commissions and other institutions or practices to restorative justice for systemic wrongdoing, it will be important to examine how they negotiate and mediate the tension between these goals.

TRUTH COMMISSIONS AND THE POLITICS OF MEMORY

Truth commissions and other official commissions of inquiry have become increasingly prominent tools for reckoning with systematic atrocity and political violence. These institutions have generally been promoted, designed, and evaluated in accordance with human rights legalism and a therapeutic approach to restorative justice. Truth commissions were initially seen as a second-best alternative to trials, in contexts where trials were not feasible. For proponents of human rights legalism, truth commissions are valuable as a basis for establishing some degree of accountability even where they cannot punish offenders. However, they are also problematic from the legalistic standpoint. To the extent that truth commissions *do* establish individual accountability by sharing findings with courts or "naming names," they may jeopardize basic standards of due process.[12] Under the influence of Chilean and South African leaders, truth commissions came to be seen as vehicles for advancing reconciliation and restorative justice. They would do so by opening spaces for victim testimony and perpetrator confession, by investigating and

---

[12] Freeman, *Truth Commissions and Procedural Fairness.*

identifying remedies for the *effects* of violence, and by cultivating a common understanding of the past.

Although they suggest different ways of justifying and evaluating truth commissions, legalism and restorative justice have two things in common. They tend to locate the value of truth commission investigations in their role as a basis for remedy and reform in the immediate aftermath of a political transition. They also imply that the critical role of truth commission investigations centers on their role in identifying and investigating the experiences of victims and perpetrators.

The argument developed here suggests an alternative way to think about the potential contribution of truth commissions. What is unique about truth commissions, and what sets them apart from other forms of transitional justice, is their commitment to examining systemic patterns of violence and injustice. To do so, truth commissions must strive to establish a degree of critical distance from the events of the present as well as the past. Yet if they do this by depoliticizing their investigations, they obfuscate the systemic dimension of past wrongs and undermine their defining aspiration. This means that their role as a basis for historical reflection is in tension with their role as a basis for legitimating reforms and remedies in the immediate term. Instead of seeing this as a problem for truth commissions, I suggest that the critical role of these institutions as a response to political violence depends on their capacity to expose the limitations of transitional reforms or remedies. Instead of establishing their contributions to justice and reconciliation by narrowing the scope of their investigations, then, truth commissions might further these goals by expanding their investigations to encompass the themes of complicity and resistance.

One objection to this view might be that it asks too much of truth commissions. Truth commissions cannot effectively cultivate dialogue and persuade people to accept the legitimacy of their findings while simultaneously doing the work of historians, which requires distance from the pressures and demands of politics. Charles Villa-Vicencio voiced this concern in response to critics of South Africa's *TRC Report*.[13] As strategies for addressing past wrongs, truth commissions require constructive ways to address the tensions between their role as historians and their role as political actors.

One way to mediate these tensions is to recognize the remedies and findings of transitional justice institutions as not only partial, but also provisional.[14] An ongoing process of investigation may lead to the *expansion* of earlier

13 Villa-Vicencio, "On the Limitations of Academic History."
14 See Ruti Teitel for a discussion of the "partial" character of transitional justice (*Transitional Justice*).

approaches to accountability, or it may lead to substantial *revision* of earlier approaches. In Chile, for example, a new truth commission expanded on the mandate of the original truth commission by investigating cases of torture and political imprisonment not covered in the earlier mandate.[15] At the same time, Chile and Argentina have revised earlier decisions not to pursue prosecutions in response to past abuses.[16] Truth commissions address the demand for some degree of closure, which is needed to enact reform, yet must strive to do so without foreclosing the possibility of expansion and revision, and without subjugating official remembrance to the imperatives of present compromises and future goals. In this regard, the work of truth commissions could benefit from the insights of scholars who have written on the theme of provisionality in political theory. For example, Lisa Ellis (drawing on Kant) and Lisa Disch (drawing on Arendt and Kant), both associate the recognition of provisionality with strategies to establish publicity and transparency in decision making, and for recording dissenting views.[17]

Another, related objection might be that if truth commissions examine patterns of complicity and resistance, their investigations will be too unsettling and divisive. This kind of objection echoes the more general concern that "too much memory" may be destructive and paralyzing for efforts to reckon with the past. In response to this kind of objection, it is useful to consider the possibility that a process may be unsettling in the immediate term but constructive over the long term.[18] It is also worth noting that it is simply unrealistic to expect that truth commissions could challenge denial regarding systematic violence in any meaningful way without provoking some degree of hostility and opposition.

[15] The National Commission on Political Imprisonment and Torture (known as the Valech Commission after its chair, Bishop Sergio Valech) completed its final report in 2005. Its mandate was to identify victims and make recommendations for reparations. The final report is available here: http://www.comisionprisionpoliticaytortura.cl/listado_informes.html

[16] According to the latest figures compiled by Human Rights Watch, 482 former military personnel and civilian collaborators are facing charges for enforced disappearances, extrajudicial executions, and torture; 256 have been convicted, and 38 were serving prison sentences. A majority of the five judges on Chile's Supreme Court now believe the blanket 1978 amnesty imposed by the military government is inapplicable to crimes against humanity and that crimes against humanity are not subject to a statute of limitations. See Human Rights Watch, *Chile: Events of 2008* (New York, 2008). Available: http://www.hrw.org/en/node/79211. In 2005, the Supreme Court of Argentina voted to nullify the amnesty laws past under Alfonsin. International Center for Transitional Justice, "Argentina 20 Years Later: Transitional Justice Regains Momentum" (New York, 2005).

[17] See Elisabeth Ellis, *Kant's Politics: Provisional Theory for an Uncertain World* (New Haven and London: Yale University Press, 2005); Disch, *Hannah Arendt and the Limits of Philosophy*.

[18] See Payne, *Settling Accounts*.

To this set of responses, the argument developed here also adds the point that by restricting their investigations to the experiences of victims and perpetrators, truth commissions may exacerbate, rather than alleviate, the unsettling and paralyzing effects of memory politics. Even where truth commissions and war crimes tribunals systematically avoid claims regarding pervasive complicity, their verdicts are often meant to be, or are perceived as, symbolic judgments of those who were supporters of a regime. Yet where such investigations remain bound to a victim-perpetrator framework, they imply either blanket exoneration or condemnation. Truth commissions could better address the theme of complicity by developing more nuanced categories of judgment that would accommodate variation and complexity in establishing responsibility.

I am not suggesting that truth commissions should stop identifying victims and perpetrators of the injustices that they examine, nor am I suggesting that they should stop examining the experience and effects of helpless victimization and the responsibility of individuals who organize atrocities. Instead, I am suggesting that truth commissions might *also* attend to the gray zone of complicity, which is difficult to judge or to understand in relation to these categories. Given their more flexible standards of evaluation, which are designed to examine systemic patterns of violence, truth commissions are uniquely suited to investigate what Levi referred to as the "gray zone" of responsibility.

For the same reason, truth commissions are also in a position to investigate the theme of resistance, which has been almost entirely neglected in contemporary transitional justice institutions and debates. By investigating or acknowledging the role of resistance, it is feared, truth commissions might simply intensify partisan divides or glorify violence and abuses committed in the name of resistance. Thus, truth commissions have recategorized stories of resistance as experiences of victims or perpetrators. In so doing, they abandon the lessons that might be learned from the experience of resistance, along with the moral obligation to acknowledge those who suffered as the result of protest or principled action. Yet they do little to offset the Manichean logic that may be associated with memories of resistance. Alternatively, truth commissions might incorporate the theme of resistance independently of the victim-perpetrator framework, while acknowledging multiple forms of resistance, as well as the shades of gray in stories of resistance. Truth commissions could examine factors associated with resistance, but also condemn abuses committed in the name of resistance. They could examine factors associated with successful resistance, but also uncover lost and buried stories of unsuccessful resistance. They could examine creative forms of nonviolent resistance. They could counter the concern that transitional justice institutions have obfuscated the role of women as political agents by investigating the role of women and women's groups in various kinds of protest against systemic brutalities and political violence.

This suggests an alternative avenue by which truth commissions might foster accountability and reconciliation while broadening theoretical and policy debates on the politics of memory. By examining the phenomenon of resistance, truth commissions might support the work of international criminal justice by providing evidence to counter pervasive claims that it was "impossible to know what was happening," and the defense that no one could have done anything other than to support or comply with orders to commit systematic brutalities. By investigating the theme of resistance, truth commissions could also support efforts to promote reconciliation and restorative justice. Stories of those who defected from positions of insider privilege in order to protest abuses, or those that worked across lines of division in solidarity with targeted groups, may establish evidence that could be used to challenge group-based demonization and destructive attributions of collective guilt. Such examples might also provide a more promising basis for guidance in the pursuit of political reconciliation than what are often very awkward efforts to establish a narrative of common victimization.

A drawing by Käthe Kollwitz entitled, "After the Battle," depicts a woman standing in what seems to be a sea of dead bodies. She is struggling to bear the weight of a single corpse while gently illuminating it with the light of a small lantern. All around her, piles of other bodies are barely discernible in the remaining shadows. Contemporary responses to political violence are sometimes framed in grandiose and even Orwellian terms, with their claims to promote truth, reconciliation, and justice. As serious efforts to reckon with past wrongs, however, they are limited and laborious. They require people to engage in painful efforts to recall experiences of tremendous suffering. They shed light on certain kinds of experiences and losses while relegating others to the shadows. Acknowledging such limitations need not be a cause for cynicism or despair. Buried in the histories of the most horrifying atrocities are examples of those who protested and struggled in ways that may have been grand gestures of sacrifice or modest acts of refusal. Such examples may illuminate possibilities for hope, political engagement, and community in the future, without obfuscating the role of complicity, passivity, and helplessness in the brutalities of the past.

Select Bibliography

Adorno, Theodor W. "What Does Coming to Terms with the Past Mean?" translated by Timothy Bahti and Geoffrey Hartman. In *Bitburg in Moral and Political Perspective*, edited by Geoffrey Hartman, 114–29. Bloomington, IN: Indiana University Press, 1986.

Aeschylus. *The Oresteia*, translated by Robert Fagles. New York: Penguin, 1966.

African National Congress. Submission of the African National Congress to the Truth and Reconciliation Commission in Reply to the Section 30 (2) of Act 34 of 1996 on the TRC "Findings on the African National Congress." October 1998.

Akhavan, Payam. "Justice and Reconciliation in the Great Lakes Region of Africa: The Contribution of the International Criminal Tribunal for Rwanda." *Duke Journal of Comparative and International Law* 7 (1997): 325–48.

"Justice in the Hague, Peace in the Former Yugoslavia? A Commentary on the United Nations War Crimes Tribunal." *Human Rights Quarterly* 20 (1998): 737–816.

Amnesty International. *Rwanda: A Question of Justice*. London: Amnesty International Secretariat, 2002.

Amstutz, Mark. "Restorative Justice, Political Forgiveness, and the Possibility of Reconciliation." In *The Politics of Past Evil: Religion, Reconciliation, and Transitional Justice*, edited by Daniel Philpott, 151–88. Notre Dame, IN: Notre Dame University Press, 2006.

The Healing of Nations: The Promise and Limits of Political Forgiveness. New York: Rowman and Littlefield, 2006.

Anderson, Benedict. *Imagined Communities*. London: Verso, 1983.

Aoláin, Fionnuala Ní, and Colm Campbell. "The Paradox of Transition in Conflicted Democracies." *Human Rights Quarterly* 27 (2005): 172–213.

"Political Violence and Gender During Times of Transition." *Columbia Journal of Gender and Law* 15, no. 3 (2006).

Arendt, Hannah. *The Human Condition*. Chicago: University of Chicago Press, 1958.

The Origins of Totalitarianism. New York: Harcourt Brace Jovanovich, 1966.

"Introduction: Walter Benjamin: 1892–1940." In *Illuminations*, edited by Hannah Arendt. New York: Schocken, 1968.

Men in Dark Times. New York: Harcourt Brace Jovanovich, 1968.

Between Past and Future: Eight Exercises in Political Thought. New York: Viking, 1969.

"Thinking and Moral Considerations: A Lecture," *Social Research* 38 (1971): 417–46.

Crises of the Republic. New York: Harcourt, Brace and Company, 1972.

Eichmann in Jerusalem: A Report on the Banality of Evil. New York: Penguin Books, 1965.

Lectures on Kant's Political Philosophy, edited by Ronald Beiner. Chicago: University of Chicago Press, 1982.

"Personal Responsibility under Dictatorship." In *Responsibility and Judgment*, edited by Jerome Kohn, 17–48. New York: Schocken Books, 2003.

"Introduction *into* Politics." In *The Promise of Politics*, edited by Jerome Kohn, 93–200. New York: Random House, 2005

"The Eichmann Case and the Germans: A Conversation with Thilo Koch" In *The Jewish Writings*, edited by Jerome Kohn and Ron H. Feldman, 485–9. New York: Schocken Books, 2007.

Aristotle. *Nichomachean Ethics*, translated by Martin Ostwald. New York: MacMillan, 1962.

Arthur, Paige. "How 'Transitions' Shaped Human Rights: A Conceptual History of Transitional Justice." *Human Rights Quarterly* 31, no. 2 (2009): 321–67.

Asmal, Kader, Louise Asmal, and Ronald Suresh Roberts. *Reconciliation through Truth: A Reckoning of Apartheid's Criminal Governance.* Cape Town: David Philips Publishers, 1996.

Asmal, Kader. "Truth, Reconciliation, and Justice: The South African Experience in Perspective." *The Modern Law Review* 63, no. 1 (2000).

Backer, David. "Exit, Voice & Loyalty in Transitional Justice Processes: Evidence on Victims' Responses to South Africa's Truth and Reconciliation Commission." Paper presented at the annual meeting of the American Political Science Association, Chicago, IL, 2004.

Barnett, Michael, and Martha Finnemore. "The Politics, Power, and Pathologies of International Organizations." *International Organization* 53, no. 4 (1999): 699–732.

Bass, Gary Jonathan. *Stay the Hand of Vengeance: The Politics of War Crimes Tribunals.* Princeton, NJ: Princeton University Press, 2001.

Beiner, Ronald. "Hannah Arendt on Judging." In *Hannah Arendt's Lectures on Kant's Political Philosophy*, edited by Ronald Beiner, 89–157. Chicago: University of Chicago Press, 1982.

Political Judgment. London: Metheune and Company, 1983.

Bell, Christine, and Catherine O'Rourke. "Does Feminism Need a Theory of Transitional Justice? An Introductory Essay." *International Journal of Transitional Justice* 1, no. 1 (2007): 23–44.

Benhabib, Seyla. "Judgment and the Moral Foundation of Politics in Arendt's Thought." *Political Theory* 16 (1988): 29–51.

Benjamin, Walter. *Illuminations*, translated by Harry Zorn, edited by Hannah Arendt. New York: Schocken, 1968.

Berat, Lynn, and Yossi Shain. "Retribution or Truth-Telling in South Africa? Legacies of the Transitional Phase." *Law and Social Inquiry* 20 (1995): 177.

Bickford, Louis. "Unofficial Truth Projects." *Human Rights Quarterly* 29, no. 4 (2007): 994–1035.

Bilsky, Leora. "When Actor and Spectator Meet in the Courtroom: Reflections on Hannah Arendt's Concept of Judgment." In *Judgment, Imagination, and Politics*, edited by Ronald Beiner and Jennifer Nedelsky, 257–86. New York: Rowman and Littlefield, 2001.

Booth, W. James. "The Unforgotten. Memories of Justice." *American Political Science Review* 95 (2001): 777–791.

"Communities of Memory: On Identity, Memory and Debt." *American Political Science Review* 93 (1999).

Communities of Memory: On Witness, Identity, and Justice. Ithaca, NY: Cornell University Press, 2006.

Boraine, Alex. *A Country Unmasked: Inside South Africa's Truth and Reconciliation Commission.* Oxford: Oxford University Press, 2000.

"Truth and Reconciliation in South Africa: The Third Way." In *Truth v. Justice: The Morality of Truth Commissions*, edited by Amy Gutmann and Dennis Thompson, 141–57. Princeton, NJ: Princeton University Press, 2000.

Boraine, Alex, Janet Levy, and Ronel Scheffer, eds. *Dealing with the Past.* Cape Town: IDASA, 1994.

Boraine, Alex, and Janet Levy, eds. *The Healing of a Nation?* Cape Town: Justice in Transition, 1995.

Borer, Tristan Anne. *Challenging the State: Churches as Political Actors in South Africa 1980–1994.* Notre Dame: University of Notre Dame Press, 1998.

"A Taxonomy of Victims and Perpetrators: Human Rights and Reconciliation in South Africa." *Human Rights Quarterly* 25, no. 4 (2003): 1088–1116.

"Reconciling South Africa or South Africans? Cautionary Notes from the TRC." *Africa Studies Quarterly* 8, no. 1 (2004): 19–37.

Borgwardt, Elizabeth. "A New Deal for the Nuremberg Trial: The Limit of Law in Generating Human Rights Norms." *Law and History Review* 26, no. 3 (2008): 679–705.

Braithwaite, John. *Restorative Justice and Responsive Regulation.* Oxford: Oxford University Press, 2002.

Brody, Reed. "Justice: The First Casualty of Truth?" *The Nation*, April 30, 2001.

Brown, Wendy. *Regulating Aversion: Tolerance in the Age of Identity and Empire.* Princeton, NJ and Oxford: Princeton University Press, 2006.

Brown, Wendy, and Janet Halley, eds. *Left Legalism/Left Critique.* Duke University Press, 2002.

Brudholm, Thomas. *Resentment's Virtue: Jean Améry and the Refusal to Forgive.* Philadelphia: Temple University Press, 2008.

Brysk, Alison. *The Politics of Human Rights in Argentina: Protest, Change, and Democratization.* Palo Alto, CA: Stanford University Press, 1994.

Human Rights and Private Wrongs: Constructing Global Civil Society. New York: Routledge, 2005.

Carpenter, R. Charli. *Innocent Women and Children: Gender, Norms, and the Protection of Civilians.* New York: Ashgate, 2006.

Cassesse, Antonio. "Is There a Need for International Justice?" Paper presented at the Summer Session of the Academy of European Law. Florence, Italy, 1997.

Chapman, Audrey and Patrick Ball. "The Truth of Truth Commissions: Comparative Lessons from Haiti, South Africa, and Guatemala." *Human Rights Quarterly* 23 (2001): 1–43.

Chapman, Audrey R., and Patrick Ball. "Levels of Truth: Macro-Truth and the TRC." In *Truth and Reconciliation in South Africa: Did the TRC Deliver?* edited by

Audrey R. Chapman and Hugo Van der Merwe, 143–68. Philadelphia: University of Pennsylvania Press, 2008.

Chesterman, Simon. *Just War or Just Peace? Humanitarian Intervention and International Law.* Oxford: Oxford University Press, 2001.

Christodoulidis, Emilios, and Scott Veitch. "Reconciliation as Surrender: Configurations of Responsibility and Memory." In *Justice and Reconciliation in Post-Apartheid South Africa*, edited by Francois du Bois and Antje du Bois-Pedain. New York: Cambridge University Press, 2008.

Clark, Ann Marie. *Diplomacy of Conscience: Amnesty International and Changing Human Rights Norms.* Princeton, NJ and Oxford: Princeton University Press, 2001.

Clark, Phil. *The Gacaca Courts, Post-Genocide Justice and Reconciliation in Rwanda: Justice without Lawyers.* New York: Cambridge University Press, 2010.

Cobban, Helena. "The Legacies of Collective Violence." *Boston Review* (2002).

Cohen, David. "Beyond Nuremberg: Individual Responsibility for War Crimes." In *Human Rights in Political Transitions*, edited by Carla Hesse and Robert Post, 53–92. New York: Zone Books, 1999.

Cohen, Stanley. "State Crimes of Previous Regimes: Knowledge, Accountability, and the Policing of the Past." *Law and Social Inquiry* 20, no.1 (1995): 7–49.
   States of Denial: Knowing About Atrocities and Suffering. Cambridge: Polity Press, 2001.

Coles, Romand. "Moving Democracy." *Political Theory* 32, no. 5 (2004): 678–705.

Conot, Robert E. *Justice at Nuremberg.* New York: Carroll and Graf Publishers, 1983.

Constitutional Court of South Africa. *S. v. Makwanyane and Another* (6) BCLR 665 (1995).

Constitutional Court of South Africa, *Azanian Peoples Organization (AZAPO) and Others v. President of the Republic of South Africa* (8) BCLR 1015 (1998).

Crocker, David. 2001. Transitional Justice [Book Review]. *Ethics and International Affairs.*

Culbert, Jennifer. "The Banality of Death in Eichmann," *Theory and Event* 6, no. 1 (2002).

De Brito, Alexandra Barahona, Carmen Gonzaléz-Enríquez, and Paloma Aguilar, eds. *The Politics of Memory: Transitional Justice in Democratizing Societies.* Oxford: Oxford University Press, 2001.

De Greiff, Pablo. "Trial and Punishment: Pardon and Oblivion: On Two Inadequate Policies for the Treatment of Former Human Rights Abusers." *Philosophy and Social Criticism* 22 (1996): 93–111.

De Lange, Johnny. "The Historical Context, Legal Origins, and Philosophical Foundation of the South African Truth and Reconciliation Commission." In *Looking Back, Reaching Forward: Reflections on the Truth and Reconciliation Commission of South Africa*, edited by Charles Villa-Vicencio and Wilhelm Verwoerd, 2–13. Cape Town: University of Cape Town Press, 2000.

De Ridder, Trudy. "The Trauma of Testifying." *Track Two: Constructive Approaches to Community and Political Conflict* 6, no. 3–4 (1997).

Des Forges, Alison, and Timothy Longman. "Legal Responses to the Genocide in Rwanda." In *My Neighbor, My Enemy: Justice and Community in the Aftermath of Mass Atrocity*, edited by Eric Stover and Harvey M. Weinstein, 46–68. Cambridge: Cambridge University Press, 2004.

Dietz, Mary. *Turning Operations: Feminism, Arendt, and Politics*. New York and London: Routledge, 2002.

Dienstag, Joshua Foa. "'The Pozsgay Affair' Historical Memory and Political Legitimacy." *History and Memory* 8, no. 1 (1996): 142–64.

Digeser, Peter. *Political Forgiveness*. Ithaca, NY: Cornell University Press, 2001.

Disch, Lisa. *Hannah Arendt and the Limits of Philosophy*. Ithaca, NY: Cornell University Press, 1994.

Dougherty, Beth K. "Searching for Answers: Sierra Leone's Truth and Reconciliation Commission." *African Studies Quarterly* 8, no. 1 (2004): 39–47.

Douglas, Lawrence. *The Memory of Judgment: Making Law and History in the Trials of the Holocaust*. New Haven, CT and London: Yale University Press, 2001.

Doxtader, Erik. "Easy to Forget or Never (Again) Hard to Remember? History, Memory, and the 'Publicity' of Amnesty." In *The Provocations of Amnesty: Memory, Justice, and Impunity*, edited by Charles Villa-Vicencio and Erik Doxtader, 121–55. Trenton, NJ: Africa World Press, 2003.

Drumbl, Mark. "Pluralizing International Criminal Justice." *Michigan Law Review* 103 (2005).

 Atrocity, Punishment, and International Law. New York: Cambridge University Press, 2007.

Elshtain, Jean Bethke. "Politics and Forgiveness." In *Burying the Past: Making Peace and Doing Justice after Civil Conflict*, edited by Nigel Biggar, 45–63. Washington DC: Georgetown University Press, 2003.

Elster, Jon. *Closing the Books: Transitional Justice in Historical Perspective*. Cambridge: Cambridge University Press, 2004.

Esquith, Stephen L. "Re-enacting Mass Violence." *Polity* 4 (2003): 513–34.

 "An Experiment in Democratic Political Education." *Polity* 36 (2003): 73–90.

Euben, Peter. *The Tragedy of Political Theory: The Road Not Taken*. Princeton, NJ: Princeton University Press, 1990.

Feher, Michel. "The Terms of Reconciliation." In *Human Rights in Political Transitions: Gettysburg to Bosnia*, edited by Carla Hesse and Robert Post, 325–38. New York: Zone Books, 1999.

Feitlowitz, Marguerite. *A Lexicon of Terror: Argentina and the Legacies of Torture*. New York: Oxford University Press, 1999.

Ferarra, Alessandro. *The Force of the Example: Explorations in the Paradigm of Judgment*. New York: Columbia University Press, 2008.

Finnemore, Martha. *The Purpose of Intervention: Changing Beliefs about the Use of Force*. Ithaca, NY: Cornell University Press, 2003.

Fiss, Owen. "The Death of a Public Intellectual." *The Yale Law Journal* 104, no. 5 (1995): 1187–1200.

Fletcher, Laurel E., and Harvey M. Weinstein. "Violence and Social Repair: Rethinking the Contribution of Justice to Reconciliation." *Human Rights Quarterly* 24, no. 3 (2002): 573–639.

 "A World unto Itself? The Application of International Justice in the Former Yugoslavia." In *My Neighbor, My Enemy: Justice and Community in the Aftermath of Atrocity*, edited by Eric Stover, and Harvey M. Weinstein, 29–48. Cambridge: Cambridge University Press, 2004.

Franke, Katherine. "Gendered Subjects of Transitional Justice." *Columbia Journal of Gender and Law* 15, no. 3 (2006).

Freeman, Mark. *Truth Commissions and Procedural Fairness.* Cambridge: Cambridge University Press, 2006.

Friedrich, Jörge. "Nuremberg and the Germans." In *War Crimes: The Legacy of Nuremberg,* edited by Belinda Cooper, 87–106. New York: TV Books, 1999.

Gibson, James L. *Overcoming Apartheid: Can Truth Reconcile a Divided Nation?* New York: Russell Sage Foundation, 2004.

Godobo-Madikizela, Pumla. *A Human Being Died That Night: A South African Story of Forgiveness.* Boston and New York: Houghton Mifflin Company, 2003.

    "Radical Forgiveness: Transforming Traumatic Memory beyond Hannah Arendt." In *Justice and Reconciliation in Post-Apartheid South Africa,* edited by Francois du Bois and Antje du Bois-Pedain, 37–61. New York: Cambridge University Press, 2008.

González-Enríquez, Carmen. "De-communization and Political Justice in Central and Eastern Europe." In *The Politics of Memory: Transitional Justice in Democratizing Societies,* edited by Alexandra Barahona de Brito, Carmen González-Enríquez, and Paloma Aguilar, 218–47. Oxford: Oxford University Press, 2001.

Govier, Trudy. *Forgiveness and Revenge.* New York: Routledge Press, 2002.

Graybill, Lynn. *Truth and Reconciliation in South Africa: Miracle or Model?* Boulder, CO: Lynne Rienner, 2002.

Grossman, Dave. *On Killing: The Psychological Cost of Learning to Kill in War and Society.* New York: Back Bay Books, 1996.

Guatemalan Commission for Historical Clarification. *Guatemala Memory of Silence: Report of the Commission for Historical Clarification,* 1996.

Gutmann, Amy, and Dennis Thompson. "The Moral Foundations of Truth Commissions." In *Truth v. Justice,* edited by Robert I. Rotberg and Dennis Thompson, 22–44. Princeton, NJ and Oxford: Princeton University Press, 2000

Gunnell, John G. *Between Philosophy and Politics: The Alienation of Political Theory.* Amherst: University of Massachusetts Press, 1986.

Habermas, Jurgen. "Hannah Arendt's Communication Concept of Power," *Social Research* 44 (1977): 3–24.

    A Berlin Republic: Writings on Germany, translated by Steven Randall. Lincoln, NE: Nebraska University Press, 1997.

Hadley, Michael L., ed. *The Spiritual Roots of Restorative Justice.* Albany, NY: State University of New York Press, 2001.

Hart, H.L.A. "Positivism and the Separation of Law and Morals." *Harvard Law Review* 71, no. 4 (1958): 593–629.

Hayner, Priscilla. *Unspeakable Truths: Confronting State Terror and Atrocity.* New York: Routledge, 2001.

Herf, Jeffrey. *Divided Memory: The Nazi Past in the Two Germanys.* Cambridge. MA: Harvard University Press, 1997.

Hertel, Shareen. *Unexpected Power: Conflict and Change among Transnational Activists.* Ithaca, NY: Cornell University Press, 2006.

Hesse, Carla, and Robert Post, eds. *Human Rights in Political Transitions: Gettysburg to Bosnia.* New York: Zone Books, 1999.

Hopgood, Stephen. *Keepers of the Flame: Understanding Amnesty International.* Ithaca, NY and London: Cornell University Press, 2006.

Human Rights Center, International Human Rights Law Clinic, University of California, and Centre for Human Rights, University of Sarajevo. *Justice, Accountability, and Social Reconstruction: An Interview Study of Bosnian Judges and Prosecutors*, 2000.

Human Rights Watch. *Chile: Events of 2008*, 2008.

Hund, John, and Malebo Kotu-Rammopo. "Justice in a South African Township: The Sociology of *Makglotla*." *The Comparative and International Law Journal of South Africa* 16 (1983): 179–209.

Hunt, Lynn. *Inventing Human Rights: A History*. New York: W.W. Norton, 2007.

Huyse, Luc. "Justice after Transition: On the Choices Successor Elites Make in Dealing with the Past." *Law and Social Inquiry* 20, no.1 (1995): 51–77.

Ignatieff, Michael. "Articles of Faith." *Index on Censorship* 5 (1996): 110–22.

  Human Rights as Politics and Idolatry. Princeton, NJ: Princeton University Press, 2001.

International Center for Transitional Justice. "Argentina 20 Years Later: Transitional Justice Regains Momentum." New York, 2005.

International Military Tribunal. Trial of the Major War Criminals before the *International Military Tribunal*, 1947.

Isaac, Jeffery. "A New Guarantee on Earth: Hannah Arendt on Human Dignity and the Politics of Human Rights." *American Political Science Association Review* 90 (1996): 61–73.

Jackson, Robert H. "Report to the President from Justice Robert H. Jackson, Chief Counsel for the United States in the Prosecution of Axis War Criminals." *Department of State Bulletin*, June 10, 1945.

  Opening Statement. *Trial of Major War Criminals before the International Military Tribunal*, vol. 1. Nuremberg: International Military Tribunal, 1947.

  Critique of Judgment (1790), translated by Werner S. Pluhar. Indianapolis, IN: Hackett, 1987.

Jaspers, Karl. *The Question of German Guilt*, translated by E.B. Ashton. New York: Dial Press, 1947.

  Lebensfragen der Deutschen Politik. Munich: Deutschen Tagenbuch Verlag, 1963.

Jochnik, Chris, and Roger Normand. "The Legitimation of Violence: A Critical History of the Laws of War." *Harvard International Law Journal* 35 (1994): 49–95.

Kagan, Robert. *Adversarial Legalism: The American War of Law*. Cambridge, MA: Harvard University Press, 2003.

The Kairos Document: Challenge to the Church: A Theological Comment on the Political Crisis in South Africa. Grand Rapids, MI: Eerdemans, 1985.

Kant, Immanuel. *Kant: Political Writings (Cambridge Texts in the History of Political Thought)*, translated by H.B. Nisbett, edited by H.R. Reiss. Cambridge: Cambridge University Press, 1991.

Keck, Margaret, and Kathryn Sikkink. *Activists beyond Borders: Advocacy Networks in International Politics*. Ithaca, NY: Cornell University Press, 1998.

Keenan, Alan. *Democracy in Question: Democratic Openness in a Time of Political Closure*. Palo Alto, CA: Stanford University Press, 2003.

Kelsall, Tim. "Truth, Lies, Ritual: Preliminary Reflections on the Truth and Reconciliation Commission in Sierra Leone." *Human Rights Quarterly* 27 (2005): 361–91.

Kelsen, Hans. "Will the Judgment in the Nuremberg Trial Constitute a Precedent in International Law?" *The International Law Quarterly* 1, no. 4 (1947): 153–71.

Kinsella, Helen. "Gendering Grotius: Sex and Sex Difference in the Laws of War." *Political Theory* 34, no. 2 (2006): 161–91.

Kirchheimer, Otto. *Political Justice: The Use of Legal Procedure for Political Ends.* Princeton, NJ: Princeton University Press, 1961.

Kiss, Elizabeth. "Moral Ambition within and beyond Political Constraints: Reflections on Restorative Justice." In *Truth v. Justice: the Morality of Truth Commissions,* edited by Robert I. Rotberg and Dennis Thompson, 68–98. Princeton, NJ and Oxford: Princeton University Press, 2000.

Klusmeyer, Douglas. "Hannah Arendt's Critical Realism: Power, Justice, and Responsibility." In *Hannah Arendt and International Relations: Reading across the Lines,* edited by Anthony F. Lang, Jr. and John Williams. New York: Palgrave McMillian, 2005.

Korey, William. *NGOs and the Universal Declaration of Human Rights: "A Curious Grapevine."* New York: St. Martin's Press, 1998.

Kritz, Neil, ed. *Transitional Justice: How Emerging Democracies Reckon with Former Regimes.* Washington DC: U.S. Institute of Peace, 1995.

Kundera, Milan. *The Book of Laughter and Forgetting.* New York: Harper Perennial, 1999.

Kurasawa, Fuyuki. *The Work of Global Justice: Human Rights as Practices.* Cambridge: Cambridge University Press, 2007.

LaPlante, Lisa, and Kimberly Theidon. "Truth with Consequences: Justice and Reparations in Post-Truth Commission Peru." *Human Rights Quarterly* 29, no. 1 (2007): 228–50.

Lauren, Paul Gordon. *The Evolution of International Human Rights: Visions Seen.* Philadelphia: University of Pennsylvania Press, 1998.

Lebow, Richard Ned. *The Tragic Vision of Politics: Ethics, Interests, and Orders.* New York: Cambridge University Press, 2003.

Leebaw, Bronwyn. "Legitimation or Judgment? South Africa's Restorative Approach to Transitional Justice." *Polity* 34, no.1 (2003): 23–51.

"The Politics of Impartial Activism: Humanitarianism and Human Rights." *Perspectives on Politics Perspectives* 5, no. 2 (2007): 223–38.

"The Irreconcilable Goals of Transitional Justice." *Human Rights Quarterly* 30, no. 1, (2008): 95–118.

Levi, Primo. *The Drowned and the Saved,* translated by Raymond Rosenthal. New York: Vintage Books, 1989.

Survival in Auschwitz translated by Stuart Woolf. New York: Collier, 1993.

Llewellyn, Jennifer, and Robert Howse. "Institutions for Restorative Justice: The South African Truth and Reconciliation Commission." *University of Toronto Law Journal* 49 (1999): 355–88.

Long, William J., and Peter Brecke. *War and Reconciliation: Reason and Emotion in Conflict Resolution.* Cambridge, MA: MIT Press, 2003.

Longman, Timothy. "Justice at the Grassroots? Gacaca Trials in Rwanda." In *Transitional Justice in the Twenty-First Century: Beyond Peace versus Justice,* edited by Naomi Roht-Arriaza and Javier Marriezcurena, 206–28. New York: Cambridge University Press, 2006.

Luban, David. *Legal Modernism: Law, Meaning, and Violence.* Ann Arbor, MI: University of Michigan Press, 1997.

Lynch, Cecelia. *Beyond Appeasement: Interpreting Interwar Peace Movements in World Politics.* Ithaca, NY: Cornell University Press, 1999.

"Acting on Belief: Christian Perspectives on Suffering and Violence." *Ethics and International Affairs* 14 (2000).

Maier, Charles. *The Unmasterable Past: History, Holocaust, and German National Identity.* Cambridge, MA: Harvard University Press, 1988.

Malamud-Goti, Jaime. "Transitional Governments in the Breach: Why Punish State Criminals?" *Human Rights Quarterly* 12 (1990): 1–16.

Maluleke, Tinyiko Sam. "The South African Truth Commission Discourse: A Black Theological Evaluation." *Journal of Black Theology* 12 (1998): 35–58.

Mamdani, Mahmood. "Reconciliation without Justice." *Southern Review* 10, no. 6 (1996): 22–5.

"A Diminished Truth." In *After the TRC: Reflections on Truth and Reconciliation in South Africa*, edited by Wilmot James and Linda Van De Vijver, 58–61. Claremont, South Africa: David Philip Publishers, 2000.

"Amnesty or Impunity? A Preliminary Critique of the Report of the Truth and Reconciliation Commission of South Africa (TRC)." *Diacritics* 32, no. 3–4 (2002): 33–58.

Mani, Rama. *Beyond Retribution: Seeking Justice in the Shadows of War.* Cambridge: Polity Press, 2002.

Markell, Patchen. "The Rule of the People, Arendt, Arche, and Democracy." *American Political Science Review* 100 (2006): 1–14.

McAdams, A. James, ed., *Transitional Justice and the Rule of Law in New Democracies.* Notre Dame, IN: University of Notre Dame Press, 1997.

McCarthy, Thomas. "Vergangenheitsbewältigung in the USA: On the Politics of Memory and Slavery." *Political Theory* 30 (2002): 623–48.

McClure, Kirstie. "The Odor of Judgment: Exemplarity, Propriety, and Politics in the Company of Arendt." In *Hannah Adendt and the Meaning of Politics*, edited by Craig Calhoun and John McGowan, 53–84. Minneapolis, MN and London: University of Minnesota Press, 1997.

McEvoy, Kieran. "Beyond Legalism: Toward a Thicker Understanding of Transitional Justice." *Journal of Law and Society* 34, no. 4 (2007): 411–40.

Medearis, John. "Lost or Obscured? How V.I. Lenin, Joseph Schumpeter, and Hannah Arendt Misunderstood the Council Movement." *Polity* 36, no. 3 (2004): 447–76.

Meintjes, Sheila, and Beth Goldblatt. "Gender and the Truth and Reconciliation Commission," A Submission to the Truth and Reconciliation Commission (May, 1996).

Meister, Robert. "Forgiving and Forgetting: Lincoln and the Politics of National Recovery." In *Human Rights in Political Transitions*, edited by C. Hesse and R. C. Post. New York: Zone Press, 1999.

"Human Rights and the Politics of Victimhood." *Ethics and International Affairs* 16, no. 2 (2002): 91–108.

"Ways of Winning: The Costs of Moral Victory in Transitional Regimes." In *Modernity and the Problem of Evil*, edited by Alan D. Schrift. Bloomington: Indiana University Press, 2005.

Mendeloff, David. "Truth-Seeking, Truth-Telling, and Post-Conflict Peacebuilding: Curb the Enthusiasm?" *International Studies Review* 6 (2004):355–80.

"Trauma and Vengeance: Assessing the Psychological and Emotional Effects of Post-Conflict Justice" *Human Rights Quarterly* 31, no. 3 (2009): 592–623.

Méndez, Juan E. *Truth and Partial Justice in Argentina: An Americas Watch Report.* New York and Washington, DC: Americas Watch, 1987.

"In Defense of Transitional Justice. In *Transitional Justice and the Rule of Law in New Democracies*, edited by James A. McAdams, 1–26. South Bend, IN: University of Notre Dame Press, 1997.

"Accountability for Past Abuses." *Human Rights Quarterly* 19, no. 2 (1997) 255–82.

"National Reconciliation, Transnational Justice, and the International Criminal Court." *Ethics and International Affairs* 15 (2001): 25–44.

Meron, Theodor. "The Humanization of Humanitarian Law." *The American Journal of International Law*, 94, no. 2 (2000): 239–78.

Merry, Sally Engle. "The Social Organization of Mediation in Nonindustrial Societies: Implications for Informal Community Justice in America." In *The Politics of Informal Justice*, edited by Richard Abel. New York: Academy Press, 1982.

Human Rights and Gender Violence: Translating International Law into Local Justice. Chicago and London: University of Chicago Press, 2006.

Mertus, Julie. "Truth in a Box: The Limits of Justice through Judicial Mechanisms." *The Politics of Memory: Truth, Healing, and Social Justice*, edited by Ifi Amadiume and Abdullahi An-Na'im. London: Zed Books, 2000.

Miller, Zinaida. "Effects of Invisibility: In Search of the Economic in Transitional Justice." *International Journal of Transitional Justice* 2, no. 3 (2008): 266–91.

Minow, Martha. *Between Vengeance and Forgiveness: Facing History after Genocide and Mass Violence.* Boston: Beacon Press, 1998.

"The Hope for Healing: What Can Truth Commissions Do?" In *Truth v. Justice: The Morality of Truth Commissions*, edited by Robert I. Rotberg and Dennis Thompson, 235–60. Princeton, NJ and Oxford: Princeton University Press, 2000.

Moon, Claire. *Narrating Political Reconciliation: South Africa's Truth and Reconciliation Commission.* Lanham MD: Rowman and Littlefield, 2008.

Morsink, Johannes. *The Universal Declaration of Human Rights: Origins, Drafting and Intent.* Philadelphia: University of Pennsylvania Press, 1999.

Mouffe, Chantal. "Democracy in a Multipolar World." *Millennium Journal of International Studies* 37, no. 3 (2009): 549–61.

Muttukumaru, Christopher. "Reparation to Victims." In *The International Criminal Court: The Making of the Rome Statute*, edited by Roy S. Lee, 262–69. The Hague: Kluwer Law International, 1999.

Neier, Aryeh. "What Should Be Done about the Guilty?" *The New York Review of Books* 37, no. 1 (1990): 32–5.

War Crimes: Brutality, Genocide, Terror, and the Struggle for Justice. New York: Random House, 1998.

"Rethinking Truth, Justice and Guilt after Bosnia and Rwanda." In *Human Rights in Political Transitions: Gettysburg to Bosnia*, edited by Carla Hesse and Robert Post, 39–52. New York: Zone Books, 1999.

Nevins, Joe. "Truth, Lies, and Accountability." *Boston Review*, 2007.

Nino, Carlos S. "The Duty to Punish Past Abuses of Human Rights Put into Context: The Case of Argentina." *Yale Law Journal* 100 (1991): 2619–25.
  Radical Evil on Trial. New Haven, CT: Yale University Press, 1998.
Norval, Aletta. "Memory, Identity, and the (Im)possibility of Reconciliation: The Work of the South African Truth and Reconciliation Commission." *Constellations* 5, no. 2 (2002): 250–65.
Olsen, Tricia, Leigh Payne, and Andrew Reiter. *Transitional Justice in Balance: Comparing Processes, Weighing Efficacy*. Washington D.C: U.S. Institute of Peace Press, 2010.
Orentlicher, Diane. "Settling Accounts: The Duty to Prosecute Human Rights Violations of a Prior Regime." *Yale Law Review* 100 (1991): 2539–615.
  "Settling Accounts Revisited: Reconciling Global Norms with Local Agency." *The International Journal of Transitional Justice* 1 (2007): 10–22.
Osiel, Mark. *Mass Atrocity, Collective Memory, and the Law*. New Brunswick, NJ: Transaction Press, 1997.
  Mass Atrocity, Ordinary Evil, and Hannah Arendt: Criminal Consciousness in Argentina's Dirty War. New Haven, CT and London: Yale University Press, 2001.
  "The Banality of Good: Aligning Incentives against Mass Atrocity." *Columbia Law Review* 105, no. 6 (2005): 1751–1862.
Owens, Patricia. *Between War and Politics: International Relations and the Thought of Hannah Arendt*. Oxford: Oxford University Press, 2007.
Parodi, Carlos. "Apologies under U.S. Hegemony." In *Age of Apology: Facing up to the Past*, edited by Marc Gibney, Niklaus Steiner, Jean-Marc Coicaud, and Rhoda Howard-Hassman, 171–86. Philadelphia: University of Pennsylvania Press, 2007.
Payne, Leigh. *Settling Accounts: Neither Truth nor Reconciliation in Confessions of State Violence*. Durham, NC and London: Duke University Press, 2008.
Phakathi, Timothy Sizwe, and Hugo Van der Merwe. "The Impact of the TRC's Amnesty Process on Survivors of Human Rights Violations." In *Truth and Reconciliation in South Africa: Did the TRC Deliver?* edited by Audrey R. Chapman and Hugo Van Der Merwe, 116–42. Philadelphia: University of Pennsylvania Press, 2008.
Peskin, Victor. *International Trials in Rwanda and the Balkans: Virtual Trials and the Struggle for State Cooperation*. New York: Cambridge University Press, 2009.
Peskin, Victor, and Mieczylslaw P. Boduszynski. "International Justice and Domestic Politics: Post-Tudjman Croatia and the International Criminal Tribunal for the Former Yugoslavia." *Europe-Asia Studies* 55, no. 3 (2003): 1117–42.
Phelps, Teresa Godwin. *Shattered Voices: Language, Violence, and the Work of Truth Commissions*. Philadelphia: University of Pennsylvania Press, 2004.
Philpott, Daniel, ed., *The Politics of Past Evil: Religion, Reconciliation, and Transitional Justice*. Notre Dame, IN: Notre Dame University Press, 2006.
Philpott, Daniel. "Religion, Reconciliation, and Transitional Justice: The State of the Field." *Social Science Research Council Working Papers*, 2007.
  "What Religion Brings to the Politics of Transitional Justice." *Journal of International Affairs*, 61, no. 1 (2007): 93–110.
Pion Berlin, David. "To Prosecute or to Pardon? Human Rights Decisions in the Latin American Southern Cone. *Human Rights Quarterly* 16, no.1 (1993): 105–30.

Through Corridors of Power: Institutions and Civil-Military Relations in Argentina. University Park, PA: The Pennsylvania State University Press, 1997.

Pitkin, Hannah Fenichel. "Justice: On Relating Private and Public." *Political Theory* 9 (1981):327–52.

The Attack of the Blob: Hannah Arendt's Concept of the Social. Chicago and London: University of Chicago Press, 1998.

Plato. "The Apology," translated by Hugo Treddenick. In *The Last Days of Socrates*, edited by Hugo Treddenick, 31–71. London: Penguin, 1954.

Power, Jonathan. *Like Water on Stone: The Story of Amnesty International.* New York: Penguin, 2002.

Principles of International Law Recognized in the Charter of the Nuremberg Tribunal and in the Judgment of the Tribunal, 1950.

Ptacek, James A., ed. *Restorative Justice and Violence against Women* (Oxford: Oxford University Press, 2010).

Pupavac, Vanessa, "International Therapeutic Peace and Justice in Bosnia." *Social and Legal Studies* 3, no. 3 (2004): 377–401.

Renan, Ernst. "What is a Nation?" translated by Martin Thom. In *Nation and Narration*, edited by Homi K. Bhabha, 8–22. London: Routledge, 1990.

Rigby, Andrew. *Justice and Reconciliation: After the Violence.* Boulder, CO: Lynne Rienner Publishers, 2001.

Risse Thomas, and Kathryn Sikkink. "The Socialization of International Human Rights Norms." In *The Power of Human Rights: International Norms and Domestic Change*, edited by Thomas Risse, Stephen C. Ropp, and Kathryn Sikkink, 1–38. New York: Cambridge University Press, 1999.

Robin, Corey. *Fear: The History of a Political Idea.* Oxford: Oxford University Press, 2006.

Roht-Arriaza, ed. *Impunity and Human Rights in International Law and Practice.* New York and Oxford: Oxford University Press, 1995.

Roht Arriaza, Naomi. "The New Landscape of Transitional Justice." In *Transitional Justice in the Twenty-First Century: Beyond Truth Versus Justice*, edited by Naomi Roht-Arriaza and Javier Marriezcurrena, 1–16. Cambridge: Cambridge University Press, 2006.

Ron, James, Howard Ramos, and Kathleen Rodgers. "Transnational Information Politics: NGO Human Rights Reporting 1986–2000." *International Studies Quarterly* 49 (2005): 557–87.

Roniger, Luis, and Mario Sznajder, *The Legacy of Human Rights Violations in the Southern Cone: Argentina, Chile, and Uruguay.* Oxford: Oxford University Press, 1999.

"The Politics of Memory and Oblivion in Redemocratized Argentina and Uruguay," *History and Memory* 10, no. 1 (1998): 133–69

Ross, Amy. "The Politics of Truth in Transition: Latin American influences on the South African Truth and Reconciliation Commission." *Politique Africaine* 92 (2003):18–38.

"The Creation and Conduct of the Guatemalan Commission for Historical Clarification." *Geoforum* 37, no. 1 (2006): 69–81.

Ross, Fiona. *Bearing Witness: Women and the Truth and Reconciliation Commission.* London: Pluto Press, 2003.

Rosser, Emily. "Depoliticised Speech and Sexed Visibility: Women, Gender and Sexual Violence in the 1999 Guatemalan *Comisión para el Esclarecimiento Histórico* Report." *International Journal of Transitional Justice* 1, no. 3 (2007): 391–410.

Roth, Brad. "Peaceful Transition and Retrospective Justice: Some Reservations. A Response to Juan Méndez." *Ethics & International Affairs* 15 (2001):45–50.

"Anti-Sovereigntism, Liberal Messianism, and Excesses in the Drive against Impunity," *Finnish Yearbook of International Law* 12 (2003):17–45.

Roth, Kenneth. "Human Rights in the Haitian Transition to Democracy." In *Human Rights in Political Transitions: Gettysburg to Bosnia*, edited by Carla Hesse and Robert Post, 93–134. New York: Zone Books, 1999.

"Defending Economic, Social and Cultural Rights: Practical Issues Faced by an International Human Rights Organization." *Human Rights Quarterly* 26, no. 1 (2004): 63–73.

"The Power of Horror in Rwanda," *Los Angeles Times*, April 9, 2009, Opinion Section.

Roth, Kenneth, and Allison Des Forges. "Justice or Therapy?" *Boston Review*, 2002.

"Rwanda: Academic Scholars Call for ICTR to Fulfill Mandate and Prosecute RPF/RPA Members," *World News Journal*, June 1, 2009.

Sachs, Albie. "Fourth DT Lakdawala Memorial Lecture." Presented at the Institute of Social Sciences Nehru Memorial Museum and Library Auditorium, New Delhi, India, December 18, 1998.

"His Name Was Henry," in *After the TRC: Reflections on Truth and Reconciliation in South Africa*, ed. Wilmot James and Linda Van De Vijver, 94–100. Claremont, South Africa: David Philip Publishers, 2000.

Sachs, Albie, and Gita Welch. *Liberating the Law: Creating Popular Justice in Mozambique*. London: Zed Books, 1990.

Sanford, Victoria. *Buried Secrets: Truth and Human Rights in Guatemala*. New York: Palgrave, 2003.

Sarat, Austin, ed., *Law, Violence, and the Possibility of Justice*. Princeton, NJ: Princeton University Press, 2001.

Sarkin, Jeremy. "An Evaluation of the TRC's Amnesty Process," in *Truth and Reconciliation in South Africa: Did the TRC Deliver?* edited by Audrey R. Chapman and Hugo Van der Merwe, 93–115. Philadelphia: University of Pennsylvania Press, 2008.

Schaap, Andrew. *Political Reconciliation*. New York: Routledge, 2005.

Scharf, Wilfried, and Baba Ngcokoto. "Images of Punishment in the People's Courts of Cape Town 1985–1987: From Prefigurative Justice to Populist Violence." In *Political Violence and the Struggle in South Africa*, edited by. N. Chubani Manganyi and Andre du Toit, 341–71. London: McMillan, 1990.

Scheingold, Stuart. *The Politics of Rights: Lawyers, Public Policy, and Political Change*. New Haven, CT: Yale University Press, 1974.

Schmitt, Carl. *The Concept of the Political*. Chicago: University of Chicago Press, 1996.

Shane, Scott. "To Investigate or Not? Four Ways to Look Back at Bush." *The New York Times*, February 21, 2009, Week in Review Section.

Shaw, Rosalind. "Rethinking Truth and Reconciliation Commissions: Lessons from Sierra Leone." U.S. Institute of Peace Special Report 130, February 2005.

Shriver, Donald. *An Ethic for Enemies: Forgiveness in Politics.* Oxford: Oxford University Press, 1995.

Sikkink, Kathryn, and Carrie Booth Walling. "The Impact of Human Rights Trials in Latin America." *Journal of Peace Research* 44, no. 4 (2007): 427–45.

Simmons, Beth. *Mobilizing for Human Rights: International Law in Domestic Politics.* New York: Cambridge University Press, 2009.

Sjoberg, Laura. *Gender, Justice, and the Wars in Iraq: A Feminist Reformulation of Just War Theory.* New York: Lexington, 2006.

Slovo, Joe. "Negotiations: What Room for Compromise?" *African Communist* (1992): 36–40.

Smith, Bradley F. *Reaching Judgment at Nuremberg.* New York: Basic Books, 1977.

Smith, Michael Joseph. *Realist Thought from Weber to Kissinger.* Baton Rouge: Louisiana State University Press, 1986.

Snyder, Jack, and Leslie Vinjamuri. "Trials and Errors: Principle and Pragmatism in Strategies of International Justice." *International Security* 28 (2003/4): 5–44.

Sriram, Chandra Lekha. "Revolutions in Accountability: New Approaches to Past Abuse." *American University International Law Review* 19 (2003): 304–429.

  Confronting Past Human Rights Violations. London and New York: Frank Cass, 2004.

  "Transitional Justice Comes of Age: Enduring Lessons and Challenges." *Berkeley Journal of International Law* 23, no. 2 (2005): 101–18.

Steinberger, Peter J. *The Concept of Political Judgment.* Chicago and London: University of Chicago Press, 1993.

Stover, Eric. "Witnesses and the Promise of Justice in the Hague." In *My Neighbor, My Enemy: Justice and Community in the Aftermath of Mass Atrocity,* edited by Eric Stover and Harvey M. Weinstein. Cambridge: Cambridge University Press, 2004.

  The Witnesses: War Crimes and the Promise of Justice in The Hague. Philadelphia: University of Pennsylvania Press, 2005.

Strang, Heather, and John Braithwaite, eds., *Restorative Justice: Philosophy to Practice.* Burlington, VT: Ashgate, 2000.

Stuart, Brian. "Truth Probe 'Could Name Ministers.'" *Citizen.* February 25, 1995.

Subotic, Jelena. *Hijacked Justice: Dealing with the Past in the Balkans.* Ithaca, NY: Cornell University Press, 2009.

Tambo, Oliver. "Statement on Signing Declaration, On Behalf of the ANC and Umkohnto We Sizwe, Adhering to the Geneva Conventions of 1949, and Protocol I of 1977." Headquarters of International Committee of the Red Cross, Geneva, November 29, 1980.

Taylor, Telford. *The Anatomy of the Nuremberg Trials.* New York: Knopf, 1992.

Teitel, Ruti G. "Nuremberg and Its Legacy, Fifty Years Later." In *War Crimes: The Legacy of Nuremberg,* edited by Belinda Cooper, 44–54. New York: TV Books, 1999.

  "Bringing the Messiah through the Law." In *Human Rights in Political Transitions: Gettysburg to Bosnia,* edited by Carla Hesse and Robert Post, 177–94. New York: Zone Books, 1999.

  Transitional Justice. New York: Oxford University Press, 2000.

  "Humanity's Law: Rule of Law for the New Global Politics." *Cornell International Law Journal* 35 (2002): 355–87.

"Transitional Justice Genealogy." *Harvard Human Rights Journal* 16 (2003): 69–94.

"Bringing Transitional Justice Home: President Obama's Dilemma about the Past Administration's Human Rights Abuses – What Is to Be Done and Who Will Be the Judge?" (December 16, 2008).

Thiele, Leslie Paul. "Judging Hannah Arendt: A Reply to Zerilli," *Political Theory* 33 (2005).

The *Heart of Judgment: Practical Wisdom, Neuroscience, and Narrative*. New York: Cambridge University Press. 2006.

Thucydides. *The History of the Peloponnesian War: Revised Edition*, edited by Rex Warner, translated by M.I. Finley. New York: Penguin Classics, 1954.

Torpey, John. "Introduction: Politics and the Past." In *Politics and the Past: On Repairing Historical Injustices*, edited by John Torpey. Lanham, Maryland: Rowman and Littlefield, 2003.

Tutu, Desmond. "Chairperson's Foreward," in *Truth and Reconciliation Commission of South Africa Final Report*, Volume 1. Cape Town: Juta, 1998.

Tutu, Desmond Mpilo. *No Future without Forgiveness*. New York: Doubleday, 1999.

Truth and Reconciliation Commission of South Africa. *Truth and Reconciliation Commission of South Africa Report*, Volumes 1–7. Cape Town: Juta, 1998.

Truth and Reconciliation Commission of Peru, *Final Report*, 2003.

U.N. Economic and Social Council. Commission on Human Rights. *The Administration of Justice and the Human Rights of Detainees: Question of the Impunity of Perpetrators of Human Rights Violations*, October 2, 1997 (E/CN.4/Sub.2/1997/20/Rev.1).

U.N. Economic and Social Council. Commission on Human Rights, *Promotion and Protection of Human Rights, Impunity: Note by the Secretary General*, February 27, 2004 (E/CN.4/2004/88).

United Nations Security Council. The Rule of Law and Transitional Justice in Conflict and Post-Conflict Societies: Report of the Secretary General. S/2004/616. August 23, 2004.

Uvin, Peter, and Charles Mironko. "Western and Local Approaches to Justice in Rwanda." *Global Governance* 9 (2003): 219–31.

Valls, Andrew. "A Truth Commission for the United States?" *Intertexts* 7, no. 2 (2003): 157–70.

Van Antwerpen, Jonathan. "Moral Globalization and Discursive Struggle: Reconciliation, Transitional Justice, and Cosmopolitan Discourse." In *Globalization, Philanthropy, and Civil Society*, edited by David Hammack and Steven Heydemann, 95–136. Bloomington IN: Indiana University Press, 2009.

Van der Merwe, Hugo, and Audrey R. Chapman. "Conclusion: Did the TRC Deliver?" in *Truth and Reconciliation in South Africa: Did the TRC Deliver?* edited by Audrey R. Chapman and Hugo Van der Merwe, 241–280. Philadelphia: Pennsylvania University Press, 2008.

Van der Merwe, Hugo, Victoria Baxter, and Audrey R. Chapman, eds. *Assessing the Impact of Transitional Justice: Challenges for Empirical Research*. Washington, DC: USIP Press, 2009.

Verdeja, Ernesto. *Unchopping a Tree: Reconciliation in the Aftermath of Political Violence* Philadelphia: Temple University Press, 2009.

Villa, Dana. *Politics, Philosophy, Terror: Essays on the Thought of Hannah Arendt.* Princeton, NJ: Princeton University Press, 1999.

Villa-Vicencio, Charles. *A Theology of Reconstruction: Nation-Building and Human Rights.* Cambridge: Cambridge University Press, 1992.

"A Different Kind of Justice: The South African Truth and Reconciliation Commission." *Contemporary Justice Review* 1 (1998): 407–28.

"Restorative Justice: Dealing with the Past Differently" In *Looking Back, Reaching Forward: Reflections on the Truth and Reconciliation Commission of South Africa*, edited by Charles Villa-Vicencio and Wilhelm Verwoerd, 68–76. Cape Town: University of Cape Town Press, 2000.

"On the Limitations of Academic History: The Quest for Truth Demands both More and Less." In *After the TRC: Reflections on Truth and Reconciliation in South Africa*, edited by Wilmot James and Linda Van de Vijver, 21–31. Athens, OH: Ohio University Press, 2001.

"Restorative Justice: Ambiguities and Limitations of a Theory." In *The Provocations of Amnesty: Memory, Justice, and Impunity*, edited by Charles Villa-Vicencio and Erik Doxtader, 30–50. Cape Town: David Philip Publishers, 2003.

Vinjamuri, Leslie, and Aaron P. Boesenecker. "Religion, Secularism, and Nonstate Actors in Transitional Justice." In *The New Religious Pluralism*, edited by Thomas Banchoff, 155–94. Oxford: Oxford University Press, 2008.

Walzer, Michael. *Just and Unjust Wars: A Moral Argument with Historical Illustrations.* New York: Basic Books, 2000.

Arguing about War. New Haven, CT: Yale University Press, 2006.

Wechsler, Lawrence. *A Miracle, a Universe: Settling Accounts with Torturers.* Chicago: University of Chicago Press, 1990.

Williams, Paul R., and Michael P. Scharf. *Peace with Justice? War Crimes and Accountability in the Former Yugoslavia.* Lanham, MD: Rowman and Littlefield, 2002.

Wilson, Richard A. *The Politics of Truth and Reconciliation in South Africa: Legitimizing the Post-Apartheid State.* Cambridge: Cambridge University Press, 2001.

Wolin, Sheldon. *Politics and Vision: Continuity and Innovation in Western Political Thought.* Princeton, NJ: Princeton University Press, 2004.

Young-Bruehl, Elisabeth. *Hannah Arendt: For the Love of the World.* New Haven, CT and London: Yale University Press, 1982.

Zalaquett, José. "Balancing Ethical Imperatives and Political Constraints: The Dilemma of New Democracies Confronting Past Human Rights Violations." *Hastings Law Journal* 43 (1992): 1425–38.

Zehr, Howard. *Changing Lenses: A New Focus for Crime and Justice.* Scottsdale, PA: Herald Press, 1990.

Zerilli, Linda. "'We Feel our Freedom': Imagination and Judgment in the Thought of Hannah Arendt." *Political Theory* 33 (2005): 155–88.

Index